P9-AGO-740

RADICAL FICTIONS AND THE NOVELS OF NORMAN MAILER

Radical Fictions and the Novels of Norman Mailer

Nigel Leigh

St. Martin's Press   New York

© Nigel Leigh 1990

All rights reserved. For information, write:
Scholarly and Reference Division,
St. Martin's Press, Inc., 175 Fifth Avenue, New York, NY 10010

First published in the United States of America in 1990

Printed in the People's republic of China

ISBN 0–312–03464–4

Library of Congress Cataloging-in-Publication Data
Leigh, Nigel, 1955–
    Radical fictions and the novels of Norman Mailer / Nigel Leigh.
        p.   cm.
    Bibliography: p.
    Includes index.
    ISBN 0–312–03464–4
    1. Mailer, Norman—Criticism and interpretation.   2. Mailer,
    Norman—Political and social views.   3. Radicalism in literature.
    I. Title.
    PS3525.A4152Z735   1990
    813'.54—dc20   89–4564
                                                         CIP

Contents

Acknowledgements

I would like to thank my teacher, Dr Richard Francis (Manchester University), for his persistent enthusiasm for and criticism of my work on Mailer, without which this study would not have found its true form. Dr Rob Procter (Edinburgh University), Paul Temple (Hatfield Polytechnic) and Tony Marjoram (Melbourne University) started the whole business off a long time ago. Norman Mailer's critical endorsement of the approach in my study as 'novel yet central' to his work kept me going. Professor Maria Vittoria D'Amico permitted me to devise courses based on the contents of this book in the American Literature Department at Catania University, Italy. Dr Dawn Trouard of Akron University, Ohio, was a helpful critical presence as Fulbright Lecturer at Catania University and a generous supplier of American research materials. Godfrey Kearns (Manchester University) and Professor Brian Lee (Nottingham University) confirmed my best suspicions about my work and Professor Arnold Goldman provided some perceptive reactions to drafts of portions of the research. Professor Stephen Fender (Sussex University) kindly accepted an article for the *Journal of American Studies* based on a section of the manuscript which did not fit in with the final version of the book. Dr Clive Bloom (Middlesex Polytechnic) took the book seriously at a crucial moment and helped speed the plough. Dr Judie Newman (University of Newcastle upon Tyne) gave the right bits of advice at the right time. In New York, Brendan Fearon was unstinting in his hospitality. Eileen Grimes not only typed the original manuscript but made a number of invaluable suggestions. Other names that cannot go without mention are those of Dr Dennis Cashman, Louis Kushnick, Wendy Jarvis and Dr Jim Aulich.

This book is dedicated to the memory of Emma Langley; to my family, Nora Leigh, Edward Leigh and David Leigh; and to Rosina M. Caruso-Clarke.

The author and publishers wish to thank Mr Norman Mailer and his agent, Scott Meredith Literary Agency, Inc., 845 Third Avenue, New York, NY 10022, USA, for permission to reproduce the extracts for the works of Norman Mailer.

Preface

... we continue to ignore the problem of power. After all, we had to wait until the nineteenth century before we began to understand the nature of exploitation, and to this day, we have yet to fully comprehend the nature of power. It may be that Marx and Freud cannot satisfy our desire for understanding this enigmatic thing which we call power, which is at once visible and invisible, present and hidden, ubiquitous. Theories of government and the traditional analyses of their mechanisms certainly don't exhaust the field where power is exercised and where it functions. The question of power remains a total enigma. Who exercises power? And in what sphere? We now know with reasonable certainty who exploits others, who receives the profits, which people are involved, and we know how these forces are reinvested. But as for power. ... We know that it is not in the hands of those who govern. But, of course, the idea of the 'ruling class' has never received an adequate formulation, and neither have other terms, such as 'to dominate', 'to rule', 'to govern', etc. The notions are far too fluid and require analysis. We should also investigate the limits imposed on the exercise of power – the relays through which it operates and the extent of its influence on the often insignificant aspects of the hierarchy and the forms of control, surveillance, prohibition, and constraint. Everywhere that power exists, it is being exercised.

(Michel Foucault)

Mailer's drive seems to be toward power of a religio-political kind. He is a Messiah without real hope of paradise on earth or in heaven and with no precise mission except that dictated by his own ever changing temperament.

I'm not sure finally that he should be a novelist at all, or even a writer, despite formidable gifts. ... One of the sad results of the collapse of the Judeo-Christian ethical and religious systems has been the displacement of those who are absolutist by temperament and would in earlier times have been rabbis, priests, systematic philosophers. ... Those who once would have been fulfilled in Talmudic debates ... have turned to writing novels.

(Gore Vidal)

You know we've been sitting smugly on Freud and Jung for 70 years but we don't know a damn thing about human nature.

(Norman Mailer)

I want to know how power works, how it really works, in detail.

(Norman Mailer)

A number of critics have acknowledged the importance of political ideas in Norman Mailer's novels. Alfred Kazin has labelled Mailer the 'chronicler of power in the grand realistic mode' and Christopher Lasch has insisted that Mailer 'is not only a writer, he is a political and cultural radical'. But no critic has yet pursued such observations to provide a systematic account of the relationships between Mailer's radical politics and the development of his fiction. This book examines Mailer's attempt to cultivate a political epistemology, a theme of power, in his novels, and charts in detail the progress of a radical argument that can be traced from *The Naked and the Dead*, through *Barbary Shore, The Deer Park, An American Dream* and *Why Are We in Vietnam?*, to *Ancient Evenings*.

In each of Mailer's six novels from 1948 to 1983 a restless, constantly evolving radical agenda is shown to be in operation. Chapter 1 identifies a dilemma about the nature and meaning of power in *The Naked and the Dead* in which Marxist-influenced structural values suppress a content that hints at contrary epistemologies incompatible with the novel's prescribed leftism. Chapter 2 details Mailer's deep, though temporary, absorption with various aspects of Marxist history, theory and practice and the consequences this has for the fiction of *Barbary Shore*. Chapter 3 narrates a growing dissatisfaction with ideological styles of thought in *The Deer Park* and shows how Mailer attempts to define the terms of a cultural or counterpolitical radicalism which remains, so far as this novel is concerned, obscure and unconvincing.

Chapter 4 observes in *An American Dream* a successful transition to a personal version of therapeutic radicalism which draws on mythopoeic and aesthetic rather than conventional political elements. Chapter 5 describes how in *Why Are We in Vietnam?* Mailer's radical vision strengthens its mythopoeic and aesthetic ideas in order to restore or conserve endangered values and categories of experience. The final chapter clarifies the role of ancient history and the dynamics of radical nostalgia in *Ancient Evenings*, establishing it as a mythopoeic epic with social implications.

This is not a comprehensive survey and no attempt is made to discuss the full range of Mailer's enormous literary output. For the most part, the close textual analysis which dominates much of the literary-based criticism of Mailer's fiction is avoided in favour of a perspective suggested by the history of ideas and a preoccupation with what Irving Howe describes as 'what happens to the novel when it is subjected to the pressure of politics'. Each of the novels has a separate identity from the others, a different politics and unique formal characteristics. But beneath the conceptual structurings of politics, ideology, counterpolitics, myth and literary form lies Foucault's 'enigmatic thing which we call power'. The transformation in Mailer's sensibility from 1948 to 1983, as it is available to us in his fiction, is from ideological radicalism to mythopoeic radicalism. The issues around or through which this change takes place, though, remain constant. As Mailer pointed out to me a few years ago: 'I don't suppose I've written anything that is not concerned with power – power in relationships, power in the world, impotence in the world, all those themes, and I believe you can take it effectively right through my work.'

1

The Dilemma of Power in *The Naked and the Dead*

I

The critic Stanley Gutman describes *The Naked and the Dead*[1] as 'an attempt to present a dilemma of power from a variety of perspectives'.[2] But the dilemma Gutman points to is much more extensive than his observation allows; it is not, as he suggests, a theme of the novel which is under authorial control but a conflict of political values which affects the whole balance of the book. A deep argument in Mailer's mind about the nature and meaning of power permeates all aspects of *The Naked and the Dead*, and it cannot be resolved. For this reason, the novel does not so much present as embody a dilemma of power.

The Naked and the Dead appears to be an anti-fascist novel written from an avowedly socialist perspective, and Mailer has never absolutely contradicted this view. He has consistently encouraged a simple understanding of the book as a straightforward, even conventional, war novel. His observations minimize the effort involved in its construction: 'I doubt if ever again I will have a book which is so easy to write.'[3] However, close examination of the text reveals a remarkable degree of moral, political and aesthetic confusion. As the critic Robert Solotaroff notes, *The Naked and the Dead* is a 'tangle of stale borrowings and exhilarating discoveries, obligations and assertions, shrewdnesses and gaucheries'.[4] The outstanding conflicts and tensions of the novel are not those between the main characters – General Edward Cummings, Lieutenant Robert Hearn and Sergeant Sam Croft – but those between two incompatible spheres of influence which contribute to the creation of the text. While Mailer may claim that the novel was unproblematic in its construction, the finished product presents the reader with serious problems of coherence. Much in the text prevents it from being approached in the manner that Mailer and such critics as Philip Bufithis – who sees the novel

1

as 'tightly unified' – have encouraged. The ideological thrust of certain passages is blatantly inconsistent with Mailer's asserted, though unparticularized, socialism; other passages are not even liberal in outlook; and many sections exist uncomfortably with anti-fascist declarations. As Solotaroff puts it, 'ideologically the novel has about as much jungle as Anopopei'[6] (the island on which the novel is set). The mistake Solotaroff makes, once he has correctly established that 'some strange fumes' have worked their way into Mailer's 'conventionally leftist nostrils',[7] is to label the novel's 'majority view' liberal and its 'minority view' radical.[8] Disharmony in the text derives not from a clash between liberalism and radicalism but from a conflict between the conscious literary-political interests of Mailer's leftist ideology, which effectively dominate *The Naked and the Dead*, and the repressed, though deeply felt, mythic concern with styles of vitalism and voluntaristic conceptions of self and power.

Everything known about the writing of *The Naked and the Dead* is redolent of clarity of purpose, extensive planning and rigid programme. Mailer concedes that it was pieced together 'mechanically'[9] with the aid of notes, dossiers on each character and charts indicating who required scenes with other characters. 'The structure is sturdy', Mailer says. As a new convert to a broad, ecumenical brand of socialism on the literary left, he adopts an impersonal attitude towards his material: 'I wished at the time to protect a modest condition. Many of my habits, even the character of my talent, depended on my humility.'[10] A social usefulness is aspired to through writing: 'I was a socialist after all, and I believed in large literary works which were filled with characters, and were programmatic, and had large theses, and were developed, let's say, like the Tolstoyan novel.'[11] From socialism Mailer derives a preconceived world view and a clear agenda of effects to be realized in *The Naked and the Dead*: a stress on determinism, a description of class relationships, a sense of historical process and a core anti-fascist thesis. It is a fiction from a writer whom Mailer himself later described as a 'young ideologue – his mind . . . militant with positions fixed in concrete'.[12]

Under the immediate influence of American fiction from the 1930s, *The Naked and the Dead* illustrates Mailer's desire to adapt the social and political concerns of Dos Passos, Farrell and Steinbeck to Second World War and post-war conditions: 'Before I was seventeen I had formed the desire to be a major writer. . . . I read and reread *Studs Lonigan, USA* and *The Grapes of Wrath*. Later I would add Wolfe and Hemingway and Faulkner and to a small measure Fitzgerald; but Farrell, Dos Passos and Steinbeck were the novel for me.'[13] Dos Passos' *USA* trilogy provides a technical model for an enormous collective novel, a tapestry-like social canvas capable of incorporating the whole diversity of America's pluralistic culture. It demonstrates how society can be treated as a vast social machine, its parts dismantled piece by piece in literary analysis. Through repeated study of these writers of the 1930s Mailer inherited the naturalism which became the aesthetic and philosophical foundation of *The Naked and the Dead*, referred to by the critic Jerry H. Bryant and others as the last of the thirties novels.[14] On this naturalistic principle, coupled with his emergent socialism, Mailer can show individuals, however outstanding, and classes of individuals in the context of large external forces that are, in the final analysis, unsusceptible to human agency. In strictly ideological terms this means, as Solotaroff points out, that the novel has 'a strong Marxist orientation with its generally prevailing social determinism, its emphasis on class structure, class consciousness, and historical process, and its critique of the American ruling class'.[15]

The method of composition used for *The Naked and the Dead*, Mailer's declared political preferences and the novel's literary models have a common denominator in determinism. The inflexible structure of the book formalizes determinism and establishes restrictive terms for the fictional world Mailer is able to create. The time machine, the most distinctive formal feature of the novel, illustrates this principle. Through a series of flashback vignettes, detailed profiles and histories of the characters introduce massive amounts of background material. As a whole, these sections form a collage of social observation (often written in a crude unexpanded note form) in the familiar manner of Dos Passos. Personalities are demonstrated to be inexorably the end products of social processes. Red Valsen's time machine is called 'THE WANDERING MINSTREL':

In 1931 all the voyages in the hobo jungle.
But the itinerary is various:
Freight trains out of Montana through Nebraska into Iowa.

Handouts at farmhouses for a day's work.
The harvest and working in a granary.
Manure piles.
Sleeping in parks, being picked up for vagrancy. (p. 194)

In these passages, where the tone is heavily naturalistic, there is
a dependence on a borrowed experimentalism which is designed
to make the novel larger, denser and more substantial. But, as
Solotaroff recognizes, this device 'offers no advance in exploring
the possibilities of the novel'.[16] Although it distracts the reader
from a basic shallowness in the characterization of all but the
most important figures, it is, as Bufithis says, 'noninnovational'.[17]
Accumulations of detail are merely heaped on to the basic
narrative.

The time machine is an instrument of structure whose purpose is to depict American society in terms compatible with
Mailer's leftism. The textures of the fiction itself are much
less controlled. No fundamental connection is made between
peacetime class conflict and military hierarchy, and the obvious
class conflict between officers and men is largely passed over.
The opportunity to recapitulate the fictionalized class struggle of
the previous decade is not taken up. Although Lieutenant Robert
Hearn offers a fragmented socialist critique in the novel, there is
no palpable suggestion of a socialist model of society. Rather,
socialism functions primarily as a source of technical values for
The Naked and the Dead; it is coded into the structure of the
book. Through the time machine the discrete entities of 'time'
accrete to convey an overall impression of rigid class, racial
and ethnic differentiation in the mid-twentieth-century United
States. History is a mechanism which fixes characters to their
environments, nails them down to a reality which is shown to be
static and unchanging. The sturdy structure unfolds programmati-
cally, creating enclosed spaces as it proceeds, into which Mailer
can insert 'mechanically' his researched sociological materials.
Some critics have praised the structure of *The Naked and the
Dead*. According to Barry Leeds, 'the most impressive thing
about Mailer's performance . . . is the structural effectiveness
of the novel. The control of such a massive weight of material
is not often within the ability of so young an author'.[18] But the
rigidities of this inorganic frame lend enormous support to one
side of the dilemma of power in the novel – the leftist ideological

majority view – while effectively suppressing those contradictory ideas which, although they are not part of Mailer's programme, represent some of the most exciting and personal aspects of the book. In other words, the engineered scaffolding of *The Naked and the Dead* supports an image of the novel which does not adequately represent the complicated attitudes towards politics and power contained in the text.

II

To understand why this situation prevails, it is necessary to examine the intellectual climate in which Mailer wrote his first novel. The possible emergence of a domestic fascism on the right wing of the American political scene was a genuine fear within leftist circles in the years immediately following the Second World War, during which Mailer worked on successive drafts of the manuscript finally published as *The Naked and the Dead*. As the conservative revival (1947–54) got under way, internal fascism became the compelling issue of the vestigial left. Conservatives were on the offensive everywhere in American political life, unifying rightist schisms under the banner of vigorous anti-communism. Winning the war against fascism functioned to delegitimize the left's extended period of hegemony, which was based on a broad anti-fascist appeal. When, in 1946, tensions developed between the United States and the Soviet Union, communism rapidly assumed fascism's role as the object of national political hostilities. Out of phase with this new political *Geist*, the left reacted noisily, berating the new tone in American politics, depicting US foreign policy and the State Department as inclined towards an indigenous form of fascism.

The Naked and the Dead places these issues into a fictional context only slightly dissembled by the Pacific location, generic features and historical details. Its predominant political theme is a reaction to the resurgence of conservative and rightist power as viewed by an increasingly beleaguered and institutionally feeble leftist culture. The most precise link between the post-war political scene and the fiction of *The Naked and the Dead* is Henry Wallace. Defecting from the mainstream Democratic Party under Truman, Wallace established the short-lived radical Progressive Party in

1947. The formation of this party was in large measure the result of the anxiety that a fascist takeover in American government was potentially imminent. Wallace observed a growing restriction of civil liberties in the United States and an 'increasing drift towards a disastrous and domestic fascism'.[19] Correspondingly, American foreign policy, particularly towards the Soviet Union, had become dangerously reactionary: 'Our government is violating our most fundamental principles in almost every section of the globe.'[20] Central to Wallace's political vision (which critics then and now characterize as near-paranoid) was an antagonism to the inordinate power of the military–industrial complex and anti-democratic elites within institutions. 'Wall Street and the Military have taken over',[21] announced Wallace's running mate in the 1948 presidential election. The campaign was organized around an attack on 'those who while sharing in the privileges of our imperfectly democratic society seek to undermine its fabric',[22] and it included a specific measure to 'end the dominance of the military in American foreign policy, thus invoking the wise policy of Clemenceau who said war is too important to be left up to the generals'.[23]

Mailer not only supported Wallace, as did a great many American writers; he became an active party worker in the 1948 campaign, shortly after completing *The Naked and the Dead*. In the opinion of his biographer Hilary Mills, Mailer 'vehemently supported'[24] Wallace; and Norman Podhoretz recalls seeing Mailer for the first time as a campaigner, 'a slight, thin, nervous figure speaking bumblingly for Wallace'.[25] When many of the campaign staff withdrew as a result of hysteria over putative communist control over Wallace's platform, Mailer remained as a party worker. A press release issued after the publication of *The Naked and the Dead* underlines the function of this type of political commitment: 'At this particular period I don't think a writer can avoid being political to a great degree. There's been a regrettable tendency in the last decade in America to be unpolitical as writers, and I think it's partially accountable for the poverty of American letters in this period.'[26] Wallace provided a vehicle for Mailer's urge to practise politics as a writer. It is not simply that Wallace's anti-Cold War stance dovetailed with Mailer's desire for rapprochement with communism, as was the case with most of Wallace's literary supporters. *The Naked and the Dead* demonstrates that, at least two years before the 1948 campaign, Mailer took seriously the

Wallacite prediction that America was in danger of becoming fascist.[27]

The first draft of *The Naked and the Dead* was a straightforward narrative about the experiences of a reconnaissance patrol, and its theme was a natural outgrowth of Mailer's experience in the Pacific theatre of the war. Only in later revisions of the manuscript, written during 1946 and 1947, did the anti-fascist thesis for which the novel is famous emerge and become foregrounded. The introduction of two new characters, General Cummings and Sergeant Croft, mark the incorporation into *The Naked and the Dead* of a set of influences and political situations which obtained only after the war had ended. They reflect Mailer's contemporary political concerns, not a historical preoccupation with the war itself. In recasting the book, Mailer updated it, with Cummings and Croft dramatizing in fiction the dark Wallacite fear that the Second World War had incubated and anticipated a period of totalitarianism in American history. Mailer, like Wallace, adopts a prophetic stance in response to the recession of leftist influence, divining a 'reactionary's century' (p. 74) just around the corner. No attempt is made to write about the international nature of the war: there are few allusions to Japan (the single Japanese character, Wakara, is given only a few pages); Germany and Italy are merely mentioned in passing. Instead, Mailer invests the material with the crises of the post-war United States to the extent that it becomes, in the words of Cummings' time machine, 'a peculiarly American statement' (p. 344), primarily concerned with the enemy located within and not outside the United States. Thus the anti-fascism of the novel is an early example of what Allen Ginsberg has labelled Mailer's 'paranoid sociology',[28] exposing a conspiracy of right-wing values thriving in a major US institution which threatens to contaminate the rest of public life.

Lieutenant Hearn, the nearest thing in the novel to a witness or narrator, realizes almost immediately that General Cummings is fascistic: 'a tyrant with a velvet voice, it is true, but undeniably a tyrant' (p. 69). Superficially he is respectable, with the 'ruddy, complacent and hard appearance of any number of American senators and businessmen' (p. 71), but closer examination reveals a 'certain vacancy in the face'. Hearn feels as if the General's 'smiling face were numb'. Mailer uses physical appearance to establish class credentials, but then subverts the image of

Cummings as an ordinary class agent representative of a certain order of American society: 'There was the appearance and yet it was not there.' Beneath the social masks Hearn detects something which is much less explicit, 'the unique urge that drove him' (p. 72). Throughout the novel there is a reluctance to use the word 'fascist'. This may be a sign of Mailer's political wisdom, since, as Michel Foucault has pointed out, the term is often used only as a 'floating signifier, whose function is essentially that of denunciation'.[29] The procedures of every form of power are suspected of being fascist. However, as Stanley Gutman points out, Cummings himself may resist the term because he is 'too shrewd to commit himself to a specific ideology'.[30] Either way, the routes of analysis are kept open by Mailer's preference for the ambiguous label 'reactionary' (p. 74). The relationship the General strikes up with Hearn is based on the conviction that the Lieutenant is also reactionary: ' "You've got a great future as a reactionary, " the General said.' Cummings welcomes the notion of a right-wing state run along militaristic lines. The island of Anopopei is his dictatorship; on it 'he controlled everything' (p. 75). His leadership is authoritarian, aimed at dominating all within its sphere: 'he was thinking of nothing at all but the campaign and the night ahead. It made the General another man, definitely the nerve end with no other desire than to find something to act upon' (p. 94). His frame of reference is radically and reductively behaviouristic. In a spirit of pure calculation, relationships are reckoned as actions and their reactions.

The General's world view is wholly antithetical to the American system of government and the democratic liberal ideology that underpins it:

> We have the highest standard of living in the world, as one would expect, the worst individual fighting soldiers of any power. Or at least in their natural state they are. They're comparatively wealthy. They're spoiled, and as Americans they share most of them the peculiar manifestation of our democracy. They have an exaggerated idea of the rights due to themselves as individuals, and no idea at all of the rights due to others. . . . (p. 151)

To Cummings' mind, the American model of open society is decadent; the individual freedoms it rests upon are excessive, dysfunctional and harmful to the idea of system. Americans 'in their natural state' are anathema to him. Cummings favours a more conditioned American, acknowledged not as a moral agent (free) but reductively as a central nervous system, an ergonomic and biological unit: 'I don't care what kind of man you give me, if I have him long enough I'll make him afraid.' By temperament he is a social engineer, and, operating with a conception of human behaviour as plastic, he holds out the ideal of modifying individuals through environmental factors to achieve major societal change. The army is his social laboratory: 'To make an army work, you have to have every man fitted into a fear ladder. . . . The army functions best when you're frightened of the man above you, and contemptuous of your subordinates.' There is no moral aspect to this experiment; cultural transformation is treated only as a series of related technical problems. Thus, for Cummings, the Second World War is not interpreted in terms of relative ideological positions (fascism, democracy) but as 'power concentration' (p. 152). It is part of a movement towards the desirable goal of increased consolidation of political power: 'The machine techniques of the century demand consolidation, and with that you've got to have fear because the majority of men must be made subservient to the machine, and it's not a business they instinctively enjoy.'

The route to an American society based on consolidation is through social engineering and the social–biological redefinition of the subject. In Cummings' vision this means relocating human value in the soft machinery of the central nervous system and removing it from abstract, subjective mental states (faiths, moralities, aesthetics). His critique is therefore against the politicized mental state of freedom:

> In the army the idea of personality is just a hindrance. Sure, there are differences among men in any particular army unit, but they invariably cancel each other out, and what you're left with is a value rating. Such and such a company is good or poor, effective or ineffective for such and such a mission. I work with grosser techniques, common denominator techniques. (p. 156)

Stripped of local differentiations, personality is a more or less organized habit system which happens to stabilize or dominate behaviour. Behaviour itself is not fixed, natural or organically

definitive but endlessly susceptible to modification by 'grosser
techniques'. The preferred type of individual can be manufac-
tured to meet the particular requirements of a social system.
In this capacity, Cummings is demiurgic; he arrogates ultimate
powers to himself in order to design a culture:

> 'You know if there is a god, Robert, he's just like me.'
> 'Uses common denominator techniques.'
> 'Exactly.' (p. 157)

Thus, for Cummings, with godlike distance from his behaviouristic social experiment, chess is an 'inexhaustible . . . concentration of life' (p. 155), while for Hearn, the left-liberal secular
humanist, 'there's nothing remotely like it in life'.

Mailer's emphasis is prophetic. The threat Cummings represents
(implicit in his name) lies in the future under post-war conditions.
The failure of European models of dystopian militarized cultures
does not deter the General. Europe was simply too small for real
development. America, by contrast, offers the greatest opportunity for success, a vast *Lebensraum* and a plenitude of material
resources. As a vision, this is a perverse variation of the classic
American dream of unchecked possibility, legitimized not by the
customary democratic ideology but by right-wing militarism. It's
a dream of unlimited rationalism, control and rigid distributions
of power:

> 'There are countries which have latent powers, latent resources,
> they are full of potential energy, so to speak. And there are
> great concepts which can unlock that, express it. As kinetic
> energy, a country is organization, coordinated effort, your
> epithet fascism.' He moved his chair slightly. 'Historically
> the purpose of the war is to translate America's potential
> into kinetic energy. The concept of fascism, far sounder
> than communism if you consider it, for it's grounded firmly in
> men's actual natures, merely started in the wrong country, in a
> country which did not have enough intrinsic power to develop
> completely. In Germany with that basic frustration of physical
> means there were bound to be excesses. But the dreams, the
> concept was sound enough. . . . Our vacuum as a nation is

filled with released power, and I can tell you that we're out of the backwaters of history now. (pp. 275–6)

This prediction is written from the vantage point of 1946–7, and, although readers of the first edition of *The Naked and the Dead* were not in a position to assess its accuracy, they were certainly able to appreciate the foundations on which it was based. In accordance with this, Cummings goes on to complete the Wallacite scenario:

Your men of power in America, I can tell you, are becoming conscious of their real aims for the first time in our history. Watch. After the war our foreign policy is going to be far more naked, far less hypocritical than it has ever been. We're no longer going to cover our eyes with our left hand while our right is extending an imperialist paw. (p. 276)

Certain critics, Robert Solotaroff included, find the General's politics problematic:

But what are we to make of the spectre of power-mad generals who are about to take over the United States? It's hard to know just how powerful 'fascism' was twenty-five years ago precisely because it was already taking more subtle forms than the plotting of a coup d'état of the generals through force or election. The warning against Cummings is another unsuccessful borrowing, in this case the appropriation of popular front appeals from the late thirties.[31]

As I have tried to show, Mailer's treatment of Cummings and the dynamic of his politics are nowhere near as redundant as this view suggests. Rather than a stale borrowing (like, say, the time machine) Cummings is actually one of the more relevant aspects of *The Naked and the Dead's* left liberalism, entirely continuous with the central concerns of American radicalism in the period. This is made even clearer in one of Mailer's first ever interviews: 'The chances are there's not a single general in the U. S. army who's like him. But there could be. He articulates a kind of unconscious bent in the thinking of the army brass and top rank politicians. He's an archetype of the new man, the coming man, the one who's really dangerous.'[32]

Cummings' political perspective is supported by an essentially behaviouristic social psychology, and he is particularly absorbed by ideas about conditioning. Classical conditioning, the system of involuntary stimulus-response bonds associated with I .P. Pavlov, is articulated in the 'fear ladder' doctrine. (Pavlov's famous experiment is described in *The Naked and the Dead*, p. 20). But Cummings also theorizes using the more sophisticated concept of operant conditioning in which behaviour is controlled through much subtler, less coercive forms of manipulation. Mailer's familiarity with both these concepts and his use of them in the creation of a right-wing personality almost certainly derives from B. F. Skinner's pioneering *Behaviour of Organisms*.[33] Skinner's own goal as a psychologist has been to arrive at an understanding of the prediction and control of human behaviour without resorting to speculations about unverifiable mental states. His basic theory, stated in *The Behaviour of Organisms*, is that behaviour is an elastic phenomenon: desirable behaviour patterns can be 'reinforced'; undesirable behaviour can be punished. Skinner taught at Harvard during Mailer's time as an undergraduate, and his own novel *Walden Two*,[34] published in the same year as *The Naked and the Dead*, depicts an entire society controlled by operant conditioning techniques, taking Mailer's idea of the army as a 'preview of the future' (p. 277) a stage further.

Mailer's use of behaviourism, which began to dominate American schools of psychology after the Second World War, gives a convincing modern accent to the archetype of the immoral, mad scientist, the sinister controller with tidy rationalist solutions to human problems. It allows Mailer to refurbish the myth for post-war political conditions. Thomas Pynchon does something very similar in his much later novel *Gravity's Rainbow*. Pynchon deals at great length and in formidable detail with Pavlovian theory and practice in wartime Europe, and like Mailer he is highly critical of what he perceives as the sterile anti-introspective manipulations of the behaviouristic enterprise. Pynchon's Cummings-figure, Edward Pointsman, 'the graying Pavlovian', is opposed by Roger Mexico:

> Like his master I. P. Pavlov before him, he [Pointsman] imagines the cortex of the brain as a mosaic of tiny on/off elements. Some are always in bright excitation, others darkly inhibited. The contours, bright and dark, keep changing. But each point is allowed

only the two states: waking or sleep. One or zero. 'Summation', 'transition', 'irradiation', 'concentration', 'reciprocal induction' – all Pavlovian brain mechanics – assumes the presence of these bi-stable point. But to Mexico belongs the domain between zero and one – the middle Pointsman has excluded from his persuasion – the probabilities.[35]

The relationship between Pointsman and Mexico recalls that between Cummings and Hearn. Mexico's unfocused rebellion against Pointsman's 'system' is shown to be finally ineffective; he is a 'failed counterforce'.[36] In *The Naked and the Dead* the anti-fascist struggle embodied by Robert Hearn is a resistance to scientific control mechanisms, the alteration of states of mind and feeling on a societal scale. Skinner and Wallace are combined usefully by Mailer to create the imaginative substance of an indigenous fascism which exists only in left-liberal anxieties. Both contribute to the portrait of the emerging reactionary personality. Wallacite perceptions about the political realities of foreign policy and civil liberties are blended with the conceptual hardware of behaviourism to produce a political psychology appropriate to dramatizing an 'unconscious bent'.

The failed counterforce of *The Naked and the Dead* is Hearn, who not only represents a broad inclination towards Marxist values but also carries much of Mailer's personality. As Solotaroff notes, he is the character 'whose thought most resembles that of the author at the time of writing'.[37] The first indication of an invitation to see Hearn as a Mailer surrogate lies in the Lieutenant's education, which corresponds with what is known about Mailer's university training.[38] But closer examination shows that Mailer is connected to this character at a deeper level. This is coded in the text through Hearn's peculiar role as a Jew. Since Mailer has never affiliated himself to Jewish-American culture in the manner of Bellow, Malamud or Roth, it is not surprising that he should associate himself with a non-Jewish figure in his fiction. In fact in this respect Leslie Fiedler has labelled Mailer an 'anti-Jew'.[39] The striking feature of *The Naked and the Dead* is that the WASP with whom Mailer identifies is given a quasi or crypto-Jewish status.

Despite Hearn's occasional anti-semitic comments, his physical appearance and its effect on others belong to the cultural stereotype of Jewish alienation. He is socially uncomfortable and distrusted by those around him:

Hearn had done little to make friends. He was a big man
with a shock of black hair, a heavy immobile face. His brown
eyes, imperturbable, stared out coldly above the short blunted
and slightly hooked arc of his nose. His wide thin mouth was
unexpressive, a top ledge to the solid mass of chin, and his voice
was sharp with a thin contemptuous quality, rather surprising in
so big a man. He would have denied it at times but he liked very
few people, and most men sensed it uneasily after talking to him
for a few minutes. He was above all the kind of man other men
love to see humiliated. (p. 61)

The hair, nose, voice and capacity for subjection – the particular
mixture of physical and psychological attributes – draws upon
the cultural mythology of Jewish rather than WASP experience.
This is compounded by Hearn's self-perception of being somehow
Jewish. Shortly after being rejected by the leader of the radical
John Reed Club for being a 'bourgeois intellectual' (p. 209), he
notices his reflection in a shop window: 'He stares at himself
for a moment, regarding his dark hair and hooked blunted nose.
I look more like a Jew-boy than a midwestern scion. Now if I'd
had blond hair, Al really would have searched himself' (p. 294).
Perceived as Jewish by the larger culture, he internalizes a
correlating sense of ethnic alienation.[40] The decision to present
Hearn in such obscure terms is curious, since Jewishness is by
no means integral to the themes of *The Naked and the Dead* and has
no force in the novel's relationships. It does, however, serve to
draw Hearn closer to Mailer's own background, and it is crucial
therefore that Hearn is only a pseudo-Jew. The lack of obligation
to *bona fide* Jewish materials can be seen in the distance Mailer
keeps from the legitimate Jews of the novel. Roth and Goldstein
bear no resemblance to the author and are handled with limited
sympathy. Their Jewishness has the same value as Gallagher's
Irishness, Martínez's Mexicanness or Czienwicz's Polishness: it
refers us to a narrowing, marginalizing cultural experience of ethnicity without transcendance. Roth and Goldstein are hyphenated
Americans who exist too much on the wrong side of the hyphen
to enlist Mailer's own identification. They remain trapped in the
perceptual prison of ethnicity. What Mailer requires here is a
species of vestigial Jewishness in a major character to match
his own complex position.

Mailer's proximity to Hearn performs a vital function. It assists

in the creation of a morally and emotionally sympathetic character who is able to counteract the personal and political excesses
of the other two major characters in the novel. Hearn witnesses,
interprets and opposes the reactionaries on Mailer's behalf. In
addition, he solves the technical problem of linking the novel's
two present-tense spheres: Command Headquarters (Cummings'
world) and the military frontier (Croft's world). As Barry Leeds
points out, Hearn 'is the crucial structural device. . . . It is
significant that during the first half of the novel he spends
most of his time in the reader's view, talking to the General'.[41] In
the unfolding narrative Hearn cements the disparate elements of
the book together and remains the only character rendered with
both realistic authority and psychological depth.[42] He provides
the nearest thing in the text to a constant point of view. The
minor characters have a sociological reality but, despite the use
of stream-of-consciousness, no interior complexity. Cummings
and Croft, while they are complex imaginative creations, derive
from a remoter region of Mailer's mind. Hearn occupies a middle
position, part of the novel's naturalism and realism, yet a reliable
guide to the farther reaches of right-wing theory and practice. His
world view provides a positive point of resistance to the fascism of
Cummings and Croft and to power in a much more generalized
sense. As Solotaroff points out, he is 'the most formidable
single human enemy'[43] that either the General or the Sergeant
encounters. Through Hearn, Mailer can advance the argument
that power is fundamentally structuralistic and expressive of
domination, coercion and manipulation. In a continuing debate
with Cummings which, as Jean Radford observes 'constitutes
one of the most thoroughgoing and sophisticated discussions of
political issues to be found in any war novel',[44] Hearn cleaves to
the belief that the essential nature of power is repressive and that
enlightenment is emancipation from power relations. To achieve
freedom, the repression of power must first be overcome. Thus
the army, which is *ipso facto* a coercive systemic power, is a model
of society that is anathema to Hearn's moral-political code.

As an officer Hearn recognizes his own participation in this
system, and he wages his own personal subversive campaign
against it:

There was a kind of guilt in being an officer . . . but it was
a convenient thing to forget and there were good textbook

reasons, good enough to convince yourself if you wanted to be quit of it. Only a few of them still kicked the idea of guilt around in their heads. . . . An officer had some excuse only if he were in combat, as long as he remained here he would be dissatisfied with himself, contemptuous of the other officers, even more contemptuous than was normal for him. (p. 67)

Hearn is first encountered performing a minor act of rebellion, behaving insolently towards a ranking officer (Major Conn) who holds right-wing views on Jews, negroes, trade unionists and women (p. 64). This strikes Hearn's persistent political note: a desire to submerge his left-liberal views to as few imperatives of hierarchy as possible. The lesson Cummings tries to inculcate in him is twofold: that the left-liberal perspective is 'clap-trap' (p. 72), and that Hearn does not believe in it. Purveying fascist self-knowledge, Cummings threatens to deradicalize Hearn's mind: 'The General's point was clear enough. He was an officer, and in functioning as an officer for long enough time he would assume, whether he wanted to or not, the emotional prejudices of his class. The General was reminding him that he belonged to that class' (p. 145). As Hearn correctly observes, this is a 'Marxist lesson with a reverse twist'. The Lieutenant, who struggles to maintain his 'isolated position on the left' (p. 146), proves a rebellious student of Cummings. To erode Hearn's recalcitrance, Cummings evolves a critique on the weakness of the Marxist theory of power: 'The root of all the . . . ineffectiveness comes right sprang out of the desperate suspension in which they have to hold their minds' (p. 150). Marxism is pervaded by intellectual flaws: 'If you ever followed anything through to the end, not one of your ideas would last an instant.' For Cummings, left-wing thought confuses the 'is' with the 'ought'; idealism displaces analysis and reinstates sentiment. 'I probably have the normal allotment of decent impulses' is Hearn's feeble riposte. It becomes increasingly impossible to maintain any ideological position consistent with a negative view of power while producing an adequate response to the ruthlessness and vigour of fascist power. Nevertheless, Hearn's representation of left liberalism is stubbornly carried through. (Hearn is not, as a consensus of critics seems to believe, a straightforward liberal.[45]) The will not to succumb remains the one thing that cannot be analysed away. Reluctantly he concedes that America 'might easily go fascist' (p. 274) after the war.

Although Hearn produces the simulacrum of an alternative position, he seems constantly vulnerable to Cummings'
personality. His time machine implies that he is a political
dilettante who has merely 'played around' (p. 152) with Marxism.
As Solotaroff puts it, he has 'flirted with such left wing causes
as communism and the non-communist labor movement but
retreated from each'.[46] Confronted with a deficiency in his
theoretical knowledge, he is, as Jean Radford notes, 'thrown
back into self-denigration and theoretical impotence',[47] and his
arguments modulate into facetiousness. Hearn's vagueness and
lack of confidence in his ideas leave him without protection
against Cummings' militant theorizing and its corollary, the power
at his personal command. This results in Hearn's collapse into a
behaviouristic interpretation of his relationship with the General
which connects with the Pavlovian imagery of the text:

> He had been the pet, the dog the master, coddled and curried,
> thrown sweetmeats until he had the presumption to bite the
> master once. And since then he had been tormented with the
> particular absorbed sadism that most men could generate only
> toward an animal. He was a diversion for the General, and he
> resented it deeply with a cold speechless anger that came to
> some extent from the knowledge that he had acquiesced in the
> dog role, and even had the dog's dreams, carefully submerged,
> of someday equalling the master. And Cummings had probably
> understood even that, had been amused. (p. 269)

At this moment the relationship between Hearn and Cummings
alters crucially. Hearn ceases to represent the left-liberal argument
against fascism and illustrates the need for a more humane politics
of the left under the threat presented by systems based on naked
structuralistic power. His absorption with the perversely coded
relationship with the General promotes only impulsive anomic
acts, such as the dropping of the remains of a cigarette on the floor
of Cummings' tent (pp. 269–70). Hearn aims only for a symbolic
effect continuous with his anti-power argument. Opposition is
registered but a measure of innocence is retained. What Hearn
misjudges is the degree to which the symbol might accumulate
meaning in an imagination keyed to the minutest nuances and
calibrations of power. Cummings' zealous overinterpretation
makes bizarre connections between Hearn, the cigarette, the

troops in his command and the Japanese enemy. The cigarette comes to threaten the army as a preview of the future, the bureaucratic pattern of the totalitarian dream: 'Hearn was an embodiment of the one mistake, the one indulgence he had ever permitted himself, and it had been intolerable to be with him since then' (p. 273). Material punishments and extravagant long-term repercussions result from Hearn's small gesture, and his immediate abasement brings him to an uncompromising truth that will not be argued away:

> The Right was ready for a struggle, but without anxiety this time, with no absorbed and stricken ear listening to the inevitable footsteps of history. . . . History was in the grasp of the Right, and after the war their political campaigns would become intense. One big push, one big offensive, and history was theirs for this century, perhaps the next one. The League of Omnipotent Men. (p. 334)

Cummings' decision to place Hearn in Sergeant Croft's reconnaissance platoon thrusts him into the novel's other sphere. This small male community is under the complete control of the Sergeant, who commands the fear of each of his men. Hearn's presence in the platoon disturbs its natural order and Croft resents the intrusion: 'Hearn was his foe' (p. 371). But the resentment of the unwelcome superior officer is ameliorated by a sense of military structure: he cannot 'acknowledge his own animosity, for he had been grounded in the army too long. To resent an order, to be unwilling to carry it out, was immoral' (p. 372). Articulating the apportionments of systemic authority, Croft is completely adapted to the culture of control; and as a militarist he recognizes Hearn's lack of adjustment to the hierarchy. The Lieutenant's reasoning, self-explaining style of leadership (based on mentalism, not behaviourism) is anathema to him: 'a platoon leader didn't buddy' (p. 368). Hearn is thus considered 'womanish and impractical'. The platoon, attuned to an authoritarian style, is confused by an officer who is a 'nice guy' (p. 384). In Croft, Hearn encounters a second fascist or reactionary: 'For an instant he felt as if he had peered into Croft, looked down into an abyss. He turned away, gazed at his hands. You couldn't trust Croft. Somehow there was reassurance in stating it so banally' (p. 421). Like Cummings, he is a power moralist, which to the left liberal is 'the wrong kind of command, a frightening command' (p. 425).

In Croft's sub-world Hearn struggles to maintain his damaged values, but under extreme conditions and after exposure to Cummings he registers his own capacity for depravity: 'When he searched himself he was just another Croft.' Yet there remains a seed of optimism, since 'the world, by all the logics, should have turned Fascist and it hadn't yet' (p. 493). In fact he is pushed beyond passive resistance to a reluctant embrace of power, of 'power over', an advocacy of repression, albeit in the service of overcoming a more pernicious repression:

> If the world turned Fascist, if Cummings had his century, there was a little thing he could do. There was always terrorism. But a neat terrorism with nothing sloppy about it, no machine guns, no grenades, no bombs, nothing messy, no indiscriminate killing. Merely the knife and the garotte, a few trained men and a list of fifty bastards to be knocked off, and then another fifty. (p. 494)

The Lieutenant's lingering liberal inclination is still towards non-intervention: 'Rely on the blunder factor. Sit back and wait for the Fascists to louse it up.' His more radicalized, proto-Marxist self sees the need for action: 'For whatever reason you had to keep resisting.' What this amounts to is a temporary *de facto* acceptance of the methods of the enemy (terrorism based on a power morality of sorts) in order to achieve an enlightened social goal.

However, nothing practical results from Hearn's formulations. His unceremonious removal from the novel in a single sentence ('A half hour later, Lieutenant Hearn was killed by a machine gun bullet which passed through his chest' – p. 506) abruptly terminates the left-liberal inquiry into power. Critics such as Solotaroff, who make the mistake of seeing Hearn as a simple liberal, cannot cope with the Lieutenant's final developments. His terrorist campaign is seen as 'at odds with what the novel seems to be saying about the weakness of liberalism'.[48] Thus Solotaroff is forced to conclude that 'Hearn is no longer a liberal by the time he is killed.'[49] Jennifer Bailey ignores Hearn's terrorism to conclude that Mailer is 'confirming the ineffectiveness of liberal ideology when Hearn is suddenly killed'.[50] But Hearn must be understood by reference to the discourse on power shared by liberalism and Marxism which emphasizes repression. Michel Foucault highlights this when he refers to certain points in common between the 'liberal conception of political power . . . and the Marxist conception'.[51] The link between the ideologies is that

> Power is essentially that which represses. Power represses nature, the instincts, a class, individuals. Though one finds this definition endlessly repeated in present day discourse, it is not that discourse which invented it – Hegel first spoke of it, then Freud and later Reich. In any case it has become almost automatic in the parlance of the times to define power as the organ of repression.[52]

This, of course, is Hearn's central argument in *The Naked and the Dead*, and, above all, he is Mailer's sympathetic representative of the 'parlance of the times'. Therefore the political implications of his death are overwhelmingly pessimistic. The character closest to Mailer's own personality, the person Gutman calls the 'potential hero'[53] of the novel, and the reader's guide has been removed as a result of the conspiracy of values between Cummings and Croft. The most enlightened position in the novel has been shown to be insubstantial. The dramatic manner of Hearn's death underscores the immediacy and potency of the potential domestic right-wing threat as perceived by Mailer, Wallace and the American left. It is a death that takes away *The Naked and the Dead's* most consistent point of view and the anti-power argument, signifying a backward step into barbaric social relations and the military nightmare of a 'renaissance of real power' (p. 75).

III

The fundamental disagreement in Mailer's mind about the nature, meaning and value of power is indicated by the presence in *The Naked and the Dead* of a number of tentative, repressed and unstructured ideas which contradict the novel's sturdy frame, anti-fascist thesis and left-liberal perspective – its 'majority view', to use Solotaroff's phrase. These contradictory influences hint at epistemologies not officially on offer in the novel, but added together they constitute a 'minority view' or, in Foucault's highly suggestive term, a 'subjugated knowledge', a content that has been 'buried and disguised in a functional coherence or formal systemisation'.[54] When Mailer breaks away from the planning, the formal logic of the book, he creates what Foucault calls an 'insurrection of subjugated knowledge', which introduces different kinds of access to the characters and their situation. The most important feature of Mailer's subjugated knowledge is that it is not wholly negative on the subject of power.

In taking a more positive view of power the novel departs from its socialist inspired realism and ideologically informed naturalism and moves towards a purer, more extreme species of naturalism. As Harold Kaplan points out, the major theme of naturalistic culture is the 'rivalry between mechanist and vitalist power and the need to see vitalist power and its symbols as the only alternative to the role of merely physical energy'.[55] Merely physical energy in *The Naked and the Dead* is represented not only by the environment but also by the behaviouristic theories of physical energy which underpin Cummings' reactionary views and prophecies. An extreme naturalistic pro-power interpretation of Hearn's death, hinted at in the text, implies that the Lieutenant is actually destroyed by physical energy – what Richard Poirier calls 'the conglomerates that fill space and determine the apportionments of time'[56] – rather than the General's influence. On this view, Cummings and Croft are only associated with Hearn's death, not contributing factors. The death has nothing to do with ideology. A distinction must be made between the logic of the thesis and that of the subjugated knowledge, between Cummings and Croft as structural vectors of military power (in which they are certainly fascistic) and as vital forces separate from the mechanics of either Mailer's literary structurings or those of the military hierarchy. Seen as the only source of vitalist power in a naturalistic world, they are not without an heroic dimension. As Norman Podhoretz observes, Cummings and Croft 'are the only characters who point to anything like an adequate response to life as we see it in the novel'.[57]

Cummings and Croft possess a charisma absent from all the other characters. However, Mailer is severely limited in how far this quality can be explored thematically, since the novel's overall programme precludes any endorsement of the right-wing values he is attacking. Thus his responsiveness to these characters is subject to complex checks and balances. Although the reader may suspect that Mailer is on a 'mystic kick',[58] it remains dissembled and unclear. What can be gathered from Mailer's restricted approaches to the mystical theme of charismatic power is a dimly apprehended politics quite at odds with the novel's *de jure* left liberalism, and an interest not with structure but with agency (the power exercised by individuals as individuals) does emerge. For this reason, *The Naked and the Dead*'s conflict with itself embodies a current debate within the social sciences between those who perceive power as exercised by agents and those who see it as the result of structural factors. In other words, *The Naked and the Dead* is poised between voluntaristic and structuralistic conceptions of the world.[59]

A number of charismatic qualities to which Mailer is attracted are not concealed from view. The General is the first of a series of important teacher or master figures in Mailer's fiction. Hearn recognizes that he is not a 'blustering profane general of the conventional variety' (p. 278) but a more exotic phenomenon: 'he had never known anyone quite like the General, and he was partially convinced the General was a great man' (pp. 67-8). Correspondingly, Hearn is the first of a series of tyro figures in Mailer's fiction: 'the General was looking for an intellectual equal . . . to whom he could expound his non-military theories, and Hearn was the only man on his staff who had the intellect to understand him' (p. 69). A reciprocal pleasure is evident in the transmission of knowledge from master to pupil, and the educative experience is intense: 'In the two weeks since they had landed he had been in the General's tent talking with him almost every night.' At a deep level Hearn is enthralled by Cummings' personality: 'Against his self-interests, his prejudices, the General held on to him and, even more, exerted himself in unfolding the undeniable fascination of his personality.' Taken as a whole, Cummings' non-military theories and historical observations go beyond Mailer's plans to categorize him with the reactionary ideologies of fascism and behaviourism. In fact it is this basic originality, the fact that Cummings cannot be reduced to a particular system, which so impresses Hearn. The Lieutenant is obliged to struggle to comprehend Cummings, and only after he is removed to work under a more bureaucratic officer does he appreciate the charismatic nature of the General's authority: 'Without the disturbing and fascinating intimacy the General had granted him in his first weeks as an aide, the job had become reduced quickly to its onerous humiliating routine' (p. 257). From Cummings' perspective, Hearn's eventual death

represents the loss of an apprentice; it marks his incomplete rite
of passage, his failure to liberate himself from stale conventions
and break through into the reality of power to which the General's
shamanistic teachings were guiding him. What Hearn should have
achieved through this relationship is what the writer on primitive
religions Mircea Eliade calls a 'ritual death':

> the neophyte, when he dies to his infantile, profane and
> unregenerate life to be re-born into a new, sanctified existence
> is also re-born to a mode of being which makes knowledge,
> consciousness and *wisdom* possible. The initiate is not only
> new-born; he is a man who is *informed*, who knows the
> mysteries, who has had revelations of a metaphysical order.[60]

In the initiatory context there is always a symbolism of death and
new birth. But the act of dying is above all 'a recommencement,
never an end. In no rite or myth do we find the initiatory death
as something *final*, but always as the condition *sine qua non* of
a transition to another mode of being, a trial indispensable to
regeneration; that is to the beginning of a new life'.[61] Cummings,
the master of initiation, overestimates Hearn's 'aptitude for power'
(p. 274), and the neophyte fails to return from the mystical journey
(the reconnaissance platoon) on which he has been sent. Unable
to become *informed*, he experiences a literal rather than a symbolic
or ritual death.

In these subjugated mystical and mythical areas Mailer exhibits
considerable sympathy for Cummings' extraordinary consciousness, charismatic perception of reality and lack of affinity with
the profane rationalism of military organization:

> The war, or rather *war*, was odd, he told himself a little inanely.
> But he knew what it meant. It was all covered with tedium and
> routine, regulations and procedure, and yet there was a naked
> quivering heart to it which involved you deeply when you were
> thrust into it. All the deep dark urges of man, the sacrifices
> on the hilltop, and the churning lusts of the night and sleep,
> weren't all of them contained in the shattering screaming burst
> of a shell, the man made thunder and light? He . . . was prepared
> to grasp the knowledge behind all this. He dwelt pleasurably in
> many-webbed layers of complexity . . . at this moment he felt

> he was living on many levels at once. . . . He felt such power
> that it was beyond job; he was calm and sober. (pp. 477–8)

It is the reality beneath routine, beneath ideology, that intrigues
Mailer. As a soldier in the First World War Cummings discovers
'that his mind must work on many levels' (p. 351) and becomes
oriented towards a reality 'which his mind must unravel'. Hearn
is attracted specifically to this mystic quality: 'If it were not for
the General he would have asked for a transfer long before the
division had come to Anopopei. . . . It was the riddle of what
made the General tick that kept Hearn on' (p. 69). At the bottom
of his extraordinariness is a belief in the pre-eminence of power:
'Man's deepest urge is omnipotence' (p. 277). All other things are
a distraction from this impulse to achieve godliness: 'When we
come kicking into the world we *are* God, the universe is the limit
of our senses. And when we get older, when we discover that
the universe is not us, it's the deepest trauma of our existence.'
Acts of power are thus the self's attempt to recover crucial lost
experiences; they reconstitute a sense of the divine, of the sacred
which, according to Eliade, 'manifests itself equally as a force or
as a power'.[62]

Cummings' practice is even more impressive than his theory
or his extraordinary consciousness. Hearn observes an 'almost
unique ability to extend thought into immediate and effective
action' (p. 68). He is an ultimate *agent*, who appears to communicate with the forces that run things. Hearn

> couldn't escape the peculiar magnetism of the General, a
> magnetism derived from all the connotations of the General's
> power. He had known men who thought like the General. He
> had even known one or two who were far more profound. But
> the difference was that they did nothing or the results of their
> actions were lost to them, and they functioned in the busy
> complex mangle, the choked vacuum of American life.   (p. 75)

'Fascination', 'admiration' and 'intrigue' are terms used repeatedly
by the narrator to describe the General. What elicits this awe is
the pragmatic nature of his personal power, its refusal to remain
an intellectual force. To use Richard Poirier's phrase, Cummings
is a 'performing self'.[63] His ideas are designed to have personal
repercussions and consequences in the world. When they do not

achieve this, he suffers the agonies of the withdrawal of personal power. The failure of the military campaign is experienced as a physical malady: 'The power, the intensity of the urges within himself, inexpressible, balked, seemed to course through his limbs, beating in senseless fury against the confines of his body. There was everything he wanted to control, and he could not direct even six thousand men. Even a single man had been able to balk him' (p. 258).

Sergeant Croft creates a second major insurrection of sub-jugated knowledge. Croft's status as a reactionary in *The Naked and the Dead* is not nearly as well established in the text as Cummings', since it relies heavily on his association with Cummings' position (though they never actually meet). As Norman Podhoretz notes, 'The platoon Sergeant and the General have so much in common that they seem to be the same person in two different incarnations.'[64] In Jennifer Bailey's view they are identical in the 'unscrupulousness with which they attempt to eliminate any obstacle to their naked ambition'.[65] Although the conspiracy of values they articulate is explicitly stated only by Cummings, the Sergeant's gnomic policy statements (his ideology is not elaborated) are continuous with Cummings' social model. In Solotaroff's critical perspective, the Sergeant is an *'extension who completes Cummings' experience in somewhat the same way that Kurz completes Marlow's journey into the Heart of Darkness'*.[66] The structural left-liberal thesis of *The Naked and the Dead* suggests that the connection between Cummings and Croft is the classic political relationship of theory to practice. Cummings provides the explanatory model for Croft's spectrum of behaviour.

The alternative epistemologies of *The Naked and the Dead* reject the label of fascist for Croft. Considered independently from Cummings, he is clearly outside the political categories. Although his nature is decidedly non-liberal, it does not ultimately comply with Cummings' model or the more conventional mode of fascism established by Adorno in his definitive study *The Authoritarian Personality*. Through exhaustive clinical study Adorno sought the deep underlying trends in the fascist personality and established a number of 'dynamically related factors'[67] which constitute the organizing forces in the right-wing individual: anti-semitism, extreme concern with the power of the Jewish community, opposition to the labour unions and racial equality, pseudo-patriotism ('blind attachment to certain national cultural values'[68]), and an uncritical ethnocentric presumption that one's own culture is superior. The tendency is marked by intense hostility to outgroups: negroes, unions, political radicals, Catholics, artists, intellectuals, pacifists and homosexuals. In *The Naked and the Dead* Adorno's 'syndrome'[69] is used by Mailer – which indicates that he has a conventional image of what fascism is – but it is confined to the description of a series of secondary and tertiary characters: Majors Hobart, Dalleson and Conn ('Three variations on the same theme – p. 62) and a group of unnamed field officers who represent 'something sick, more insular than the Conn-Dalleson-Hobarts' (p. 64). The syndrome is not active in the dynamic of Croft's personality, and in a number of ways he is notably non-fascistic: he has no connection with groups on the American right, as might be expected; he is less racist, ethnocentric or anti-semitic than most of the working-class men in his command; and he is the only person to show affection for the Mexican Martínez ('He was the only man in the platoon whom Croft liked, and he felt an anxious, almost paternal care for Martínez, which was at odds with the rest of his nature' – p. 55).

Both the military hierarchy and the experience of war satisfy deep urges in Croft's character. The way in which he connects with the other men is forbiddingly cold: 'He hated weakness and loved practically nothing' (p. 135). He is directly and indirectly responsible for the deaths of a number of men within the sphere of his influence – Hearn, Roth and Wilson. Failure to observe Croft's uncompromising leadership is a perilous misprision because he is radically non-humanistic. The lives of others have little value for him and the deaths of those around him do not disturb his composure: 'He pushed and laboured inside himself and smouldered with an endless hatred' (p. 141). Two mutually reinforcing incidents in *The Naked and the Dead* establish Croft as the unquestionable enemy of the novel's left-liberal values. The first is the Sergeant's handling of the Japanese prisoner taken by the platoon: 'He realized suddenly that a part of his mind, very deeply buried, had known he was going to kill the prisoner from the moment he had sent Red on ahead. He felt quite blank now. The smile on the dead man's face amused him' (p. 168). The second is the pointless cruel killing of a wounded bird:

Croft held it for a moment. He could feel the bird's heart beating like a pulse against his palm. . . . It was no bigger than a stone yet it was alive. He wavered between compassion for the bird and the thick lusting tension of its throat. He didn't know whether to smooth its soft features or smash it in his fingers. . . . (p. 448)

The heightened language and obvious symbolism recall the cigarette incident. On discovering the cigarette squashed into the floor, Cummings trembles with 'unendurable wrath' (p. 273) and the narrator glosses, 'If he had been holding an animal in his hands at that instant he would have strangled it.' The incidents with the prisoner and the bird demonstrate the gratuitousness of Croft's violence, his abuse of the structural power he represents and a degree of propinquity with Cummings' worst impulses.

It is against this image that Mailer's pro-vitalist sympathies strive to find form and give Croft a favourable context. As Mailer later admitted, 'Beneath the ideology in *The Naked and the Dead* was an obsession with violence. The characters for whom I had the most secret admiration, like Croft, were violent people. Ideologically, intellectually, I did disapprove of violence. . . . '70 Croft's time machine, 'The Hunter' (pp. 134–41), places him firmly in a classic tradition of American literary hunters that includes Natty Bumppo, Captain Ahab, Thoreau, Faulkner's Ike McCaslin, and Hemingway. He is a specimen of the type tagged by Lawrence as 'hard, isolate, stoic and a killer'.71 Although the reconnaissance platoon is led nominally by Hearn, in the field it is Croft who emerges as the *de facto* leader, pushing titular power aside and replacing it with authority based on performance skills and the ability to inspire devotion. In Max Weber's terms the process conforms to a standard pattern: because charisma 'knows only inner determination', the holder of charisma 'seizes the task that is adequate to him' and thereby 'demands obedience and a following by virtue of his mission'.72 Croft is obsessed by Anopopei's central geographical feature, Mount Anaka: 'The mountain attracted him and inflamed him with its size. He had never seen it so clearly. . . . He stared at it now, examined the ridges, feeling an instinctive desire to climb the mountain and stand on its peak' (p. 447). He is actively engaged with the environment and the 'rule of merely physical energy'. As the environmental theorist Yi-Fu Tuan observes,

Certain aspects of nature defy every human control: these are
the mountains, deserts, and seas. They constitute, as it were,
permanent fixtures in man's world whether he likes them or
not. To these recalcitrant aspects of nature man has tended
to respond emotionally, treating them at one time as sublime,
the abode of the gods, and at another as ugly, distasteful, the
abode of demons.[73]

The scaling of the mountain becomes Croft's charismatic mission. When Hearn is killed, the platoon is liberated from its
official purpose, and the Sergeant directs it towards Anaka, a
site of no strategic military value whatsoever. At least one of
the men recognizes what is going on: '"You know that Croft,"
Polack said to Wyman, "he's an idealist, that's what the fug he
is"' (p. 606). Polack can see that Croft is behaving as if nothing
except Anaka exists beyond his mind. The mountain is his Other.
Mircea Eliade describes how in the primitive world view there
is, beyond 'organized' and 'inhabited' space, the 'unknown and
dangerous region of the demons, the ghosts, the deserts and of
foreigners – in a word, chaos or death or night'.[74] It is into this
zone of archaic consciousness that Croft propels himself in a
flight from the historical present and, ultimately, the explanatory
historicism of Mailer's left-liberal practice.

However, just as Cummings' 'more ambitious plan' (p. 602),
his pursuit of grand cultural designs, comes to pieces, the ascent
of Mount Anaka proves unsuccessful. During the attempt several
men are killed and the platoon is reduced collectively to 'dogs
terrified by a master's boot' (p. 684), recalling Pavlov and Hearn's
behaviouristic self-image. The charismatic spell under which
Croft holds the platoon is broken when a soldier accidentally
disturbs a hornets' nest. The men disperse and retreat. To the
Sergeant, the situation is tragic: 'He had lost it, had missed some
tantalizing revelation of himself. Of himself and much more. Of
life. Everything' (p. 709). In the interests of clarity and unity the
majority historicist view asserts itself over the inchoate subjugated knowledge. As a result of this self-censorship, the more
intriguing aspects of Cummings' and Croft's minds are left largely
unexplored. Thus the General and the Sergeant are not defeated,
as Jennifer Bailey argues, because 'they have extended their individual power into impossible realms far beyond the connotations
of their own experience'.[75] As Solotaroff realizes, 'Mailer *arranged*

defeats for the novel's authoritarians because he did not want to seem to be praising the strength of fascism.'[76] Even if, as Norman Podhoretz insists, Mailer discovered in the writing of *The Naked and the Dead* that his 'real values tended in an anti-liberal direction',[77] the political imperatives of the inflexible structure remain in place. (Podhoretz's conclusion that a reactionary ideology successfully displaces the text's left liberalism is not supported by the novel's conclusion.) Cummings and Croft are effectively alienated from the military system and the political future. Mailer realizes that Major Dalleson, the technological rationalist, the 'organization man',[78] is in ascendance. As Jean Radford says, in the final pages of *The Naked and the Dead* Dalleson 'already feels himself as an instrument of the system'.[79] The image the novel leaves us with therefore is of Dalleson's inane obeisance to structuralistic power.

The subjugated knowledge of *The Naked and the Dead* does not add up to much more than a veiled respect for a voluntaristic conception of power, for individuals *as* individuals, and for personal activism. The asserted elements – the bias of structure, the immediate historical paranoia, the inherited left-liberal antipathy to power – cannot be dislodged. But as a result of the competing claims of these two distinct influences the dilemma of power in *The Naked and the Dead* remains unresolved. Inevitably, as Solotaroff observes, Mailer loses 'control of the novel's symbolic lines'.[80] Finally the book is just too dependent on the model of thirties social fiction. In Richard Poirier's analysis, Mailer's 'being a literary young man forced him to lie, even while he mined his truths without knowing it. The truth was simply that perversity and power interested him far more than those efforts at health which led to limpness and defeat'.[81] The novel thus remains awkwardly poised between two styles of radicalism. What is perhaps most surprising is that in his next novel Mailer should choose to recover not the perversity and power of *The Naked and the Dead* but its leftism, pursuing a richer and more rigorous understanding of Marxist culture.

2
Marxisms on Trial: *Barbary Shore*

I

If there are large formal differences between *The Naked and the Dead* and Mailer's second novel, *Barbary Shore*,[1] there is nevertheless a close political kinship between the two books. The Marxist influence in *The Naked and the Dead* is translated in *Barbary Shore* into Marxist perspective. The only actual Marxists in the first novel – if Hearn is excluded as a left liberal or proto-Marxist – are an anonymous hobo in a time-machine section and the members of Havard's John Reed Club who expel Hearn from their group. In *Barbary Shore* Marxism is centralized. As Stanley Gutman points out, the novel is nothing less than 'an inquiry into the political, social, and historical meaning of Marxism in the twentieth century'.[2] The discourse on power is established again, this time on terms that are openly political and unencumbered by generic imperatives. Whereas Mailer had, like Hearn, only 'played around' with Marxism in *The Naked and the Dead*, here he is concerned to fulfil Walter B. Rideout's definition of the radical writer's intention to 'work out in his fiction a Marxist analysis of society'.[3] The firmness of Mailer's grip on ideological matters is reflected in the narrowness and depth of the material, his extended excursions into the left, the right, twentieth-century political history and human nature. Dense, abstract and formalized expository material confined to the shorthand form of dialogue in *The Naked and the Dead* makes up the core of *Barbary Shore*.

Mailer's precise position with regard to the ideological perspectives evoked in the novel remains unclear, unstable and changing. At certain points in the text he is broadly Marxist in sympathy; at other points a narrow Trotskyist viewpoint is endorsed; and towards the end it is strongly implied through symbols that he favours a post-Marxist radical position. However, the absence of a definitive politics in the novel does not affect its basic commitment to a radical social philosophy, and it presents us with answers to a number of important questions. When did the Russian Revolution begin to fail? Is Marxism a spent force? Ought we to be left-wing? The speculative, unsettled nature of the arguments unleashed show Mailer's mind to be no more fixed or certain than it was in his factitiously coherent first novel, but the ambiguity in the exposition of *Barbary Shore* represents an intellectual and political improvement on *The Naked and the Dead* because it is more honest. No attempt is made to subjugate ideas that threaten the overall moral and aesthetic programme of the book. In fact there is an almost complete absence of those elements of planning which safely guided the 'construction' of *The Naked and the Dead*. For better or worse, Mailer thinks thematically rather than aesthetically, without the insurance policy of sound structure. This makes the novel an invaluable source for an understanding of the details of Mailer's political development on the left (which was virtually forgotten in the 1960s and 1970s), and it demonstrates the degree to which the theme of power can intrude upon the texture of his fiction.

In 1955 Mailer said, with reference to the writing of *The Naked and the Dead*,

> I was an anarchist then, and I'm an anarchist today. In between I belonged to the Progressive Party during the Wallace campaign, and then broke off rather abruptly at the time of the Waldorf Peace Conference in 1949. What followed was a period of political wandering in the small circle of libertarian socialism. I was at the same time very radical and half-hearted about it.[4]

Reflecting again in 1963, he pointed out that he 'started *Barbary Shore* as some sort of fellow traveller and finished with a political position which was a far-flung mutation of Trotskyism'.[5] Between the writing of *The Naked and the Dead* and *Barbary Shore* Mailer became fully radicalized. Many potential radical influences had been avoided in the first novel as a result of their association with something he actively avoided in his work: 'it was and is easier to write a war novel about the Pacific – you don't have to have a feeling for the culture of Europe and the collision of America upon it. To try a novel about the last war in Europe without a sense of the past is to fail in the worst way.'[6] Only after *The Naked and the Dead* is Mailer able to cultivate the feeling for the culture of Europe and the sense of the past, and with these things comes a mandate to produce radical fictions.

The origins of this process lie in Mailer's relationship with Jean Malaquais, to whom *Barbary Shore* is dedicated. Malaquais is the prevailing influence on the novel, the source of its main ideas, its presiding consciousness and the model for one of its most important characters. Mailer met Malaquais, an anti-Stalinist Marxist philosopher-novelist, in Paris shortly after the publication of *The Naked and the Dead* (which he translated into French), and he rapidly assumed the role of Mailer's political teacher.[7] To Malaquais, Mailer seemed to be a 'boy scout, both intellectually and mentally',[8] politically ignorant and naïve:

> Norman had a classical petit-bourgeois middle class concept of elections. You elect a representative, a civil servant, as president, and if you don't like them, you vote them out of office. I told him this was nonsense, that crooks get reelected. On that score we had differences because for him an election meant democracy. But he didn't even know the difference between direct democracy and elective democracy.[9]

In Malaquais's view, Mailer possessed no significant political orientation. He knew nothing of the Russian Revolution, very little about the Moscow Trials, and at a time when many intellectuals in the United States were anti-Stalinist he was unfamiliar with their argument. As a result of these enormous gaps, Mailer, a radical manqué, became engrossed in Malaquais's foreign perspectives. Despite Malaquais's belief that there remained in his protégé a vestigial 'lingering inclination towards a pseudohumanism or liberalism',[10] Mailer publicly expressed leftist opinions on the post-war international situation in Europe.[11] The influence of Malaquais, combined with the ignominious collapse of the Wallace campaign, consolidated Mailer's radical development. If the Wallace campaign ended for a long time Mailer's attraction to collective political action, it served to open him up to a much more extreme conception of political power. Once he became a resident of New York, Malaquais assumed responsibility for Mailer's continuing education, guiding him through studies of the French and Russian Revolutions and the American working class. Significantly Malaquais did not emphasize Marx, on the grounds that Mailer was too ignorant of political theory for it to be of any value. In discussions Malaquais concentrated on his own negative concept of state capitalism (Soviet communism), which percolated through to *Barbary Shore*.

Malaquais argued that most available versions of communism were counter-revolutionary, distortions of Marx's vision. By 1949 there is strong evidence that Mailer had absorbed Malaquais's specific brand of ideology. During the Conference for World Peace at the Waldorf Hotel, Mailer made a speech which hinged on the idea of state capitalism: 'I am afraid both the United States and the Soviet Union are moving towards State Capitalism. There is no future in that. The two systems approach each other more clearly. All a writer can do is tell the truth as he sees it, and to keep on writing.'[12] Critical of socialism, Mailer nevertheless spoke from a socialist point of view, and through this critical dialectic created a niche for himself on the independent revolutionary left. What Malaquais was instrumental in doing was in guiding Mailer away from a more conventional brand of leftism or from Stalinism. As a consequence, Mailer did not come under the historical imperative to renounce or retreat from socialism. Immune from the forces which demoralized and disillusioned the conventional American left, he was free to occupy an advanced position, albeit on his own idiosyncratic terms. The fiction of *Barbary Shore* centres on this notion of socialism's 'inheritance', and the plot to which Marxist dialectics are affixed is a reworking of Mailer's own induction into the mysteries of historical materialism. The narrative is one which, according to Walter B. Rideout, the radical novel employs most frequently: the education of a central character in a social philosophy that shakes him loose from unthinking acceptance of the *status quo*. Upon learning the true nature of class society, the character experiences a conversion to political radicalism.[13] Thus *Barbary Shore* exploits both Mailer's own experience of conversion and the sacred story of initiation told and retold in the literature of radicalism.

Barbary Shore uses Malaquais in several ways. He provides the novel with a central figure in the character of the charismatic European Marxist intellectual William McLeod (the Irish name is a pseudonym which conceals East European origins).[14] Equipped with Malaquais's intellectual instruction, Mailer can approach the theme he avoided in *The Naked and the Dead* and present doctrinal issues with uninhibited relish. In addition, Malaquais can be used to rework on new terms the relationship which obtained between Cummings and Hearn. He can provide for *Barbary Shore* what *The Naked and the Dead* lacked: a model for the relationships in charismatic induction. The feeling for culture is equally a culture of feeling, and the epistemological thrill which comes from personal transmissions of knowledge drives the novel. Thus, for Mailer, the book is inseparably associated with the vision 'formed osmotically by the powerful intellectual influence of . . . Jean Malaquais'.[15]

II

There are two forms of bureaucratic power in *Barbary Shore* which are the focus of Mailer's political concern. The first is American and embodied by Leroy Hollingsworth, a representative of secret government agencies; the second is European and associated with William McLeod (or his past behaviour) and the period of Russian history from the 1917 Revolution to Trotsky's assassination and the signing of the Nazi-Soviet Pact. The first is a development of *The Naked and the Dead's* anti-fascist and anti-bureaucratic themes. The second is largely the inheritance of Malaquais.

The Naked and the Dead ends with a time machine projected prophetically towards a post-war future in which Major Dalleson will be the prototype, the coming man. Mailer's attitude towards Dalleson is derisive: 'A more imaginative man would have loathed the assignment, for it consisted essentially of composing long lists of men and equipment and creating a timetable. It demanded the same kind of patience that is needed to construct a crossword puzzle.'[16] Dull, conventional, the opposite of the charismatics, Dalleson is a stock figure: the bureaucrat.[17] Mailer sides with Cummings, who treats him with unconcealed scorn: 'Dalleson's got a mind like a switchboard he told himself. If your plug will fill one of his mental holes, he can furnish you with the necessary answer, but otherwise he is very lost.'[18] The congeries of images the Major attracts – timetables, crosswords, switchboards – evokes his closed mechanical mind. Reading reality through these restrictive cognitive maps, Dalleson never experiences the world directly. His world is uninhabited by the arcane forces which animate and obsess Cummings and Croft. Consequently he is protected against the opening-up of human vision to the degree that it will involve, as it does for Cummings and Croft, exposure to a reality that is perilously unpredictable (both men are frustrated by chance), unscheduled and unschematic.

Dalleson represents a post-war future that is essentially bureaucratic and authoritarian: rule by the officer class. Reinforcing this insight, *Barbary Shore* heralds the emergence of an American version of the police state. The historical context is again the conservative revival, during which American communism became the focus of State Department and governmental agencies' interest in national security. Written immediately prior to the Korean War and rise of McCarthyism, the novel anticipates both developments. (Ruth Prigozy's view that *Barbary Shore* is 'the most serious novel to emerge from the McCarthy period'[19] underestimates the degree to which Mailer predicts the worst excesses of McCarthyism between 1953 and 1955.) The prophetic Dalleson-figure is Leroy Hollingsworth, an undercover government agent sent to investigate the political mentor (McLeod) of the novel's narrator, the writer-manqué Michael Lovett. He also intends to secure the return of an unnamed 'little object' (p. 196) which has been appropriated by McLeod from the US Government, to whom he has defected from an American communist organization. Commentators do not agree which governmental agency employs Hoollingsworth. For Barry Leeds he is simply a 'secret policeman'.[20] Andrew Gordon also sees him as an ambiguous 'government agent'.[21] Jean Radford goes further and describes him as 'an agent for the national security organization closely resembling the FBI'.[22] In Robert Solotaroff's view, he is certainly an FBI agent,[23] and both Jennifer Bailey and Robert Begiebing agree.[24] But Philip Bufithis is less certain: he works for 'possibly the FBI or the CIA'.[25] And Stanley Gutman prefers ttto see him as 'an agent of something like the CIA'.[26]

Evidence drawn from the whole of Mailer's work suggests strongly that Hollingsworth is the first example of an obsession with the powers and activities of the CIA (formed in 1947) which is a distinctive theme of Mailer's until the 1970s. In an open letter to President Kennedy, Mailer warned against the CIA's view of Cuba.[27] In his film *Maidstone* Mailer creates a secret service, based on the CIA, which threatens the autobiographical hero played by Mailer.[28] In *St George and the Godfather* conspiracy theories are returned to: 'Aquarius [Mailer] sometimes thought it was his life's ambition to come up with evidence that the CIA was tripping on American elections.'[29] And in 1973 Mailer went so far as to create an organization called the Fifth Estate, reflecting his view that the CIA and FBI were constantly manipulating the American public:

> I want a people's FBI and a people's CIA to investigate these two. . . . If we have a democratic secret police keeping tabs on Washington's secret police, which is not democratic but bureaucratic, we will see how far paranoia is justified. . . . What happened in Dallas? What about Martin Luther King? The real story behind Watergate? How many plots are there in America? Two? Three? None?[30]

Although Mailer's counterintelligence plan did not develop, it finally emerged in Washington, first as the Committee for Action Research and then as the Organizing Committee for the Fifth Estate, and Mailer refers to it as 'the best political idea of my entire life'.[31] He also argued that there had been secret government involvement in the death of Marilyn Monroe.[32] But the crowning achievement of Mailer's longstanding preoccupation with the CIA is undoubtedly his 1976 essay 'A Harlot High and Low', which contains an epigraph from Malaquais: 'There are no answers. There are only questions.'[33] Here Mailer searches – in vain again – for a 'model' for the 'penetration of Central Intelligence'.[34]

The seeds of this obsession with the CIA and secret government stretch back to the beginnings of Mailer's work. In *Barbary Shore* Hollingsworth's character is Mailer's first attempt to penetrate the epistemology of Central Intelligence. Jean Radford's assertion that Hollingsworth 'embodies some of the qualities of Croft and Cummings'[35] misses his real affinity with Major Dalleson, and the degree to which both characters are essentially portraits of depersonalization. Hollingsworth is a jumble of contradictions: bland on the surface, bestial beneath; untidy but obsessed with order; shy yet aggressive; humble and vain; gracious and sadistic. His excessive formality ('his politeness was irritating' – p. 38) masks his true feelings, which are, to use the novel's primary image, barbaric. Without naturalness or spontaneity, Hollingsworth's overcivilized behaviour indicates its opposite, a complete absence of genuine manners. Guinevere's daughter,

Monina, penetrates through to Hollingsworth when she bites his hand:

> Hollingsworth was caught by surprise. Unguarded, a moan escaped from his mouth, his eyes opened in fright. What nightmares were resurrected? He sat helpless upon the chair, his head thrown back, his limbs rigid, a convict in the death-room, his body violated in the spasms of the current.
> I'm innocent,' he screamed. (p. 125)

The repressed, compartmentalized personality structure of the bureaucrat is neurotic. Guilt, fears of persecution and sexual chaos are concealed from public view. Beneath Hollingsworth's attempts at sexual charm lies the puerile, predatory mind of a rapist (p. 97). Beyond that there are moments when he seems 'womanish' (p. 225), and his approaches to McLeod sometimes hint at sexual attraction (something similar was implied in the Cummings–Hearn relationship in *The Naked and the Dead*). The spectrum of sexual feeling attributed to Hollingsworth argues for a lack of harmony in his nature. The elements in him do not add up; there is no integration of the different aspects of self. His mind, like Dalleson's, is a switchboard, a bureaucratized circuit of connections. Looking out through 'opaque and lifeless' (p. 40) eyes, he perceives only what he is programmed to see. As McLeod says, 'I tell myself he's got a policeman's brain, and it's only the murders he can understand' (p. 202). He cannot deal with the cryptic. He is like Kennedy's CIA, who turn 'nuances into facts, and lose other nuances, and mangle facts into falsities'.[36] In Mailer's view, Central Intelligence can only possess the zero and the one, and 'theoretical incapacities' (p. 161) prevent Hollingsworth from understanding much of what McLeod confesses with regard to the matters under investigation.

His personal culture (boondock simplicity, a taste for Westerns, pornography and ballroom dancing), hostility to metropolitan values, philistinism, and cover job as a Wall Street clerk locate him in the context of the conservative revival. To McLeod, the focus of wisdom in *Barbary Shore*, Hollingsworth is a 'madman' (p. 36); the rigid categories he operates with are the essence of 'state information' (p. 153). The confession McLeod is required to make must therefore conform to a reductive pattern:

Admits to being a Bolshevist.
Admits to being a Communist.
Admits to being an Atheist.
Admits to blowing up Churches.
Admits to being against free enterprise.
Admits to encouraging violence.
Advocates murder of President and Congress.
Advocates destruction of the South.
Advocates use of poison.
Admits allegiance to a foreign power.
Is against Wall Street. (p. 72)

Thought and behaviour are made to comply with an already-existing stencilled model. As in Dalleson's map-reading exercises on the final page of *The Naked and the Dead*, 'state information' overlays a grid on reality. McLeod's resistance to this process, given his willingness to confess, is a refusal to package the complexities of his political culture in accordance with these requirements: 'I resent Leroy for my judge and the fact that he makes a smudge on the paper and is indifferent to what I have endured I find intolerable' (p. 202). With his own intimate knowledge of bureaucratic power, he will not acknowledge its maddened rationality. Hollingsworth's 'political education' (p. 148) is thus kept on charismatic non-bureaucratic terms that are alien to his most basic procedures and taxonomies.

Hollingsworth's bland depersonalized self derives from a subservience to the structural power he represents. He is banally evil. The vacancy of self, the absence of distinguishing personal qualities, is a functional component of the model of power in which he is a vector. Through him Mailer argues that the American state, particularly in its secret aspects, is dangerous to its subjects; and in the final pages of the novel, when the rooming house in which most of the action takes place is invaded by 'agents from the country we live in' (p. 248) there is an image of internal state terror which compares with the practices of Stalin's secret police. Despite national and ideological differences, capitalism and communism are shown to exist on the same plane. Thus, at a certain point, Hollingsworth and McLeod, who has worked for both Stalin and the CIA, are interchangeable. As McLeod observes, 'the truth is that there are deep compacts between Leroy and myself, you might almost say we are sympathetic to each other' (p. 199). Hollingsworth's emergence at the end of *Barbary Shore* with the 'inheritance' of McLeod's confession (though not the sought-after 'little object') repeats the conclusion of *The Naked and the Dead* and is central to the bleak political signal Mailer is transmitting. In symbolic terms, the unreconstructed bureaucrat, immune to the influence of McLeod's confession, finds favour with both the capitalist proletariat (represented by the sexual favours of Guinevere) and its subsequent generation (represented by Guinevere's daughter). Even the mentally disturbed Trotskyist, Lannie Madison, is prepared to support Hollingsworth: 'if there is a future, it is with him' (p. 179). Only McLeod is capable of recognizing the political pattern of ascending bureaucracy and exact value of Hollingsworth's 'inheritance': '"So you come soon to power," McLeod said quietly, "but you have merely inherited a crisis, and yours is the profit of cancer"' (p. 233). Hollingsworth's emergence only extends the political bureaucracy which took hold of the century after the Russian Revolution; it simply adds to the process of political retardation.

However, the specific theme introduced by Hollingsworth is not pursued in great detail. This is partly because it repeats what has already been said about Dalleson, but primarily Hollingsworth is neglected because of Mailer's almost total preoccupation with McLeod's charismatic personality and the Marxist material only he can introduce and handle in the fiction. Thus in the second half of *Barbary Shore* Hollingsworth is used mainly to sustain a dramatic situation in which McLeod can speak at inordinate length on issues relating to the history of socialism, a role he shares with Michael Lovett, the true recipient of McLeod's inheritance. The issues evoked by Hollingsworth are either abandoned or absorbed into the larger theme of bureaucracy associated with McLeod alone. If Hollingsworth is the rising bureaucrat of the capitalist state, McLeod is an ex-bureaucrat from the communist state. Politically they are moving in opposite directions. McLeod is the novel's 'great reader' (p. 25) and 'thinking man' (p. 104), the intellectual epicentre from which the text derives. His vast amount of political experience, knowledge of Europe and feeling for culture permit him to 'understand finally the gory unremitting task of history' (p. 200). He is the only character with an overview of the world situation. The reverence in the text for McLeod's powerful intellect ('his

intelligence was acute' – p. 34) and his assumption of the role
of 'pedagogue' (p. 68) is Mailer's acknowledgement of his own
political mentor. But the patina of sophistication McLeod has is
not composed solely of knowledge or personal culture; it is also
the guilt and pessimism of accumulated experience (the realm
Cummings is about to be thrust into at the end of *The Naked and
the Dead*), and what fascinates Mailer here is the complex fate of
the radical mind.

McLeod naturally assumes the role of mentor towards the
tyro Lovett: 'In everything he did there were elements of such
order, demanding, monastic. He was unyielding and sometimes
forbidding' (p. 35). (In similar terms, Cummings refers to himself
as a 'chief monk, the Lord of my little abbey.³⁷) But Lovett resists
the destabilizing effect of the charismatic personality and admits
only to a 'left-handed fascination' (p. 25) with the older man. The
conversations between the two men are intense, abstruse and,
for Lovett, demanding. McLeod is teasingly gnomic, oblique
and mysterious. Overstretched by these encounters, Lovett
sometimes 'shunned his company' (p. 28). McLeod's ability
as an interrogator ('He had a facility for wearing one down' –
p. 26) is shown in the way he inspires involuntary admissions
and spontaneous confessions: 'I discovered myself telling him
one day about the peculiar infirmity I was at such pains to
conceal from everyone else' (p. 34); 'in his presence I could
find enthusiasm for the balm of confession' (p. 66). The crucial
difference between McLeod and Hollingsworth as interrogators is
that McLeod's scrutiny is 'so dispassionate, so balanced'. McLeod
does not abuse his personal authority.

However, McLeod's political record is as evil as General
Cummings'. What makes him morally superior to Cummings is
his repentance, charted in a vein of religious imagery beneath
the novel's ideological surface. Lovett's accusation that McLeod
is a bureaucrat touches a raw spiritual nerve:

Once I told him, 'You sound like a hack,' and McLeod
reacted with a rueful frown. 'An exceptional expression for
you to employ, Lovett,' he told me softly. 'I take it you mean
by "hack" a representative of the people's state across the sea,
but I'm wondering where you picked up the word, for it indicates a reasonable amount of political experience on your part.
(p. 35)

An enormous reservoir of guilt is contained within McLeod's personality. Joining the 'movement' when he was twenty-one and leaving when he was forty (he is forty-four in the novel's present) is described as 'nineteen years with the wrong woman' (p. 105). It is revealed that he has played an obscure but active role in Stalin's purges as a 'hangman of the Left Opposition' (p. 153). In the words of Lannie, the deranged Trotskyist, he has been 'the undertaker of the revolution' (p. 158). In fact the details of McLeod's assassinations elicit Hollingsworth's professional respect: 'one has to admire his efficiency' (p. 191). McLeod's defence of his actions hinges on the denial of self implicit in bureaucratic power; he was 'the product of a system', an instrument or extension of the state. His crimes were therefore selflessly motivated. A personal moral-political crisis only occurs on the death of Trotsky (ambiguously described in the text) and the Nazi-Soviet Pact. Defecting to the US Government, he worked in yet another bureaucratic capacity as a 'statistician' (p. 151). But this attempt to reverse his actions for the communist state 'merely succeeded in doubling it' (p. 202). Thus McLeod has been the consummate hack, operating for both ideological systems; a 'true reactionary' (p. 158), as he refers to himself. It is even implied that he was partly responsible ('just a cog' – p. 203) for Trotsky's assassination. As a bureaucrat he despised the very idea of Trotsky since it inspired guilt and self-hatred: 'the thought of him was unbearable'.

At the time of the novel's present McLeod is not politically active and no longer a 'joiner' (p. 35). Socialist experience has amounted to personal tragedy; being a state functionary has left him 'destroyed as a person' (p. 185). As an independent leftist, a 'Marxist-at-liberty' (p. 36), he searches for a non-bureaucratic alternative in writing and study. This recontemplation of the basic aims of socialism is a way of continuing to affirm Marxist politics. Precisely what sort of politics is left vague, but the gesture is hopeful: 'Thus notice the admirable path I have taken from the bureaucrat to the theoretician' (p. 202). As a writer he redeems himself, preparing articles and pamphlets for the radical conventicle. He may be a broken political spirit, a 'poor retired bureaucrat' (p. 108) who is 'completely adrift' (p. 205), but he has transcended the authoritarian influence of the state in both its communist and capitalist forms. He is no longer 'a servant of any power' (p. 195).

The radical analysis advanced by McLeod, which underlies
the whole novel, is composed of two elements. It is a *retrospective* overview of the failure of socialism in the Soviet Union
after 1917 and a *prophetic* assessment of the growing similarities
between the Russian and American states and their effect on the
world situation. Although Mailer is critical of developments in
socialism since the revolution, he does not go as far as Wilhelm
Reich and argue that all socialist revolutions are bound to fail.
He adopts the position ultimately attributable to Trotsky: 'when
the events of 1917 failed to induce similar proletarian uprisings in
the countries of the West, the revolution was doomed' (p. 228).
After initial success the revolution began to collapse in the midst
of an internal ideological debate about world revolution *versus*
revolution in one country. Through McLeod's expositions Mailer
argues that the central irony of the revolution is that its energies
became directed against the very principles it helped to liberate.
The state's legitimization of violence and terror during the purges
of those labelled counterrevolutionary marks the point at which
the abuse of power began. To avoid the formation of opposition (Mailer's 'Left Opposition'), members and officials were
liquidated. Stalin, though he is never mentioned in *Barbary
Shore*, is the embodiment of this bureaucratization of socialism,
and terror is understood wholly as a phenomenon associated
with Stalinism rather than as an instrument used throughout
the revolution to consolidate its aims. In other words, Mailer
remains sentimental about the revolution itself and isolates it
from the negative critique of socialist power. Thus he is not
prepared to trace the philosophy of mass terror to its theoretical
source in Marx's concept of the dictatorship of the proletariat,
the necessary though (ideally) transitional phase of authoritarian
hegemony. Instead he prefers the view, derived from Malaquais,
that Stalin's dictatorship is an aberration and not a development
of Lenin's systematic application of Marxist theory.

Yet the pattern of Mailer's version of the failure of socialism
arguably owes as much to Max Weber as it does to Marx.
McLeod's description is of the routinization or bureaucratization
of charisma: 'It is the fate of charisma, whenever it comes into the
permanent institutions of a community, to give way to a process
of tradition or of rational socialization.'[38] In Weber's model this
routinization process in inevitable: 'In its purest form charismatic
authority may be said to exist only in the process of originating. It

cannot remain stable, but becomes either traditionalized or rationalized, or a combination of both.'[39] Thus only in the beginning can
a revolution be genuinely revolutionary. As the cultural historian
Bernard de Jouvenal puts it, 'The beginnings of a revolution are
of an indescribable charm. The event, while it is still in suspense,
seems to open up every possibility.'[40] Mailer uses Stalin to reclaim
the revolution, celebrate the purity of its origins. No matter how
faulty its practices might be, its theory remains sound. In this way
Mailer can be both a socialist and an ardent critic of socialism.
As a result of holding this dialectical view, and because of the
historical lateness of his arrival at Marxism (he was never a member of the Communist Party), Mailer is effectively spared the kind
of destructive inner struggle experienced by older writers such
as Arthur Koestler (the influence of whose *Darkness at Noon* on
Barbary Shore is evident), André Gide (to whom Malaquais was
amanuensis) and Richard Wright. These writers were forced to
retreat from communism as a belief system, while the routinization
of the revolution's charisma implies no such personal tragedy for
Mailer.

The second part of McLeod's analysis is more apocalyptic
than the first. In the wake of the failure of socialism, 'state
capitalism' (p. 226) has emerged. Both the Soviet Union and
the United States (monopoly capitalism) are in a condition of
near-crisis. Monopoly capitalism requires the steady expansion
of markets and is committed to a programme of imperialism and
colonialism, while the Third World (which is the object of this
programme) is moving rapidly towards forms of state capitalism.[41]
The crisis of state capitalism hinges on its 'inability to raise the
standard of living' (p. 228). Socialism, 'lost in the necessity for
survival' (p. 229), has created the conditions of slave labour.
The economy has deteriorated and has no internal capacity to
improve productivity. The separate condition of each ideological
system makes war an inevitable outcome: 'I think it is reasonable
to assert that if either of the two powers is unable to solve the
economic problems without going to war, it must follow that war
will come. But what if both the Colossi suffer such contradictions?
A fortiori the inevitability receives its double guarantee' (p. 228).
Each bloc prepares for war from its own imperative to survive.
But it will be a war between two systems that have grown alike,
between 'virtually identical forms of exploitation' (p. 230). From
that moment

the rate of production is never again capable of steady
increase. The search begins for methods to stimulate it.
State competition becomes substituted, and artificial cam-
paigns between state corporations, accompanied by all the
machinery of propaganda, make exhaustive efforts to match
the requirements of armament. Piecework reappears. Such a
process is narcotic. The injection must become progressively
more intense, until the price for losing a competition becomes
the neck of a bureaucrat. The first stage of cannibalism has been
reached, and the bureaucracy finds itself obliged to dispose of
the same personnel it needs so desperately. They are a class
which comes to power at the very moment they are in the act
of destroying themselves. (p. 231)

The process is the long road to the 'concentration camp'
(p. 232) inside the state and war outside it. War becomes the
permanent condition ('the police are everywhere' – p. 230) and
the deterioration continues 'until we are faced with mankind in
barbary'(p. 233).

McLeod's analysis is an extension of the thesis put forward by
Cummings in *The Naked and the Dead* that 'this is going to be the
reactionary's century, perhaps their thousand year reign'.[42] *Barbary Shore* continues to worry this insight. Cummings and McLeod
are both theorists of forces of reaction (fascism, Stalinism) and
participants in the phenomena they describe, insiders. Although
this kind of writing against the power of the state lies within a
distinguished tradition stretching back in American literature to
Thoreau and Tom Paine, in *Barbary Shore* the critique of bureaucratic state power is problematic, not only because it is crudely
incorporated into the novel's fiction but primarily because Mailer's presentation of the material overvalues its significance. Jean
Radford is prepared to dismiss the Mailer-McLeod critique on the
grounds that it is 'couched in fairly orthodox Trotskyist terms',[43]
and readers of any persuasion will encounter difficulties. For the
anti-Stalinist left, Mailer's intellectual pyrotechnics are much too
commonplace to be engaging. Beyond the thrill of radical recognition lies only leftist *Weltschmerz*. (Malaquais found the book
basically unsatisfying.) For the popular readership, though, the
theoretical hardware which clearly intoxicates Mailer is far too
formidable, sectarian and obscurely handled to be compelling.
As McLeod himself points out, he speaks 'in the most abstract

and general terms' (p. 234). In centralizing the critique of state power and making *Barbary Shore* rest on it, the novel becomes simultaneously banal and obscure. It is difficult to see for whom this material was intended. However, Mailer luxuriates in the climate of dialectics and rigorous analysis, and from the point of view of the theme of power the novel is particularly revealing. It demonstrates the degree to which Mailer is capable of being absorbed by theoretical questions about power and how politically motivated his writing can be. In the sophistication of its politics, considerably more advanced than the vocabulary of *The Naked and the Dead*, it highlights Mailer's capacity for development and provides ample evidence of his attempt to root himself in a leftist tradition. Above all, it clarifies Mailer's urge to be a writer of didactic intentions, whose mission is to spread ideas, in this case the political ideas of McLeod's analysis.

III

McLeod's pivotal analysis is largely a negative gloss on Marxist power: socialism is man's only hope but it has been corrupted. The pessimism of this overview leaves little room for a viable conception of Marxism, although the purpose of the discourse in *Barbary Shore* is to further the aims of socialist thought. Mailer's achievement is to arrive at a critical if not a full-blown Marxist position within a fictional context and the conducive atmosphere of internal debate, and a controlling form of radical politics does emerge in the final pages of the novel. The focus of this is Lovett's politicization, the abandoning of his political neutrality and belief that the radical cause is 'hopeless' (p. 107). He divests himself of the self-image of a non-political writer 'There was my typewriter, and somehow I did not want to leave it there. Why I took it with me I hardly knew, but within the hour I had dropped it in a pawnshop and followed my impulse to the end, the name I gave was not my own and the address I wrote was a street which did not exist' (p. 240). Relinquishing his manuscript propels him from amnesia, pastlessness, into time and transforms him into a historical agent. He moves from the cultivation of sentiment to action. Through McLeod the amnesiac has made a literal recovery of consciousness. Laying the groundwork, McLeod has prepared Lovett for study (p. 251) and the continuation of his own return to theory.

The fundamental purpose of his confession has therefore been for
Lovett to bear witness. The apparent interlocutor, Hollingsworth,
is incapable of understanding and bored by the discourse. The
other symbolic witness, Lannie, is too deranged to benefit from
its information.

In addition to this programme of political re-education,
McLeod's will leaves to Lovett the 'remnants' of his 'socialist
culture' (p. 256). This symbolic transference, which echoes Mailer's relationship to Malaquais, attests to the power of charismatic
transaction. At first sight this image of individual power seems to
conflict with the preoccupation with historical materialism. As
Mailer himself points out, 'men enter into social and economic
relations independent of their wills' (p. 138). But in the context
of such proliferating bureaucracy (communist and capitalist) the
idea of intense personal relations gains radical credibility and
becomes associated with the style of Marxism which the novel
ultimately endorses: the 'heritage' of fundamental revolutionary
values connected with Trotsky and the charismatic doctrine of
permanent revolution. Here Mailer manages to locate a political
optimism which anticipates the 'rising of the Phoenix' (p. 256).

Although the independent radicalism of *Barbary Shore* is expressed poetically, it falls a long way short of providing any
basis for collective action. The suggestion is that there will be
a long period of abeyance during which the radical tradition
will persist as an underground. Lovett moves towards a personal
non-collective activism in the interstices of American society, a
secret exile which resembles that experienced by the counterforce
of Thomas Pynchon's *The Crying of Lot 49* ('How many shared
Tristero's secret, as well as its exile? What would the probate
judge have to say about spreading some kind of legacy among
them all, all those nameless, maybe as a first instalment'[44]).
Pynchon blends the same ambiguous images of inheritance and
exile to describe the structure of America's adversarial culture.
The critic Frank D. McConnell argues that Pynchon's version of
the underground network is 'more serious and more compelling
than Mailer's, precisely as his own commitment (political and
metaphysical) to the necessity of the underground is more intense.
He recognizes, as only a member of a revolutionary class can, the
inherent sorrow and danger of revolution.'[45] But the real difference
between the two conceptions of the underground is that Mailer's
is seriously ideological whereas Pynchon's is non-ideological, a

regulatory counterforce which maintains the reality of the *status quo* and is not part of a revolutionary dialectic. (In fact recent information indicates that Pynchon's notion of an underground is, at least in part, inherited from Mailer.[46]) The suggestion that Pynchon is a member of a revolutionary *class* is an ideological absurdity. Lovett's exile and inheritance are ambivalent because they connect a disillusion with socialism with an initiation into its mysteries. Finally, it is only possible to arrive at a version of Marxism that is tentative, personalized, marginal and quixotic. Lovett is the 'poor hope' (p. 256) of the left.

In the absence of a clearly defined radical politics of immediate practical relevance, *Barbary Shore* becomes an essay in powerlessness to effect social change, individual helplessness and depersonalization. As Stanley Gutman says, the novel 'hides its small hope behind a vast dream of despair'.[47] McLeod's discourse takes up the theme of alienation at the social level and is based on Marx's early economic and philosophical manuscripts (the so-called 1844 Manuscripts), which were not published until 1932. In these writings alienation is the key concept for the analysis of capitalism. (Later Marx focused on class relations and the cluster of terms used for alienations disappeared from his work.) For Robert Solotaroff the novel's 'obsessive concern with just how bad both capitalisms [American and Russian] are seems primarily to have been the product of fairly intensive readings of Marxist literature from 1948 to 1950, particularly *Das Kapital*, Trotsky's *History of the Russian Revolution*, and the latter's polemics against the Soviet state'.[48] But this indiscriminate impression fails to catch the precise radical inflections in *Barbary Shore*. Malaquais restricted Mailer's encounters with Marx's own writings, and his own radicalism followed the fashionable early Marx in its emphasis on the worker's loss of control over the process of work, the product of his labour and his eventual reification:

A man is capable of participating efficiently in the modern industrial process, with all its demands for skill, intelligence, and intense labour, only if there is a reward possible, to wit an adequate scale of living and a promise of an improved future. Deprived of the minimum of comfort and hope, workmanship must degenerate. Little balm for the labourer if factories swallow the earth, when they fail to provide him with creature comfort,

and less balm for the bureaucrat when the failure to produce
becomes increasingly more serious. (p. 299)

Marx distinguishes three types of alienation: reification, the sale
of oneself as a commodity, and the experience of estrangement.[49]
In McLeod's discourse Mailer elaborates on the first two senses
of alienation, but the primary feeling of alienation in *Barbary
Shore* generates from Lovett himself, whose experience is one
of estrangement. Like Robert Hearn, who tries to 'get by on
style', Lovett is passive, blank and lacking in personal distinction
(since there is no physical description of him, he is impossible
to visualize). His emptiness is symbolized by his amnesia: 'The
details of my own history were lost in the other, common to us
all. I could never judge whether something had happened to me
or I imagined it so' (p. 11). Until halfway through the second
chapter he remains an unnamed, unidentified voice, and, as
controller of the narrative, its registering consciousness, he is
anxious and disturbed. A war wound facilitates his perception of
himself as a 'cripple' (p. 63). The injury is not romantic but part
of a severe erosion of self: 'At times I am certain I used to lie on
the bunk and stare at a photo of myself taken in England or was
it in Africa? I would examine the face which the doctors assured
me would be almost duplicated' (p. 64). Pastless, faceless, he has
experienced a literal depersonalization and estrangement.

The half-hearted attempts made by Lovett to become a writer
are symptomatic of his damaged condition. The novel he works
on but never completes is, like *Barbary Shore*, a bleak exploration
of bureaucracy and alienation: 'I intended a large ambitious work
about an immense institution never defined more exactly than
that, and about the people who wandered through it' (p. 54).
Towards the end the novel is forgotten, no more significant
than Guinevere's banal script ideas (pp. 56–9) or Lannie's crazed
experimental poems (pp. 132–3), a symptom of the malaise of
non-connection rather than a critical tool for dealing with it.
Mailer associates Lovett with Narcissus, and his fragments of
literary self-reflection suggest alienation without transcendence.
His name alludes to this narcissistic love of one's own image:
'Her mouth curled again. "You can't love anybody Mikey, for
you're Narcissus, and the closer you come to the water the
more you adore yourself until your nose touches, and then
you're alone again"' (p. 131). Lovett's personal emancipation

comes only with the selling of his typewriter, the abandonment of his novel and the dissipation of literary ambitions. True recovery comes with political rearmament, which projects him into an underground existence (he is last seen fleeing into an alley) where he will be immune from the kind of harmful exposure to history which has caused his amnesia (alienation).

Alienation is not only present in McLeod's discourse or individual characters: it is also inscribed in the formal construction of the novel. Just as *The Naked and the Dead* begins and ends with a code image (a map of Anopopei and Dalleson's absurd map-reading classes using pin-ups), *Barbary Shore* opens and closes with a dream trope of collective estrangement:

I am a traveller. He is most certainly not myself. A plump middle-aged man, and I have the idea he has just finished a long trip. He has landed at an airfield or his train has pulled into a depot. It hardly matters which.

He is in a hurry to return home. With impatience he suffers the necessary delays in collecting his baggage, and when the task is finally done, he hails a taxi, installs his luggage, bawls out his instructions, and settles back comfortably in the rear seat. Everything is so peaceful. Indolently he turns his head to watch children playing a game upon the street.

He is weary, he discovers, and his breath comes heavy. Unfolding his newspaper he attempts to study it, but the print blurs and he lays the sheet down. Suddenly and unaccountably he is quite depressed. It has been a long trip he reassures himself. He looks out of the window.

The cab is taking the wrong route!

What shall he do? It seems so simple to raise his hand and tap upon the glass, but he feels he dare not disturb the driver. Instead he looks through the window once more.

The man lives in this city, but he has never seen these streets. The architecture is strange and the people are dressed in unfamiliar clothing.

He looks at a sign, but it is printed in an alphabet he cannot read. (pp. 12–13)

In the dream Lovett shouts at the man, 'You are wrong, I say, although he does not hear me; this city is the real city, the material city, and your vehicle is history.' The image is of anomie, confusion and future shock in an indecipherable reality.[50] On the final page of the novel, in a mood of spiralling hysteria, the image returns: 'Meanwhile vast armies mount themselves, the world revolves, the traveller clutches his breast' (p. 256). That no real progress has occurred in the course of the novel is reinforced by the pessimistic repetition of the closing incantatory words of chapter 1 at the end of the novel: 'So the blind lead the blind, and the deaf shout warnings to one another until their voices are lost' (p. 13). Both the traveller image and the incantations sustain an unrelievedly gloomy view of recent history.

Alienation is the political note the novel sounds most stridently. But this ought not to be understood only in terms of Mailer's idiosyncratic position. Rather there are distinct similarities between *Barbary Shore* and a number of other novels of the same period, notably Saul Bellow's *Dangling Man* and Ralph Ellison's *Invisible Man*. Each of these books, written as notes from an underground, charts the effects of a moral-political collapse of perspective on a marginalized hero. Mailer's *amnesia*, Bellow's *dangling* and Ellison's iinvisibility are tropes for the inner vacuities of cultural or political estrangement. Bellow presents a central character, Joseph, who finds himself bereft of all political certainties as he awaits military induction. His reaction to this is to turn inward in an attempt at self-recovery. Like Lovett, he does little but sit in his room, worry, think and attempt to write. He 'dangles' passively because no rationale can be constructed to justify action. Bellow's expository material is structured as interior monologues with an imaginary dialectical character, 'The Spirit of Alternatives', that are no more graceful than Mailer's discourse-making. However, rather than agonizing over Marxism, Joseph wrestles with his own, and Bellow's, political background in liberalism and the Enlightenment philosophers. His writings, which are left as incomplete as Lovett's novel, are a desperate examination of the promises of freedom and self-fulfilment offered by the rationalist thinkers (including Marx). 'The Spirit of Alternatives', playing the same role as McLeod, pessimistically contradicts Joseph, forcing him to accept the absurdity of his claim to a separate, distinct identity. By the end of *Dangling Man* Joseph cannot bear the weight of doubt, and his programme of self-recovery founders. Unlike Lovett, he surrenders with relief to a bureaucratic life:

Hurray for regular hours!
And for the supervision of the spirit.
Long live regimentation.[51]

Ralph Ellison's invisible man begins in and returns to the same
claustrophobic, marginal 'border area'[52] inhabited by Lovett and
Joseph, and his room is literally rather than figuratively chthonic.
Invisible Man emerges out of Ellison's complete disillusion with
Marxism (the Brotherhood of the novel) and all other political
discourses, and his hero's 'residence underground'[53] is perceived
in more sanguine terms than either Mailer's or Bellow's; it is a
hibernation, 'a covert preparation for a more overt action'.[54] But,
like Lovett and Joseph, the invisible man has not formulated the
precise action he should take: 'The next step I couldn't make, so
I've remained in the hole.'[55] Unclear whether he is 'in the rear
or the *avant-garde*',[56] he has followed the advice given to Lovett
and returned to theory: 'Here, at least, I could try to think
things out in peace.'[57] He has neither capitulated like Joseph
or activated himself like Lovett. A cultural middle way, flirted
with but ultimately rejected by Lovett and Joseph, is found in
writing. As a writer, the invisible man can deal with alienation.
Something an old schoolteacher has said to him about Joyce's
Portrait of the Artist as a Young Man is the key to his development:
'Stephen's problem, like ours, was not actually one of creating the
uncreated conscience of his race, but of creating the *uncreated
features of his face*.'[58] The creation of self, solving the problems of
one's own identity, is the prerequisite of more socially responsible
styles of behaviour. Face comes before race. Writing permits
Ellison's hero to make music out of invisibility (alienation), but
the song of self is no romantic indulgence; it is a hard-headed
preparation for a programme of action: 'Without the possibility
of action, all knowledge comes to one labelled "file and forget",
and I can neither file nor forget.'[59]

Mailer's underground man undergoes a recovery of self which
is less dramatic than the invisible man's. He has yet to create the
features of his face: 'When I stare into the mirror I am returned a
face doubtless more handsome than the original, but the straight
nose, the modelled chin, and the smooth cheeks are evidence of
a stranger's art' (p. 11). Despite his valued inheritance, he has
'much to learn' (p. 250), and he remains, in Chester Eisinger's
words, 'the victim of nameless terrors and alienation, who cannot

make a vital relationship between his ideas and the society he lives in'.[60] That this feeling comes out of Mailer's own experience has been made clearer in a recent comment on the overwhelming sense of deracination in this period:

> I was having a form of twentieth century experience which would become more and more prevalent: I was utterly separated from my roots. I was successful and alienated and that was a twentieth century condition. This went into all my work after that in one way or another and will go on forever because by now I suppose I can say that kind of personality interests me more than someone who is rooted.[61]

Ultimately *Barbary Shore* is not only a study in alienation but an alienating novel for the reader to deal with. The close attention paid to politics and power is at the expense of formal and aesthetic considerations. Although it develops, according to Mailer, 'without any plan',[62] it becomes even more arch and artificially coded than its exposition with the half-hearted introduction of Hawthornian allegorical elements which clash with the historical preoccupations.[63] No novelistic synthesis of these elements is achieved. At the bottom of this failure lies Mailer's inability to find a fictional correlative for the ideas he is working out. In his study of left-wing fiction Walter B. Rideout warns of the dangers involved for the radical novelist 'when schematized thinking of any kind is inorganically imposed on the creative process';[64] and Irving Howe has pointed out that the question of what determines the success or failure of a political novel is linked to the larger question of what art is, in the sense that no novel, finally, can succeed simply on the basis of an idea itself.[65] In the case of *Barbary Shore* it is not simply that the dialogue is artificial (as in a romance); there is an overall failure to establish links between the highly developed exposition and the sketchy story of human relationships. A gap exists between the political discussion, which is presented in the form of long, dense interior (Lovett) and exterior (McLeod) monologues, and the fictive elements of character, description, setting and plot. Mailer's preference for the former over the latter leads him to neglect the dramatic core of the novel. Thus what Rideout calls the tricky problem of 'how to combine the unburdening of capitalist fact with a convincing statement in fictional terms'[66] is never properly addressed, and the reader of whatever political persuasion balks at the formal and technical inelegance. If, as Howe argues, the novelist's task is always to show 'the relationship between theory and experience, between that ideology that has been preconceived and the tangle of feelings and relationships he is trying to present',[67] *Barbary Shore*'s inertia derives from its overemphasis on its preconceived theory.

The formal dissatisfactions of *The Naked and the Dead* arise from its 'sturdy' structure; the themes it pursues are choked by Mailer's extensive planning. *Barbary Shore*'s problem is almost the reverse: the theme overwhelms the flimsy fictional structure erected to support the book. The writing refuses to obey any imperatives of form because Mailer is totally preoccupied with the novel as a vehicle for political wisdom or, in epistemological terms, what the novelist, philosopher and critic William Gass calls the 'truth function'[68] of literature. Gass provides an eloquent caution against the novel's suitability for this kind of work:

> Fiction is not a form of meaning, nor a means of attaining wisdom. As a philosopher, to put on the other hat, I have a very dim view of the ability of literature to give us knowledge. But fortunately, it seems to me, we can read literature without taking it seriously in that direction while seriously taking it in another direction. As long as you can keep the work on the plane of making statements about the world, then the question becomes 'Are these statements wise statements, deep statements, true statements?' But in my view the integrity of the work is all that matters aesthetically. I mean, my books are made up. They're not about the world. I don't have any wisdom and I have never met a writer yet who had.[69]

The American post-modern writer Gilbert Sorrentino has expressed a similar view: 'For some reason, incomprehensible to me [the] mimetic concept has all but defined the "important" novel in this country. We love our novelists to be seers, to have Important ideas.'[70] Clearly *Barbary Shore* is committed to the truth function and Important ideas to the extent that almost everything else is forgotten, and as a designed artefact with internal consistencies it is deficient. But despite this indisputable criticism *Barbary Shore* has a fascination. As Richard Poirier, alone among critics, realizes, it is 'especially appealing to those . . . who look into the structures of a book hoping to find a clue to the author's sense of analogous social, economic, or political structures'[71] – in other words, those of us who are interested in examining the operations in the truth function of Mailer's fiction.

3

A Flight from Ideology and Transits to Narcissus in *The Deer Park*

I

Only on the surface does *The Deer Park*[1] belong to the genre of the Hollywood novel. The book makes no attempt to explain how Hollywood society fits together. The contention that Mailer 'explores the media'[2] is therefore misguided. At the deeper levels of the novel lie the interrelated political themes of self, sexuality and ideology. Hollywood plays a special role in the evocation of these matters because, as Norman Podhoretz realizes, Mailer sees in it

> The image of a society that has reached the end of its historical term, a society caught between the values of an age not quite dead and those of a new era that may never crawl its way out of the womb. The defining characteristic of such a society is a blatant discrepancy between the realities of experience and the categories by which experience is still being interpreted – a discrepancy that can make simultaneously for comedy and horror.[3]

Yet *The Deer Park* is not the novel that might have been expected from the author of *The Naked and the Dead* and *Barbary Shore*, whose major concerns were liberalism, Marxism and fascism, and the sort of radical analysis of Hollywood which the previous novels had ideally equipped him for does not take place. Only partial interest is shown in the most obvious political subject in the material, the indictment and exile of left-wing writers and directors in the film community (which had been happening since 1938); and there are few echoes of Adorno and Horkheimer's classic interpretation of Hollywood, 'The Culture Industry: Enlightenment and Mass Deception',[4] which presents American cinema as a vast amplification, mechanization and marketing of deception. Clearly the Marxist orientation of *The Naked and the Dead* and the Marxist self-reflexive subject of *Barbary Shore* have been exorcized. This absence may seem curious, but *The Deer Park* must be perceived in the context of the profound pessimism about the socialist enterprise at the conclusion of *Barbary Shore*. Jennifer Bailey argues that it is 'quite probable that Mailer began *The Deer Park* with the intention of concentrating his theme upon the political corruption of the early 1950s' and that he was 'beginning to feel pessimistic about the possibilities of political revolution'[5] during the writing of the novel. However, nothing in Mailer's prolix accounts of the genesis of *The Deer Park* confirms this view, and a close reading of *Barbary Shore* reveals Mailer sloughing off as well as taking on a Marxist world view. Marxism had been simultaneously taken on and put on trial. The final paragraphs show him effectively working through socialism to the point where it is located in the past-tense imagery of heritage, and he is already a species of post-Marxist by the end of the book.

The Deer Park does not posit a social conflict at the centre of its numerous drafts. The more dynamic tension in it is between an ideological perspective and an experimental non-ideological politics of sensibility rooted in a radically voluntaristic conception of the nature and meaning of power. The political sub-theme of the novel, which deals with the persecution of the director Charles Eitel, shows Mailer to be dissatisfied with ideology but unprepared ultimately to relinquish Marxism *tout court*. Marxism can continue as a useful analytical tool because it never represented a hopeful theory of history for Mailer. But as his socialism becomes weaker and more qualified his cultural position is even more isolated. To hold the views of the 'libertarian socialist is equivalent to accepting almost total intellectual alienation from America, as well as a series of pains and personal contradictions in one's work'.[6] What *The Deer Park* represents is Mailer's first real fictional gropings towards a truly independent radical position grounded in its own ideas rather than those of his inheritance.

II

The Congressional investigations in Hollywood provide a setting, a political background, against which Mailer can develop the theme of power. The actual historical events of the period are not foregrounded and many details remain blurred because Mailer creates only a spirit of investigation in the film industry without being concerned to describe its context. The House Committee on Un-American Activities opened in 1938 with the aim of investigating the activities of both the far left and the far right in the United States; but in Hollywood the Committee concentrated its efforts on what the historian David Zane Mairowitz describes as a 'first all-out-no-holds-barred strike against leftist infiltration'.[7] The blacklist of communists was established in 1947, two years before Mailer went to Hollywood to work for Sam Goldwyn. After 1947 right-wing pressures and the fears of financial backers forced the film industry to maintain a permanent blacklist which included even ex-communists and fellow travellers considered too risky to employ. As Mairowitz points out, the blacklist effectively ended 'the party's brief encounter with the movie colony',[8] although palpable leftist influence, measured by any standard, had been superficial. The left had never been able to get its 'message into films . . . because of the structure of the industry'.[9] Its chief significance was largely the excessive value placed on it by the Committee.

The second front against Hollywood communists began in 1951, in the period just after Mailer's departure from California. According to Mailer's biographer, Hilary Mills, Mailer was 'one of the few literary celebrities in Hollywood who had no compunction about being identified with the left'.[10] However, as Mairowitz records this period, the Korean War 'had put a scare into many liberal sympathizers, and ex-communists who came up for investigation found themselves no longer heroes but untouchables'.[11] Most of the witnesses called between 1951 and 1954, the years of *The Deer Park's* composition, were either 'voluntary repenters or were made to "see the light" when called'.[12] Because silence amounted to a presumption of guilt, a tradition of 'friendly' witnesses evolved (including such people as Walt Disney, Gary Cooper and Robert Taylor). The fictional persecution of Charles Eitel by the Committee most closely resembles the experience of the writer-director Elia Kazan, who appeared in closed sessions and refused to give names, then testified publicly.

In Mailer's fictionalized Hollywood there are two political systems at work. The first is represented by the studios, which function as courts (to follow the allusion of the novel's title) or 'little monarchies',[13] as the director John Huston has labelled them. This system generally prompts comic reactions from Mailer. According to Jean Radford, Hollywood is seen as an 'ideology factory, producing the cold war patriotism and the sentimental, escapist myths about sex, relationships and reality which dominate American consciousness'.[14] But in Mailer's satirical comedy the studios' power appears trivial and banal, and the reader is allowed to feel superior to it. It is the second political system, also described by Radford, that is truly threatening: 'Supreme Pictures is not merely an internally authoritarian organization producing films with a pernicious ideological content; it is also integrally linked to the repressive McCarthyite State, as is made clear through its cooperation with the Subversive Committee in Congress and its refusal to employ Eitel until he conforms to their political line.'[15] Although the state operates in Mailer's Hollywood in the form of the Committee, no integral link is shown to exist between the two bodies, as Radford states, and *The Deer Park* posits no deep compact between the representatives of the film companies and the government policemen. Hollywood simply responds to the desires of the Committee by blacklisting anyone tainted by investigation. Thus the studios have no real imperatives worth speaking of and do not seem to excite Mailer's imagination. Only the Committee is treated with political seriousness. As Stanley Gutman points out, 'The Committee, as Mailer portrays it, powerfully influences all aspects of American life; its interest is not in security or safety or truth, but in the suppression of the independent will of the American people.'[16]

In the characterization of Congressman Richard Crane and his two assistants Mailer continues to write from the heightened sensitivity to the bureaucratic power of the state that shaped *Barbary Shore* and *The Naked and the Dead*. The representatives of the Committee therefore refer backwards to the first two novels: 'It was Congressman Richard Selwyn Crane of the Subversive Committee, and Eitel had dreamed about Crane; often in the middle of a nightmare he could see Crane's youthful face with its *grey hair* and *ruddy cheeks*, hear the Congressman's *soft voice*' (p. 238, emphasis added). Although Gutman suggests that Crane is a 'thinly veiled Joe McCarthy',[17] there is neither a strong physical nor a strong institutional resemblance to the Senator. Closer to home, Crane has the physical attributes and manners of General Cummings: 'He was a little over medium height, well fleshed, with a rather handsome sun-tanned face and graying hair, but there were differences. His expression when he smiled was very close to the ruddy, complacent and hard appearance of any number of American senators.'[18] And, when Crane says to Eitel, 'I know you don't like me, but the curious thing is that the day I questioned you I had the feeling we could be friends under other circumstances' (p. 239), he recalls the potential for intimacy that existed between Hollingsworth and McLeod ('these are deep compacts between Leroy and myself, you might almost say we are sympathetic to each other'[19]).

Charles Francis Eitel is an extension of Mailer's inquiry into a certain kind of radical mind. While Eitel is nowhere near as severe an ideologue as McLeod, he experiences very similar problems of political faith, and both men are examples of radicals with damaged (McLeod) or lost (Eitel) Marxist idealism. Robert Begiebing is completely mistaken when he argues that Eitel's 'radicalism is totally apolitical'.[20] His path to radicalism had been the conventional one of Depression experience. Through his first wife and her European friends he 'studied radical literature and talked politics' (p. 38). Equipped with an ideology, he made a number of stunning films about social conditions in the 1930s. He 'argued about Spain, he spoke at public meetings, he helped to gather contributions' (p. 39). Eitel even travelled to Spain to make a film, although 'the year spent there was wasted'. The last interesting films he has made are a series of documentaries for the military during the war, one of which was considered too powerful to release.

With the conclusion of the war Eitel is doomed to make 'the studio's pictures' (p. 43). Making a Faustian pact with the establishment, co-opted by Hollywood, he gives in to the materialist temptation. Both artistically and politically this brings about his ruination. In the novel's present, the early 1950s, Eitel's Marxism exists only as a retrospective influence and vestigial social conscience, accompanied by a trace of aesthetic integrity which survives in the form of an uncompromising script he idealistically wishes to produce. Marx remains with him in the form of unattributed quotations: '"You know," he said, "it's not the sentiments of men which make history, but their actions"' (p. 197). But it is a Marx distilled and reduced to aphorism, and when Eitel is first seen interrogated by the Subversive Committee it is not his politics or morals that elicit our admiration; we admire his audacity, wit and sense of performance. Politics are the complicating legacy of a previous era: 'There were so many petitions he had signed, so many causes to which he had given money, first from conviction, then from guilt, finally as a gesture. It was part of the past; he was indifferent to politics' (p. 44). In spite of this condition, Eitel's personal history, his particular past, provides the strongest link between *The Deer Park* and the world created in *The Naked and the Dead* and *Barbary Shore* – and behind these texts the leftist culture of the thirties and forties. The theme of Eitel's deradicalization is crucial because it reveals Mailer attempting, at least in fictional terms, to lay that period to rest.

Political confession in both *Barbary Shore* and *The Naked and the Dead* is double-edged. Although McLeod and Eitel declare themselves to the state and assent to past mistakes, they also confess in order to inspire and educate a new political generation. For the state Eitel merely supplies, in a gesture of conformity, information it already possesses. His lapse of integrity has to be balanced against the example he sets for his protégé, Sergius O'Shaugnessy, of what not to become. Sergius comes to represent Eitel's hope for a more radical, less compromised life. The older man's accumulated wisdom is focused only on Sergius's development. If the precise content of his teaching is not socialist, it refers back to the idealism and sense of commitment of Eitel's Marxist years; and the overwhelming desire is for Sergius to reconnect with the animating spirit of the broad radical tradition from which he is now permanently alienated. Of hardcore Marxists, though, the novel is highly critical. The leftist community in Hollywood exists on the margins, unable to work because the studios will not employ its members. During the Congressional investigation Eitel and his girlfriend, Elena, are restricted to this group of 'émigrés': 'They were writers and directors and actors and even a producer or two who had refused, as he had refused, to cooperate with the Subversive Committee' (p. 170). Elena finds them 'pompous' and Eitel hates the thought of 'being classed' with them. The essence of Eitel's distaste for them lies in their ideological mental mapping:

> Eitel was always bored by people who could enter a discussion only so far, and then could go no farther, because to continue would mean that they would have to give up something they had decided in advance they would continue to believe in.

Besides he knew them so well; even years ago they had bored him when he had belonged to their committees.

An argument Mailer himself would use much later against the left's 'sound-as-brickwork-logic of the next step':[21]

[He] had heard Communists and Trotskyists expatiating on social problems and social actions for years with just this same militant, precise, executive command in analyzing the situation, the same compelling sense of structure, same satisfying almost happy dissection and mastication of the bones and tendons of the problem before them, and Mailer had in fact decided years ago, repelled by some bright implacable certainty of such full-time Marxists, that Leninism was finally good for Leninists about the way psychoanalysis was good for psychoanalysts. . . .

But Eitel, like Mailer, has a complex, ambivalent attitude towards the Marxists, which includes an acknowledgement of them ('no matter how much he disliked the émigrés and their wives, he found himself wishing that Elena was not so ignorant of everything they talked about' – p. 171). Although they have 'repulsive personalities' (p. 295), the impulse they represent is historically important and legitimate. The hostility in Mailer's attitude towards the émigrés is a reflection of his own confession of 'almost total alienation' as a libertarian socialist. He is distancing himself from the marginalization which renders the left socially irrelevant in the United States. Thus they represent the fate of ideological purists, unable to make meaningful contact with the society in which they operate. Consequently at the end of *The Deer Park* Sergius studies Marx's *Capital* and questions his status as a socialist: 'When I cut it all away, I was still an anarchist, and an anarchist I would always be' (p. 345).

Putting socialism to one side, the novel locates no ideological solutions to the problems it sets up, and for the first time in Mailer's fiction Marxism fails to function as an epistemology which makes the world more intelligible. The assumption of this anti-ideological position might be seen in the context of much of the cultural, political and sociological thought of the 1950s, particularly the work of Raymond Aaron, Edward Shils, Seymour Martin Lipset and Daniel Bell. Bell, in his book of essays entitled *The End of Ideology*, popularized the notion that in an era of consensus politics ideology was losing its meaning for much of post-war American society. (Of course, the 1960s showed this judgement to be premature, and Dolbeare and Dolbeare identified at least seven ideologies 'alive and well in the United States'[22] in the 1970s: capitalism, liberalism, reform liberalism, black liberation, the new left, American Marxism and conservatism.) But his own development is idiosyncratic. In *The Deer Park* he is beginning a transition to what he later described as a 'private mixture of Marxism, conservatism, nihilism, and large parts of existentialism'[23] which leaves him with no 'intellectual accord' with Marxism and makes him a permanent critic of ideological apprehensions of reality. It is a transition that represents a true modification of his political sensibility. At the centre of *The Deer Park* Mailer sets about answering the difficult questions this abandonment of ideological themes brings forth. What can replace ideology as a tool for explanation? What can replace ideological politics as a literary subject?

III

What replaces ideology is an absorption with the individual or self. The individual is no longer trapped in the time machine of history but potentially the instrument of his own will, his own internal desire for self-realization. Instead of being ultimately a representative of a larger group or class, he is a fundamental order of being. As Mailer has pointed out, the individuals in *The Deer Park* are 'beings', meaning 'someone whose nature keeps shifting', as opposed to characters, whose nature you 'grasp as a whole'.[24] Because the ideological drama concerning the state and the studios is decentred, the interest in character, what M. H. Abrams calls the 'moral and dispositional qualities'[25] of character, assume pre-eminence. For the first time in Mailer's fiction, character is not fate but the possible transcendence of fate. A generalized aspiration towards self-improvement permeates the novel: 'Nobody is better than he ought to be' (p. 102), announces one of the characters; 'I wish I could be better' (p. 172), intones Elena; 'If only I can give him some polish, he's going to be a very interesting person' (p. 246), declares Lulu Meyers of a third-rate actor. As Robert Solotaroff notes, 'The dynamic . . . view implicit in the novel is that the self is not only constantly changing but that it can only change for the better by some way of struggling with the world which is trying to kill it.'[26] More specifically, through Charles Eitel, Marion Faye and Sergius O'Shaugnessy Mailer explores three competing versions of selfhood (selves that are models rather than types) and works out the power relations of each.

The philosophical position of *The Deer Park* derives at least in part from Eitel, whose status as a wisdom-giver, a truth-teller, is based on his being a child of an idealized previous era, the Enlightenment. Despite his credentials as a lapsed socialist of sorts, Eitel connects more fundamentally with the old-fashioned liberal tradition. His stand against the Subversive Committee (which arouses his hostility towards those Marxist purists with whom he is accused of belonging) is rooted in his belief in the contract that is made between individual and society. The Committee's crime is that it violates the right to *due process*; its exercise of governmental power is unacceptably whimsical. Eitel, by contrast, embodies integrity, decency, dignity, honour and the rights of man. As Solotaroff says, he is 'generally associated with liberal positions through his emphasis on the power of reason, the rights of others, and the need to make generous gestures'.[27] This moral, uplifting dimension links Eitel to the reformist impulse within liberalism. For the reform liberal 'the realization that politics is a real route towards noble ends should be simultaneous with the reintroduction of morality'.[28] Above all Eitel is a moral presence in *The Deer Park*, and it is on this quality that his authority rests. Measured by his actions (which he assures us make history) he is less impressive. Although he is what Arnold Kauffman terms a 'radical liberal',[29] he remains compromised by the Hollywood establishment and the Subversive Committee. Like his fellow radical liberal Robert Hearn, he is able to analyse the threat from the political right in the United States but woefully ill-equipped to create any meaningful strategy against it. Both Hearn and Eitel illustrate what the sociologists Dolbeare and Dolbeare see as the acute dilemma of ideologies that are critical of capitalism and liberalism but nevertheless 'act entirely within their framework and on the basis of the same values'.[30] For all his high-toned moralism, Eitel does co-operate with the Committee and the studios in order to save himself. As Andrew Gordon puts it, Eitel's submission 'represents one of Mailer's deepest fears concerning power, since the director sacrifices autonomy and control over his work for the illusory power of acceptance by the authorities'.[31] His values provide no leverage upon society, the implication being, as Stanley Gutman sees, that 'the humanistic, liberal hero will continually meet defeat through the agency of overwhelmingly hostile social institutions'.[32] Eitel himself is acutely aware of his compromise and the failure of his values on the all-important practical level. His philosophy is reduced to connectionless aphorisms and clever remarks.

Eitel's self is fundamentally discredited as a model. The traditional hero, the man of good values, is found to be defunct. As the critic Richard Foster argues, 'vision, passion, and courage have dwindled in Eitel to intelligence, compassion and guilt'.[33] But Mailer's attitude towards him is complex, since there are aspects of him that have been neither corrupted nor co-opted, and it is in his relationship with Sergius that these redemptive elements of his personality emerge most forcefully. As Marion Faye realizes, Eitel is a 'frustrated teacher' who wants 'people to trust him' (p. 328). Through the instruction of Sergius, he can set his own record straight. The development of the younger man is thus keyed to the personal sacrifices of the older man, and what Robert Begiebing rightly calls the 'transfer of power' is made 'from the old man to the new'.[34] Eitel's teaching, his confession of self, compensates for the humiliating act of political confession made to the state; it is an act of 'telling' of a completely different order, one 'clearly associated here with the world-renewing force of heroic mythologies'.[35]

Eitel is the central theorist of self in *The Deer Park*. His privately expressed ideas may have little bearing on his own social behaviour (which is guided by conventional reform liberalism) but they are of immediate use to Sergius:

That was the night [Eitel] told me his theory, and although I do not want to go into theory maybe it was part of character. I could write it today as he said it, and I think in all modesty I could even add a complexity or two, but this is partly a novel about how I felt at the time, and so I paraphrase as I heard it then, for it would take too long the other way. Eitel made reference to famous people and famous books I never heard about until that evening although I have gotten around to reading them since, but the core of Eitel's theory was that people had a buried nature – 'the noble savage' he called it – which was changed and whipped and trained by everything in life until it was almost dead. Yet if people were lucky and if they were brave, sometimes they would find a mate with the same buried nature and that could make them happy and strong. At least relatively so. There were so many things in the way, and if everybody had a buried nature, well everybody also had a snob, and the snob was usually stronger. The snob could be a tyrant to buried nature. (p. 123)

Reproduced in considerable detail, the theory is presented for serious consideration. The allusion, principally to Rousseau and his 'famous books' (the *Confessions* and *Dialogues*), reinforces Eitel's status as a double confessor. The idea itself, though, can hardly be attributed to Eitel, since it is only a reformulation of Rousseau's negative social contract. Mailer simply employs Rousseau's argument for a reconstituted individual and a return to nature in order to gain critical leverage against the ideology of contract liberalism.[36] But it also invokes a notion, aptly expressed by Leslie Fiedler, which is deeply rooted in American literature:

[America] is not exclusively the product of Reason. . . . Behind its neo-classical facade is a nation sustained by a Sentimental and Romantic dream, the dream of an escape from culture and a renewal of youth. Beside the *philosophes*, with whom he seemed to accord so well that they scarcely knew he was their profoundest enemy, stands Rousseau. It is his compelling vision of a society uncompromised by culture that has left the deepest impress on the American mind.[37]

The Deer Park testifies to the continuing influence of Rousseau's vision. Within the congenial atmosphere of the novel's end-of-ideology argument Rousseau is in fact able to supplant Marx in Mailer's evolving political vision. The 'escape from culture' referred to by Fiedler is overwhelmingly in Mailer a flight from a Marxism which had been synonymous with that culture of Europe so successfully assimilated through Jean Malaquais. Eitel, though, is personally unable to carry through a recovery of self; his buried nature has been 'whipped' and 'trained'; he has become too middle-class to meet the radical standards of the anti-bourgeois Rousseau.

But this is no simple failure. The second function of Eitel's confession to Sergius is to serve as a negative model of self, illustrating which particular defeats to avoid. His excursion into socialism has left him disappointed, his operational liberal ideology has proved useless in practical situations, his personal radical dream lies just beyond reach. Sergius's responsibility is to interpret Eitel's decline correctly: 'How I'm deteriorating, oh how I'm deteriorating' (p. 210); 'In the end that's the only kind of self-respect you have. To be able to say that you're disgusting' (p. 297). It is a process that weans Sergius off models altogether and encourages him to 'do without heroes' (p. 299). The crucial development is an inner one: 'There's a law in life so cruel and so just which demanded that one must grow or else pay for remaining the same' (p.198). In aggressively organic terms Sergius is invited to observe the law of life in the example of Eitel's stunted ruin. The law itself is like charisma, which, according to Max Weber, 'may be said to exist only in the process of originating. It cannot remain stable'.[38] Robert Solotaroff calls Eitel's growth statement 'the unifying thought of Mailer's intellectual career';[39] Stanley Gutman notes how 'time and time again Mailer reformulates the necessity for growth, often in the exact words of Eitel's insight'.[40] Eitel himself is too 'other directed'[41] for personal growth, and in the end he becomes a man of the studios. In Bellow, Malamud or Updike, Eitel might have been accepted as an intriguing central consciousness to be treated with a mixture of sympathy and comedy, but Mailer is too preoccupied with the politics of individuals, with individuals as models, to succumb to Eitel's charm. Eitel, to use Solotaroff's word, is too 'essentialist'[42] for Mailer and becomes therefore the novel's sacrificial hero.

Marion Faye is 'another protégé' (p. 182) of Eitel's and, as Robert Begiebing says, 'another guiding intelligence for the hero'.[43] As a student of Eitel's, Faye has rejected the mentor but not his teaching, and at first sight he seems committed to Eitel's charismatic principle of growth and development. But as the novel progresses the radical experiment which he conducts on the self is revealed to be founded on a complete break with the sentimental concept of natural man and the organic. His policy is to deconstruct indiscriminately all his behavioural responses, natural or conditioned, and reshape them through the application of pure will. This is the most radical posture in the novel, and Mailer's interest in it has led a number of critics to insist that

Faye is the true hero of *The Deer Park*. Jean Radford refers to him as the novel's 'ultimate hero'[44] on the grounds that his 'nihilist despair'[45] is the only appropriate response to the historical condition which besets the characters. For Jennifer Bailey he is the 'only person to effect a dramatically convincing revolt against Desert D'Or's hell';[46] his is the only 'subversive philosophy'.[47] Yet Faye, a late development in the book's conception, requires much more space than the book can allow him and he therefore remains an intriguing figure of obscure motivation.

The late inclusion of Faye ('The book needed something which wasn't in the first draft, some sort of evil genius'[48]) points to the relocation of Mailer's political interest in a more offbeat style of countercultural radicalism. Accorded the status of 'philosopher' (p. 147), he perceives the decadence of the surrounding culture more clearly than anyone else. Paranoid about all external influences and societal manipulations, he attempts to reconstruct himself in his own image, pursuing, in Solotaroff's words, the 'undiluted solitude of self'.[49] The key feature of Faye's moral insurrection is his capacity for action over sentiment. Beyond his analysis, judgement and insight he has a unique dynamism which comes from putting ideas into direct practice. This distinguishes him from the bookish, theoretical Eitel, who has a limited capacity for action. Eitel is a man of history because he is the raw accumulation of experiences. Faye's unsocial contract with the world requires him to be a maker of experiences, and by extension his own history, on the basis of his own strangely reasoned decisions. To avoid 'self-swindles' (p. 148) he deliberately tests himself where he is weak (fear of the night, fear of generous impulses, fear of fellow feelings) and where he is vulnerable to societal control mechanisms (guilt, social responsibility, rule observance). In practice this means he becomes increasingly nonconformist and disconnected from the ordinary experiences of those immersed in the surrounding culture.

The practice of autonomy makes extreme demands of Faye, forcing him to work hard to maintain the severest standards of a self-discipline that is off the human scale. In effect, he obliterates the humanist in himself. This is illustrated in the scene where Faye mistreats the pathetic heroin addict Paco, who begs for help: 'first you had to get rid of your own guilt and to do that you had to kill compassion. Compassion was the queen of guilt.

So screw Paco, and Faye burned for that sad pimply slob' (p. 160). Faye's alternative self-psychiatry privileges personal action over language-based therapies, 'for words belonged to the slobs, and the slobs hid the world with words' (p. 161). Because guilt and its related emotions – the whole core of sentimentalities in human nature – are eradicated, there is no experience of repression in the conventional sense. Part of this involves actively seeking out perverse and pathological states of mind. As Sergius, a veteran, notes, 'I had killed people, I had almost been killed myself, and these were emotions [Faye] considered interesting' (p. 23). Faye is not mad. The cultivation of factitious anti-social urges within himself is part of an overall policy of imitating psychopathic actions. Psychopathy provides him with a model for behaviour. Thus Faye can only dramatize moral irresponsibility in an essentially rational attempt to organize the instincts into psychopathic patterns. Solotaroff speaks of Faye's 'all too rational will' as opposed to Sergeant Croft's 'primordial self'.[50] However, in the imagery of the novel the attempt to live out the infantile fantasy of unchecked selfishness can be seen as a twentieth-century version of Rousseau's child of nature, a debased post-Freudian reworking of Eitel's conception of natural man, replacing buried nature with the 'buried infant'.[51] In fact his psycho-political critique challenges Eitel's essentially eighteenth-century romanticism and provides a point of interrogation against conservative Freudian orthodoxies regarding the definition of neurosis.

The erosion of Mailer's ideological perspective in *The Deer Park* allows other influences to come through. Notable among these is a new concern with religious questions: 'I have some obsession with how God exists. Is He the essential God or an existential God; is He all-powerful or is He, too, an embattled existential creature who may succeed or fail in His vision?. . . . I think it began to show itself while I was doing the last draft of *The Deer Park*. Then it continued to grow. . . .'[52] This religious psychology begins with the introduction of Faye into the second draft of the novel and the network of religious imagery that accumulates around his character. Faye entertains the conceit that his father 'had been a brilliant and dissolute priest' (p. 320) and has himself experienced 'a period when he had been religious, had taken fasts, thought of entering a monastery [and] spent a week on retreat'. Sergius recognizes him as a 'religious man turned inside out' (p. 148), a saint in reverse. Instead of opposing hedonism, he pursues the 'pleasure' obtained from a 'conquered repugnance' (p. 147). This, of course, is the opposite condition from Eitel's, yet Faye struggles wilfully with the 'fury of a man looking for purity' (p. 151) to maintain his own unworldly standards. He uses marijuana, though it gives him no pleasure; he consults 'odd books' (p. 145) in the hours before dawn; he reads Tarot cards and surrounds himself with prostitutes who function as his 'disciples' (p. 151). He is a figure who strangely anticipates the historical emergence of Charles Manson, whom Mailer later described as 'one of the more incandescent sensibilities of our time'.[53] Manson, like Faye, faces the 'complexity of things'[54] in pursuit of a coherent personal ethic: 'The thing about Manson's life . . . is how hard the man worked for his ideas.'[55] The Manson-style religious vision cultivated by Faye rises out of his unredeemable sense of weariness with the world while having a vast surplus of personal energy, a toxic mixture which produces an apocalyptic sense of mission. Looking over the southern California desert, where nuclear weapons have been tested, Faye communes with himself:

> So let it come, Faye thought, let this explosion come, and then another, and all the others, until the Sun God burned the earth. Let it come, he thought, looking into the east at Mecca where the bombs ticked while he stood on a tiny rise of ground trying to see one hundred, two hundred, three hundred miles across the desert. Let it come, Faye begged, like a man praying for rain, let it come and clear the rot and the stench and the stink, let it come for all of everywhere, just so it comes and the world stands clear in the white dead dawn. (p. 161)

Faye's psychic energy is charged by a profound sense of the apocalyptic that is expressed in terms which connect the interior language of religious experience with a non-Freudian conception of the unconscious. Thus for Faye there are no public political solutions to the problems of the world; his commitment is to an ultimately spiritual – which is to say anti-humanist – purification ceremony of mass extinction, heralding the end of the material world.

Faye does not receive full endorsement in *The Deer Park*. In the final analysis he is unable to see his way clear of the tangle of decadent cultural influences, and as a social theorist he has severe

limitations because he offers so little to culture. The terminal position he is being pulled towards is a reduction to absurdity: 'Faye
had a feeling so deep in himself that this was finally the situation
where he could push beyond anything he has ever done, push to
the end as he had promised me so many nights ago, and come
out – he did not know where, but there was experience beyond
experience, there was something. Of that he was certain' (p. 323).
By the end of the novel he is in prison, caught by the police on
an insignificant violation, relegated to a marginal position. The
moral and dispositional qualities he embodies, the dialectic he
tries to create, do not cohere into anything of substance. Faye
himself acknowledges this failure. Considering the prospect of
prison after a car accident, he accommodates himself to reality:
'"It's all right," he thought, holding on to consciousness as if it
were something to grip with his battered mouth, "it's all right,
to make it, maybe I need a year like that. More education," he
tried to say, but a spasm of pain was carrying him into a coma'
(pp. 323–4). Mailer honours the attempt by Faye, the line of inquiry
he sets up, if not the actual achievement. In the context of a flight
from ideology his experiment in self-realization stands as a meaningful, though inchoate, challenge to a claustrophobic historical
situation. As Robert Begiebing argues, Faye is a 'potential agent
of regeneration'.[56] But his psychology remains elusive, slightly
beyond Mailer's intellectual grasp, and, although he becomes
less of a 'mystery' (p. 148) to Sergius, the narrator never really
understands him. The novel concludes with the hint that Faye
will somehow return, though, as Begiebing points out, 'one is
hard pressed to see what Faye is learning and what his return
will mean'.[57] Mailer, like Faye, requires 'more education'.[58]

On first appearances the model of selfhood projected by Sergius
O'Shaugnessy would seem to be the least impressive of the three
available, and in his account of the writing of *The Deer Park* Mailer
confessed to being 'unable to create a narrator in the first person
who was not overdelicate, oversensitive, and painfully tender'.[59]
But there are formal justifications for Sergius's tenderness. His
blandness, like Nick Carraway's in *The Great Gatsby*, serves to
highlight the two dominant personalities. More importantly, it
allows Mailer to dramatize Sergius's development towards full
consciousness. If Eitel is a child of the Enlightenment and Faye is
psychopathically infantile, Sergius is a *tabula rasa*; unlike them, he
has yet to become something and engage with history. Yet in this

uncondition, with 'a lot to learn' (p. 32), he embodies more fully than anyone else in the novel the central questions about the self and power. A contentless individual, he is obliged to create a self or remain a cipher. As Begiebing notes, he is moving from 'impotence and unconsciousness to potency and consciousness', the thing at stake being 'increased consciousness'.[60] Fundamentally he is preoccupied with the same problem Faye wrestles with, the inheritance of the philosophically bankrupt eighteenth and nineteenth centuries embodied by Eitel. Eitel in fact recognizes that Sergius, although he may not be aware of it, 'wants to be an intellectual' (p. 196) and that his coming of age will not only solve a personal problem of identity but also contribute to cultural advances at the level of society. Thus it is important for Sergius, in Solotaroff's words, to 'reform himself'[61] and become a member of the intellectual class.

At the beginning of *The Deer Park* Sergius is a minimal self: 'I was never sure of myself, I never felt as if I came from any particular place, or that I was like other people. Maybe that is one of the reasons I have always felt like a spy or a fake' (p. 29). Objectively he is handsome but he has no sense of inner value: 'I never believed I was convincing' (p. 13). Because he knows so little about himself, and others recognize he is 'very cold at heart' (p. 102), he adopts the epistemological premises of an actor, albeit an 'unemployed actor' (p. 28). Mailer roots this image in the text, tracing it to Sergius's father, who had 'wanted to be an actor' and invented the name O'Shaugnessy in a 'fling'. With his father's death Sergius 'began to look for a new character', becoming a 'fake Irishman' with an inadequate sense of self. Sergius improvises in a void, with no inner experience, none of the Method's affective memory. His status as an orphan (like Lovett's as an amnesiac) compounds this sense of an absence of identity.

The groundwork for Sergius's development has been laid in Korea, where he has flown bombing missions: 'Sometimes on tactical missions we would lay fire bombs into Oriental villages. I did not like that particularly, but I would be busy with technique, and I would dive my plane and drop the jellied gasoline into my part of the pattern. I hardly thought of it in any other way. From the air, a city in flames is not a bad sight' (p. 53). The bombing is an abstraction; Sergius rationalizes the experience by reducing it to 'technique' and 'pattern' and reifying the Korean villagers. The real, suppressed meaning of the bombing is revealed only through an experience at a different level:

> One morning I came back from such a job and went into the Officers' Mess for lunch. We were stationed at the airfield near Tokyo, and one of the Japanese K. P.'s, a fifteen-year-old boy, had just burned his arm in a kettle of spilled soup. Like most Orientals he was durable, and so he served the dishes with one hand, his burned hand held behind him, while the sweat stood on his nose, and he bobbed his head in little shakes because he was disturbing our service. I could not take my eyes from the burn; it ran from the elbow to the shoulder, and the skin had turned to blisters. The K. P. began to get on my nerves. For the first time in years I started to think of my father. . . .
>
> After lunch I took the Jap aside, and asked the cooks for tannic-acid ointment. There wasn't any in the kitchen, and so I told them to boil tea and put a compress on his arm. Suddenly I realized that two hours ago I had been busy setting fire to a dozen people, or two dozen, or had it been a hundred? (pp. 53–4)

Sergius's shock of recognition, his epiphany, is part of *The Deer Park*'s flight from ideology. Generalized abstractions and large patterns fail to communicate, while vivid personal experiences are an immediate (that is to say, not mediated by intervening concepts) guarantee of far-reaching truths. The Japanese boy's arm escalates Sergius's political and social awareness to the extent that it brings about nervous collapse ('I was not very sick, but it was a breakdown' – p. 56); it attests to the terror of responsibility once the distancing effect of ideologies and systemic faiths is penetrated. At this raw, personal, infra-ideological level things reach into the numb blankness of Sergius's alienation. He is rudely awakened to the existence of agency. His instinctive reaction is to retreat from this insight: 'I needed time, and I needed the heat of the sun. I do not know if I can explain that I did not want to feel too much, and I did not want to think.' But the connection is established and accretes into a psycho-social theory: 'I had the idea that there were two worlds. There was a real world, as I called it, a world of wars and boxing clubs and children's homes on back streets, and this real world was a world where orphans burned orphans. It was better not even to think of this. I liked the other world in which almost everybody lived. The imaginary world' (pp.54–5).

This is linked to Faye's uncompromising insistence on the corrupting, deluding sentimentalities of the unreal culture, and both characters strike a Thoreauvian note: the majority of people live repressed lives of quiet desperation within the ideology-encrusted 'imaginary world' of industrial civilization. The real world, by contrast, is subjective ('as I called it'), a place of violent contracts on the margins of culture. Reality is thus not immediately available on the surface of society; it has been pushed underground to lead a fugitive existence. This conception shows Mailer struggling to maintain the notions of the real and realism without recourse to ideological politics. Like Eitel's vision of nature, Sergius's reality is buried, masked, covered by layers, and it involves an accommodation to the sort of psychologized apprehension of society that is anathema to ideological radicals. There is no adherence to a full-blown psychological viewpoint; rather, psychology is used by Mailer for the repair of a damaged world view. The inchoate idea of 'two worlds' serves to protect Sergius's minimal self from the co-opting manoeuvres of the Hollywood establishment. With the connivance of the producer Collie Muneshin and Lulu Meyers, the studio head Herman Teppis attempts to buy the rights to Sergius's life for a film. Encouraged by Eitel he is able to resist the lure of their offer with his own vision: 'and all the while Collie would go on or Lulu would go on, painting my career with words, talking about the marvellous world, the real world, about all the good things which would happen to me, and all the while I was thinking they were wrong, and the real world was underground – a tangle of wild caves where orphans burned orphans' (p. 220). The underground 'tangle of wild caves' Sergius has discovered is that of the unconscious, knowledge of which can be used. Rather than a retreat from politics, the unconscious is presented as the basis of a political epistemology, a new source of energy. As Emerson had realized in the previous century, 'That which was unconscious truth, becomes, when interpreted, and defined as an object, a part of the domain of knowledge – a new weapon in the magazine of power.'[62]

As Sergius's sense of self increases, the acting imagery that surrounds him becomes progressively more Stanislavskian. The usable unconscious is incorporated into the knowledge required to create an authentic rather than a 'fake' role. As David Zane

Mairowitz observes of Stanislavsky, 'There are strong elements of social therapy in the acting system, and it is meant to give broad scope to the idea of the honest performance as a road to character-building on and off stage.'[63] In effect, during the course of the novel Sergius goes through both parts of the Stanislavskian system: he frees himself from previous conditioning, breaking down stereotyped gestures and actions, then begins to transform himself into a character, working on material locked in the unconscious. Faye follows a similar therapy but he fails to get beyond the preliminaries of the system, succeeding only in destroying his conditioning. Sergius is distinguished by his ability to 'grow' as a personality; he alone manages the self-therapy of creating a role and building a character to become, in Solotaroff's words, 'a sort of object lesson in the possibilities of living outside of the corrupt system'.[64]

Nevertheless, the method Mailer uses to resolve the issue of politics and self in Sergius's case indicates the limits of his fictive imagination, and the role which emerges out of these materials rests to an extraordinary degree on a borrowed sensibility. To 'create an adventurer [he] believed in'.[65] Mailer simply falls back on Hemingway's code, which emerges suddenly, and inorganically, in the final chapters of the novel, when Sergius studies the arcana and discipline of bullfighting in Mexico. The practical emphasis of this code (a 'few lessons in the mystical private way' – p. 340), its praxis, contrasts with Eitel's abstract talk of honour, courage and bravery – things that only ever exist at the level of language. The trouble with Eitel is that his self is inscribed in the rhetoric that Hemingway signally rejected in *A Farewell to Arms*: 'I was always embarrassed by the words sacred, glorious and sacrifice and the expression in vain. Abstract words such as glory, honour, courage, or hallow were obscene beside the concrete names of villages, the numbers of roads, the names of rivers, and numbers of regiments and the dates.'[66] As an aficionado, Sergius pulls language down to the level of experience, re-apprentices himself to action values instead of sentiments: 'So then I began a very odd six months. I travelled around with the *novillero* and his girl, and I took lessons from him' (p. 340). Like Faye, the *novillero* is located in sacred imagery: he is 'a radical priest of his art' (p. 342), bullfighting is his 'vocation'. He provides a suitable model for Sergius because he brings the teachings of Eitel and the codeless energy of Faye, sentiment and action, into alignment. Bullfighting inculcates the idea that 'life is an education which should be put to use'. Consequently Sergius is able to make a living giving bullfighting lessons, although he is 'far from good enough to be a teacher' (p. 343).

The final chapters of *The Deer Park* offer little more than a parody of the Jake Barnes/Lady Brett/Romero sections of *The Sun Also Rises*, but through imitating Hemingway Mailer acknowledges a new influence on the theme of power. (The importance of Hemingway for Mailer at this time is illustrated by the elaborate lengths Mailer went to in order to secure Hemingway's endorsement of *The Deer Park*.) What is disappointing is the degree to which the issues in the novel are resolved by the atavistic procedure of alluding backwards to the values of a previous generation of writers. Sergius simply develops a patina of Hemingway values through a series of rather blatant references. Inevitably a certain amount of fudging takes place. Just as Mailer is unable to think through the *avant-garde* personality of Faye, so he fails to clinch Sergius's much-bruited development. He is only able to connect him to the life-support system of Hemingway's *oeuvre*.

Numerous critics have noticed that something is awry in Sergius's position at the end of the novel. Jennifer Bailey sees it as primarily a formal or aesthetic problem: Mailer 'cannot find a satisfactory means of dramatizing O'Shaugnessy's ambition in his novel'. The fault lies with Mailer's intrusive intellectual hardware: 'O'Shaugnessy is shaped by Mailer's ideas on what *should* consti- tute self-creation, not by the progress of a plot which suggests that this is a process *chosen* by the protagonist. O'Shaugnessy therefore effects a moral growth that is independent of the world in which he moves.'[67] For Robert Solotaroff the fact that 'the growth of Sergius is schematically tucked away in the next-to-last chapter of the novel' is a 'stunning disproportion'.[68] In Robert Begiebing's view, because Sergius 'only begins his journey as a gatherer of forces and a hero of renewed life at the end of the novel', we are 'left with only a hope rather than an actual redemption of the world'.[69] These criticisms are fundamentally correct, but the inorganicism they point to derives not nearly so much from the unwelcome presence of ideas in the text as from an evident lack of ideas at the book's conclusion. It is a question not of artistic shortcomings but of moral-political shortsightedness; Hemingway's code functions as an intellectual *deus ex machina,* saving *The Deer Park* from complete confusion. Sergius is thus able to affirm a transcendence over his fake or minimal self:

> one must be ready to live in the hunt for the most elusive game – our real motive or motives, and not the ostensible reason – and therefore I would have to look into myself. But that was not the easiest thing to do, for what did I have to discover? (p. 316)

> ... knowing I was weak and wondering if I would ever be strong. For I touched the bottom myself, and there was a bottom that time. I returned to it, I wallowed in it, I looked at myself, and the longer I looked the less terrifying it became and the more understandable. . . . (p. 317)

The increase in the knowledge of self, of the unconscious and reality which comprises Sergius's new found narcissism, implies a true integration of self, even if Mailer is clearly unable to give it much substance:

> I found as I continued to study that there was an order in what I sought, and I read each book as a curve in some unconscious spiral of intellectual pursuit until the most difficult text at the proper moment was open, and yet the more I learned the more confident I became, because no matter the reputation of the author and the dimensions of his mind, I knew as I read that not one of them could begin to be the final authority for me, because finally the crystallization of their experience did not have the texture apposite to my experience, and I had the conceit, I had the intolerable conviction, that I could write about worlds I knew better than anyone alive. (pp. 345–6)

Yet these claims, appealing as they are, remain only assertions. Sergius's vision is all form and no content. The 'curve' of his intellectual pursuit (which recalls Cummings' curve, the form line of all cultures) is part of an unresolved dialectic ('spiral'). Placed at the end of *The Deer Park*, it is a promissory note on future work – work in which personal experience will be the guarantor of voluntaristic truth.

IV

The most obvious effect of Mailer's new preoccupation with the unconscious is the inclusion of sexuality in his political equation. In *The Naked and the Dead* sex is treated in a strictly sociological manner, as an indicator of societal health. The time machine brings characters into sexual focus to explain their behaviour in terms of problems – jealousy, cuckoldry, lust, homosexuality. More radical sexual disorders are imputed to Cummings and Croft in order to explain their distasteful political natures. In *Barbary Shore* sex is an index of large ideological categories, the cumulative sociology of the first novel giving way to stylized political allegory. The under-the-surface meaning of the main characters' sexual maladjustments is symbolic of events in society, particularly the Russian Revolution and the dysfunctions of capitalism. Thus there is a transparent political interpretation of Guinevere's (the masses') promiscuity, Hollingsworth's (the new right's) homosexuality and sado-masochism, Lannie's (the exhausted left's) hysterical lesbianism, Monina's (the new generation's) erotic precocity, McLeod's (apostate Stalinism's) impotence and Lovett's (neophyte radicalism's) unrequited sexual desire. In what Richard Poirier calls a 'sophomorically diagrammatic'[70] treatment, the secret of each character's sex life translates into an abstract political meaning.

In *The Deer Park* sexuality is both foregrounded and incorporated into Mailer's political epistemology. Redrafting the novel, altering its focus from ideology to a more plastic cultural politics based on the energies of the self, meant that it became, as Mailer says, 'more sexual in the new version'.[71] More radically, Mailer claims that sex was the novel's chief weapon, 'a cold chisel into all the dull mortar of our guilty society'. The subtitle added to the reconceived manuscript was 'A Search For the Obscene'.[72] The novel's title alludes to the decadent promiscuity of the film capital, but the subsequently abandoned subtitle suggests something else – that sex is, as David Riesman labelled it in the 1950s, the last frontier, or, as Eitel sees it, 'a dream of bounty' (p. 112). For Laura Adams the novel's 'real accomplishment as an entity . . . was to push back the frontier of sex in the serious novel'.[73] Stanley Gutman also defends Mailer's large claim for *The Deer Park*: 'The novel is permeated by sex, a fact that led many readers to disparage Mailer's seriousness and dismiss the book as an attempted

best-seller'.[74] Through his own discourse on sex, Mailer is able
to attempt to delegitimize psychoanalysis and psychiatry, jargon
systems, intellectual bureaucracies that demystify and rationalize
sexual energy. Eitel winces on Mailer's behalf at Elena's use of
words such as 'ambivalences' (p. 359) and 'transference' (p. 110),
which she has picked up from analysis. This prevents the book
from offering the kinds of rationalizations used against Cummings
and Croft, and encourages insights into the subjects of sexual
love, impotence, prostitution and homosexuality that are quite
beyond the intellectual policing of the competing discourses on
sex. Mailer's emphasis is on the resources of personal energy that
can be available to the voluntaristic individual, for whom sex is a
lever on power. As Robert Solotaroff puts it, Mailer is 'reaching
towards the formulation that more than offering up a revelation
of the state of one's psyche, one's sexual activities are themselves
decisive causes of growth or decline'.[75]

The official voice of the Hollywood establishment is that of
hypocritical conformity. Herman Teppis promotes the clichés
of 'sincere love', 'motherhood' and 'the big family right here
at Supreme Pictures' (p. 260). In Mailer's satire these sentiments
are juxtaposed with a scene in which a young vulnerable actress
is obliged to perform fellatio on Teppis in his office. In turn, this
unleashes the only truth uttered by Teppis in the novel: '"There's
a monster in the human heart," he said aloud to the empty
room' (p. 278). For a brief moment Ahab's pasteboard masks are
removed to expose the full horror of a (sexual) reality unmediated
by disingenuous rhetoric. Teppis's penis is revealed as the 'thumb
of power' (p. 277). Beneath the factoids, the subterranean 'real
world' of the novel is filled with sex: prostitution, adultery,
orgies, passion and Mexican machismo. Because sexuality is, as
Jennifer Bailey notes, a 'potentially redemptive'[76] energy, Mailer
investigates closely the sex lives of Sergius, Eitel, Elena, Faye and
Lulu Meyers in a search of a discourse of pleasure; and at the end
of the novel an all-embracing truth is arrived at:

> There are hours when I would have the arrogance to reply
> to the Lord Himself, and so I ask, 'Would you agree that sex
> is where philosophy begins?'
>   But God, who is the oldest of the philosophers, answers in
> his weary cryptic way, 'Rather think of Sex as Time, and Time
> as the connection of new circuits.' (p. 363)

According to Sergius, this insight will 'give hope to us noble humans for more than one night'. It is not a rational, systematic idea, but an imaginative leap predicated on the novel's inquiry into sexuality, cryptic because it is only the starting point of a philosophy. Most significantly, it focuses the religious imagery that has been emerging in the novel and brings it into alignment with the sexual material. The aphoristic conclusion results from Sergius hearing voices, a direct experience of the divine. For a moment history is cancelled, replaced by the numinous Time. *The Deer Park* arrives at a sexual mysticism, a beatific vision of sex through God, a closer knowledge of God's presence in sex.

Yet the most striking thing about this conclusion is the degree to which it does not seem justified by the precise sexual content of the novel. (It is known that the final paragraph came to Mailer as an afterthought under the influence of mescaline and was included in the text only days before it went to print.) As Robert Begiebing observes, 'it is necessary to bring considerable outside material to the novel itself to understand [the] relationship'[77] between sex and time. Most of the sexual experiences discussed in *The Deer Park* are of a much lower order of magnitude than the concluding principle. Sergius's sexual nature is yet another aspect of Mailer's inheritance from Hemingway. The sexually damaged hero-narrator is recognizably a Jake Barnes figure, a wounded male whose condition is alleviated by the blank, vain starlet Lulu Meyers: 'For the first time in a year I knew I would be all right' (p. 98). But overwhelming impotence merely qualifies Sergius for sexual misery under the spell of the narcissistic Lulu ('And so I passed around the house, close to desperate with my desire to see her again' – p. 253). Although Lulu gives Sergius a renewed sense of his power in the world, the potency she fosters is that not of self but of what Begiebing calls 'extrinsic considerations', and through her Sergius succumbs to 'extrinsic power in the world'.[78] Only in the final pages does Sergius become constituted in his own sexuality, making the transition to priapic machismo under the aegis of Hemingway-style discipline. The lesson learned from the *novillero* is not confined to bullfighting; the transfer of power between the two men has a sexual dimension: 'I took lessons from him and all the while he knew that his girl would spend her time with me, until finally he merely paid her expenses and usually did nothing else. The more he suffered her taste for me, the more he would plead with me to stay every time I wanted to quit them' (pp. 340–1). The *novillero* acknowledges Sergius's replenished powers, even if they are brought about at the cost of his own deterioration.

In the central sexual relationship of *The Deer Park*, between Eitel and Elena, there is an attempt to probe a love affair in all its aspects. Eitel is convinced that sex is his 'true art' (p. 106) and that good sex is the *sine qua non* of good work: 'With Elena beside him he thought for the first time in many years that the best thing in the world for him was to make a good movie' (p. 112). On the surface he appears to be keyed to the knowledge that sex is the connection of new circuits, that the quality of creativity hinges somehow on sexual experiences. But we soon learn that he is as deluded and sentimental about sex as he is about politics. Although he believes himself to be the controller of the sexual education that takes place with Elena, that he is manipulating the affair 'with confidence, aloofness, and professional disinterest' (p. 200), it is he who is ultimately subjugated: 'What he could not bear was the thought that she did not love him completely without thought or interest in anything else alive' (p. 307). In the short term sex does contribute to a revival in Eitel's sense of self; he is restored sexually; but in the long term it actually feeds into a spiralling personal disintegration which heralds his final accommodation with the Hollywood establishment. No sexual goal is achieved with Elena, and she too undergoes a collapse. Eitel begins the relationship 'warmed by the knowledge that he was good for Elena' (p. 126); by the end the education has been reduced to the jargon and conservative categories of psychoanalysis. The novel thus supports Faye's view that Eitel and Elena 'missed the connection' (p. 328). Faye has radically broken down his own sexuality, perversely contributing to the decadence he abominates. As a pimp he promotes the eschatology of connectionless eroticism and the enslavements of prostitution, which he presents as a model for the whole spectrum of human behaviour: 'No one ever loved anyone except for a rare bird, and the rare bird loved an idea or an idiot child. What people could have instead was honesty, and he would give them honesty, he would stuff it down their throats' (p. 156). The inverted idealism of his mission is to disrupt conventional love because it has become debased. Only Sergius, who refuses to sell the 'rights' to his life, escapes Faye's searching critique. All the other characters have prostituted their sexuality, work and selfhood.

A further difficulty in accepting fully the sexual conclusion of *The Deer Park* lies in the relative absence of actual sexual description. As Richard Poirier complains, 'the novel needed much more sex than [Mailer] congratulated himself for giving'.[79] Mailer is particularly coy about sexual details. On the subject of Sergius's 'wound', Mailer in 1955 is even more guarded than Hemingway in 1926: 'It had come to me shortly before I left Japan, and I had been helpless ever since. Once or twice, with girls I picked up in the bars of Desert D'Or, I had tried to cut my knot and only succeeded in tying it more tightly' (p. 24). The reluctance to approach sex directly leads to ludicrously artificial dialogue which strains to be frank about the subject yet retain a level of decorum:

'Sergius, you have the right to know. I slept with Tony Tanner.'
'But where? When?' I cried aloud, as if to learn what was most important of all.
'In a telephone booth.' (p. 233)

Mailer takes up the theme only to produce vague, distasteful images of intercourse. His language remains mandarin, purged of the obscenity necessary to connect with the 'real world'. With such moral restrictions and self-censorship the novel thus remains timid in precisely those places where it offers itself as radical. It is therefore difficult to take seriously the infamous problems the novel created for the New York publishing houses. Despite Mailer's essentially self-serving arguments and citations of example in *Advertisements for Myself*, the differences between the sexual passages in the penultimate and those in the final versions of the novel are minor and, for the most part, insignificant. The novel's reputation as sexually advanced is therefore unwarranted, resting only on Mailer's cunning promotion of the repressive actions of Putnam and Rinehart and the shrill coda attached to reprints of the text.

The notion that *The Deer Park* has a philosophy of sex, a discourse on the subject, is not borne out by a close examination of the novel. The best that can be said is that the sexual discourse Mailer does develop in the late 1950s and early 1960s has its origins in the final, ill-fitting paragraph in which we are invited to link sex and time. Here, though, a perspective has not been placed on the sexual material which would have provided greater imaginative access to the key areas largely neglected in the novel: rape, orgasm, contraception, various kinds of intercourse, maleness, femininity, masturbation and peripheral sexualities. For the most part these things are not approached (the portrait of the homosexual Teddy Pope is a caricature), and it is difficult to believe that Mailer is able to distinguish between sexual phenomena that are decadently symptomatic of the prevailing culture and those that contribute to the new sexual frontier. The orgies, 'parties carried to a conclusion' (p. 243), seem to offer an epistemology ('We'll all know more when we're done'), but their meaning is ambiguous and duplicitous. It is even possible that, given the pessimism regarding so much of the sexual material at the centre of the novel, Faye's radical disengagement from sexuality is the most appropriate position available. With no 'new circuits' in evidence we are left with sex as an open-ended question. As Jennifer Bailey notes, 'the sexual theme illustrates the genesis of Mailer's revolution, for which he still had to find a suitable form'.[80] We have the desire for a radical change in which sexual love will become, in Richard Poirier's phrase, 'a species of political action',[81] but not the thing itself. For Poirier this is not really possible until Mailer completely abandons his 'somewhat priggish Marxism';[82] only when this has occurred can he be free to work out the ramifications of his own theory of sex.

The Deer Park is certainly free of the sorts of dilemmas and complexities that complicate the literary forms of *The Naked and the Dead* and *Barbary Shore*; and, for the most part, the truth function, what the German writer Günter Grass calls 'content-as-resistance',[83] is kept under strict control. But Mailer had been dissatisfied with early versions of the novel because composing it in 'fine style' had left it 'timid' and 'inhibited',[84] wilfully lacking in risktaking content. As Poirier argues, it 'revealed to [Mailer] the crippling limitations of the form he had to this point given his career'.[85] Redeveloping the manuscript, Mailer tried to give it more substance, more of a truth function, more content-as-resistance (it 'lost its polish, became rough'[86]). Yet Mailer's roughing-up has a limited effect and *The Deer Park* remains the least burdened by political thought of any of his novels. The craft-conscious form keeps it (as Mailer said of the first version) 'well written but minor'.[87] The failure is not of technique, as many critics have argued, but of vision. Mailer projected himself into the book without a preformed position, hoping, as Solotaroff puts it, to discover the truth 'as he invents his fiction'.[88] But working out his ideas under such restrictive formal constraints creates an inert finished product. As Mailer later confessed, he did not have 'the guts to stop the machine, to give myself another two years and write a book which would go a little further'.[89]

Like Hollywood society, *The Deer Park* is caught between an age not quite dead and a new era that, in Norman Podhoretz's words, 'may never crawl its way out of the womb'. Emancipated from ideology it may be, but it is far from constituted in any mature alternative and ends up, as John Aldridge observes, having 'no morality at all'.[90] Nevertheless, in the context of American radicalism it does fulfil two important functions. On the one hand, it does what American radicals have consistently done in the twentieth century, to twist the left away from Marxism inch by inch. On the other, it clears the ground for a more distinctively American politics of self, sexuality and myth, in which 'politics as politics' can be supplanted by 'politics as a part of everything else in life'.[91]

4

The Radical Geography of Self and Society in *An American Dream*

I

A politics that is part of everything else is not achieved overnight, and Mailer spent almost ten years after the publication of *The Deer Park* carrying through a programme of political re-education. During this period, roughly between 1955 and 1965, he produced no novel, concentrating his writing instead on much more ratiocinative and intellectually discursive forms: essays, cultural criticism, reviews, political journalism, and lengthy interviews or self-interviews (a form he made almost entirely his own). Collected together in *Advertisements for Myself* and *The Presidential Papers*, this large body of work charts in detail the thoroughgoing reworking of Mailer's philosophical, political and epistemological position. In the most important writings of this period – 'The White Negro', 'The Political Economy of Time' and 'The Metaphysics of the Belly' – the stymied radical mind can be observed in a dialectical argument with itself, pushing towards an open, essentially freelance radicalism constructed from a highly personal mixture of literature, psychoanalysis, politics and religion. The 'lingering Leninist'[1] of *The Deer Park* becomes in *An American Dream*[2] a 'therapeutic revolutionary',[3] a social theorist of an anti-politics or counterpolitics that has distinct affinities with such exotic radicals as Wilhelm Reich, Herbert Marcuse, Norman O. Brown and Michel Foucault.

As has been shown, the impulse in this direction operated in *The Deer Park*, although without any worked-out position. Only with 'The White Negro' in 1957 are two crucial areas of literary-political research, repression and alienation, tackled fully without the aid of an ideological framework. The ruling idea in Mailer's own perspective, his newer radical thought, is, as Richard Poirier has pointed out, the notion of social distances:

84

Everywhere in Mailer and Lawrence, in Brown and Reich, are metaphors having to do with the geography of depth, of margins, and of movements outward. It we are to believe the radical geography of the self and society there is something buried in each of us, buried in the corporate self; and it follows that these saving remnants may reside in those who have benefited least from technological systems and who are therefore least corrupted. . . .[4]

In 'The White Negro' Mailer assembles a contemporary version of the aboriginal or mythical American self for the twentieth-century urban frontier. A revolutionary *individual*, he has the power to alter society because he exists, in Mailer's radical pun, 'without roots'.[5] Retaining his qualitative alienation as something of value, rather than integrating with society, he constructs his own self-reliant therapies for the psycho-political technologies of repression: 'Orgasm is his therapy – he knows at the seed of his being that good orgasm opens his possibilities and bad orgasm imprisons him.'[6] There is a striking readiness on Mailer's part to recommend cutting away from society towards extreme psychic states and the 'uncharted journey into the rebellious imperatives of self',[7] reviving, in effect, the problematic forms of voluntarism that comprise the subjugated knowledge of *The Naked and the Dead*. But in 1957, unlike 1948, Mailer is able to recover a distinctly social value from apparently anti-social behaviour and assemble what amounts to a consciousness for liberation.

The radical geography of self and society is even more pronounced in *The Presidential Papers*, a pervasive condition encompassing the whole of post-war American history: 'Our history has moved in two rivers, one visible, the other underground; there has been the history of politics which is concrete, practical and unbelievable . . . and there is the subterranean river of untapped, ferocious, lonely and romantic desires, the concentration of ecstasy and violence which is the dream life of the nation.'[8] Recognizably an extension of Lovett's underground existence and Sergius's 'real world', the key idea of this collection of essays is an attempt to produce a plastic cultural politics capable of reaching downwards to untapped energies and reconnect the individual to society in a radically transformative way. It is a process that will disrupt the banal, profane powers at the centre of institutional life and establish the much-bruited new circuits of *The Deer Park*'s coda, restoring, as Robert Begiebing puts it, 'a "wholeness" and balance to the self and society'.[9] The promise of such an 'existential politics'[10] is that romantic desires, ecstasy and violence form a usable psychic surplus that, once unrepressed, can be applied socially: 'if there is a strong ineradicable strain in human nature, one must try not to suppress it or anomaly, cancer and plague will follow. Instead one must find an art into which it can grow.'[11]

As the post-Marxist Mailer begins to blur ethical and aesthetic categories (Poirier sees this blurring as characteristic of the new literary radicalism), fiction increases its significance as a forum for the examination of the hypothetical 'dream life of the nation'. In *An American Dream* this can be seen in the focus on an individual whose life is transformed by circumstances into a radical romance of margins and movements outwards, a search for the saving remnants that will not only secure his own redemption but also, in the larger dialectic, emancipate the 'everything else' that is implied by Mailer's politics of culture. Through Stephen Richards Rojack and the fictional textures of *An American Dream* the margins are brought to bear on central political questions about the contracts and transgressions of individual and society.

II

Traditionally radicalism has been reluctant to recognize the importance of personal liberation for political struggles. The notable exceptions to this rule are those, such as Wilhelm Reich and Herbert Marcuse, who have seized on psychoanalysis as a possible revolutionary doctrine. For both Reich and Marcuse the revolutionary's classic aim of public social correction modulates into a transitional phase of private self-transformation, the individual's deconstruction of the repressive aspects of his own social existence at the micro-level. Following a quite different route from the neo-conservative Daniel Bell, Reich and Marcuse, like Mailer himself, arrive at their own version of the end-of-ideology argument. Their alternative vehicle for social change and regulation is the transgressing individual, who is not merely radical in social behaviour but also his own source of 'Power-knowledge',[12] an empiricist unmediated by a body of rationalist theory or codes of practice, as in Marxism. In radical psychoanalytic terms, the transgressing individual is free and by that fact alone revolutionary. Existing dangerously outside the mental structures that spring from the economy, he has a genuinely critical consciousness. 'The White Negro' is a classic statement of the counterpolitical argument for self-transformation, and it immediately places Mailer among those who have managed to view psychoanalysis as a revolutionary or critical doctrine. Attempting to, in his words, construct the 'radical bridge from Marx to Freud',[13] Mailer offers us his revolutionary individual, the psychopath, in response to traditional radicalism's post-war impasse: 'despair of the monotony and bleakness of the future has become so engrained in the radical temper that the radical is in danger from all imagination'.[14]

The psychopath questions the conventional political relationship of theory to practice, particularly the role of the theorizing intellectual as the immediate catalyst for social change. As Foucault defines the situation, 'The intellectual spoke the truth to those who had yet to see it, in the name of those who were forbidden to speak the truth: he was conscience, consciousness, and eloquence.'[15] In 'The White Negro' the intellectual does not represent the masses or his minority group or express the stifled views of the collectivity in order to stimulate greater consciousness. Mailer's self-reliant philosophical psychopath (not to be confused with his plain counterpart) does not require theoretical mediation: 'What characterizes almost every psychopath and part psychopath is that they are trying to create a new nervous system for themselves.'[16] He operates on his repression directly, without recourse to ideological construct, 'codifying, at least for himself, the suppositions on which his inner universe is constructed'.[17] Its politics inhere in a spontaneous reclamation of identity and energy from the pejorative categories of mainstream psychoanalysis. The psychopath (itself such a category) knows instinctively that 'to express a forbidden impulse actively is far more beneficial to him than merely to confess the desire in the safety of the doctor's room'.[18] Along with Reich and Marcuse, Mailer takes radical psychoanalysis onto the streets, and in doing so transforms the concepts of individual sickness, collective health and cure, making them counterpolitical rather than technical-medical issues. 'The White Negro' is an extremist celebration of libertarian values, an intoxicating and enabling piece of mythmaking; *An*

American Dream is less reckless, an extended fictional exploration of some of its consequences. The part-psychopath narrator-hero of the novel, Rojack, has radicalizing experiences and unmediated increases in consciousness forced upon him, and there is nothing he fears more than release from the repression that keeps him, by societal standards at least, a sane, adjusted member of the community. Rojack is an important test case for psychoanalytical counterpolitics because, unlike the characters in *The Deer Park*, he is not a model but a reluctant radical called into service by circumstances. As Stanley Gutman rightly stresses, it is precisely because Mailer 'seems more concerned with Rojack as a complex human being and less concerned with the need to create in him a reflection of a philosophic system that Rojack is a more successful characterization than his predecessor, Marion Faye'.[19]

The central image of society cultivated by *An American Dream* is that of an establishment. Through a system of interlocking metaphors of copulation and incest, centring on Rojack's father-in-law Barney Kelly, and a related metaphor system concerned with espionage, centring on Rojack's wife Deborah, Mailer creates a condensed but highly suggestive picture of capitalist culture controlled by a sophisticated network that forms what C. Wright Mills labelled the power elite, 'an intricate set of overlapping cliques [sharing] decisions having at least national consequences'.[20] Mailer's establishment, like Mills's, is institutional, and as the novel progresses more of its cohesive influence is revealed; by the end it appears to be a conspiracy that includes the university, the police, the media, government, the secret services, the Mafia and the leisure class. As a unified image of society it is yet another example of Mailer's paranoid sociology, stretching back through his exposure of the film industry, the government's persecution of leftists, to the fear of a fascist takeover in the United States. In *An American Dream* the establishment has been created under the specific conditions of capitalist philosophy: America has fulfilled itself only with the aid of a market economy, and the profane, materialistic result of the nation's idealism has brought about a corporate reality. Rojack's participation in the establishment takes two forms. First, he has a set of social roles at the centre of institutional life, as a university professor, an ex-Congressman and a television personality. More crucially, though, his marriage to Deborah makes him an intimate of the Kelly family, which is at the hub of the vast conspiracy in society. Deborah's malignity is therefore not simply personal; she is a 'society bitch' (p. 128), and Rojack's existence in the marriage implies larger contracts ('I did not have the strength to stand alone' – p. 24). Both the public and the private are networked to the establishment's sphere of influence.

Rojack's crisis in the opening pages of *An American Dream* derives from a fundamental alienation from the American establishment and its particular claim on reality: 'I had learned to speak in a world which believed in the *New York Times*: Experts Divided on Fluoridation, Diplomat Attacks Council Text, Self-Rule Near for Bantu Province, Chancellor Outlines Purpose of Talks, New Drive for Health Care for Aged. I had lost my faith in all that by now'. . . . (p. 40). The problem is one of adjustment to the profane, rational version of the social dream with its emphasis on personal success, wealth, commodities, fame – what Eric Fromm labels the *having* as opposed to the *being* mode of existence. When we first encounter Rojack, his alienation is advanced and its roots stretch back as far as the Second World War. Although he has achieved establishment status, he has been moving farther and farther from the centre. Like Sergius, he feels like an 'actor' (p. 14), his personality is 'built upon a void'. Like Mailer himself, he has abandoned conventional ideological politics:

> Thus I quit my place in politics almost as quickly as I gained it, for by '48 I chose to bolt the Democratic Party and run for office on the Progressive ticket. Henry Wallace, Glen Taylor and me. I had reasons for the choice, some honourable, some spurious, but one motive now seems clear – I wanted to depart from politics before I was separated from myself forever by the distance between my public appearance which had become vital on television, indeed nearly robust, and my secret frightened romance with the moon. About the month you decide not to make a speech because it is the week of the full lunar face you also know if still you are sane that politics are not for you and you are not for politics. (pp. 14–15)

Rojack is not heroic in the style of the white negro; he is merely an uprooted, deracinated and alienated self. Andrew Gordon sees him as an 'obsessional neurotic'[21] in crisis, and Philip Bufithis acknowledges his 'dissolution of self',[22] but above all he is repressed, exhibiting what Reich calls 'character resistance'.[23] In his own judgement Rojack is 'finally a failure' (p. 15) and a coward (p. 200); his ego is without 'armature' (p. 23). If he cannot find protection from the deeper experiences of self that appear to threaten him, he may 'topple like clay'.

Yet it is precisely such an experience that has provided the solid foundation for Rojack's rejection of the corporate establishment. During the Second World War he had killed four German machinegunners single handed, and the death of the soldiers has a peculiar religious-political meaning for him: 'It was all in his eyes, he had eyes I was to see once later on an autopsy table in a small town in Missouri, eyes belonging to a redneck farmer from a deep road in the Ozarks, eyes of blue, so perfectly blue and mad they go all the way in deep into celestial vaults of sky, eyes which go all the way to God. . . . '(p.12). To Rojack, the soldiers represent 'German-Protestant rectitude', and Mailer interprets the killings as an act of rebellion against proto-capitalism, what Weber calls the *spirit* of capitalism. The Germans' eyes transmit the methodological accumulation and rationalism at the bottom of the Protestantism which underlies contemporary or late capitalism as embodied by the American establishment. Although Rojack is half-Protestant and part of the establishment, he has existed since the war in a semi-alienated state, lost in a 'private kaleidoscope of death' (p. 14) ushered in by the dying soldiers, whose 'eyes had come to what was waiting on the other side, and they told me then that death was a creation far more dangerous than life. I could have had a career in politics if only I had been able to think that death was zero, death was everyone's emptiness. But I knew it was not.' Death seems to be an epistemology that stands in polar opposition to capitalism; knowledge of it, as Jean Radford observes, produces a 'rejection of politics and other forms of the American Dream of power'.[24] When Rojack later murders Deborah, society's bitch, he again attacks the 'good old protestant centre of a mad nation' (p. 136). Her eyes are thus 'equal to the German' (p. 42). Through this act of killing, the prisoner of capitalist materialism destroys a particular image of the world, which opens a door that offers a glimpse to something beyond: 'heaven was there, some quiver of jewelled cities, shining in the glow of tropical dusk, and I thrust against the door once more . . . and *crack* the door flew open . . . and I was through the door . . . I was floating. I was as far into myself as I have ever been and universes wheeled in a dream' (p. 36). The murder is a hysterical attempt by the self to get free of the miasma of social existence. While it is, as Stanley Gutman says, 'ostensibly . . . an act of liberation',[26] an attempt, in Richard Poirier's elegant construction, to 'escape from the world as it is contrived and structured by conspiracies of power',[25] the result is far from liberating. Added to Rojack's increase in consciousness is a multiplying sense of confusion: 'I looked deeper into the eyes of the mirror as if they were keyholes to a gate which gave on a palace, and I asked myself "Am I now good? Am I evil forever?"' (p. 42). His social self, what Reich calls pejoratively 'character', has disintegrated, leaving him an unstable consciousness: 'I was in some far gone state: no longer a person, a character, a man of habits, rather a ghost, a cloud of loose emotions which scattered on the wind' (p. 57). The contract between self and society is abrogated; the self in isolation is terrifyingly free, unhinged.

The questions this opens up had been touched upon as early as *The Naked and the Dead*, but, as Andrew Gordon notes, between that novel and *An American Dream* Mailer's 'conception of history had become radically altered'.[27] Whereas in the first novel voluntaristic individuals are perceived as never less than dangerous to society, in 'The White Negro' the psychopath's danger to society is part of his contribution to culture. Moral lines are no longer easy to establish. As Ruta, the German maid in *An American Dream*, puts it, 'the more you learn the more you know there are never any answers, just more questions' (p. 213). The precise degree to which the individual is a source rather than a vehicle for power becomes ambiguous. Mailer captures the complexity of this in his essay on the CIA (which is known as the 'Agency'), where he presents a series of 'epistemological models'[28] for the penetration of the individual's true role. The idea of the double agent is the key metaphor to explain philosophical uncertainty:

The human brain is divided: into the right lobe and a left lobe; a bold side and a cautious one; a moralist and a sinner; a radical and a conservative; a live lover and a dead one; a wit and an idiot; a hard worker and a sloth. We are all ourselves, and to some degree we are the opposite of ourselves. Consider the overlays of personality which accompany these shifts of identity when a cover story is added. . . . The mind reels. The scenarios do a dervish. . . . All clear boundaries of identity are lost.[29]

Rojack confronts this dilemma because he is plagued by the doubleness of his agency. The individual, he recognizes, is the centre of a field of forces, and the 'secret of sanity is the ability to hold the maximum number of impossible combinations in one's mind' (p. 150). Deracinated, pushed to the margins of culture – radicalized, individual responsibilities become even more acutely felt. Mailer is fond of labelling this condition *existential*, but it is a mistake to conclude from this that he is greatly influenced by such European thinkers as Sartre, Kierkegaard and Heidegger. The term is used with little rigour or stringency and is rather unstable in its meaning.[30] Mailer himself concedes that 'the general concept of existentialism'[31] is not really his intellectual territory and admits to appropriating it in order to 'adventure out on a few thoughts'. Nevertheless, his use of the term consistently emphasizes the individual's problem of knowledge, his epistemological gaps, and the uncertainties of agency: 'we find ourselves in an existential position whenever we are in a situation where we cannot foretell the end.'

Mailer's idiosyncratic existentialism validates ignorance. The lack of knowledge so detrimental to the political vision of *The Deer Park* is transformed here into an area of research, a philosophical position in its own right. The condition of not knowing is honorific; epistemological gaps are existential. Reich locates the origins of repression in man beginning to think about himself instead of obeying his instincts. Following Reich, Mailer argues for 'turning the conscious mind back upon its natural sub-servience to the instinct',[32] and, in turn, the psychopath converts 'his unconscious experience into much conscious knowledge'.[33] (Both Reich and Mailer reverse the naïve intellectualism of the liberal tradition which blames human problems on ignorance.) Rojack's position is existential because he can locate no categories for his actions as he performs them; he is caught in an 'exercise in epistemology',[34] a search for an adequate hypothesis to meet the terms of his psychic alienation:

> And I lay back on my seat and felt something close to nausea because mystery revolved around me, and I did not know if it was hard precise mystery with a detailed solution, or a mystery

fathered by the collision of larger mysteries, something so hopeless to determine as the edge of a cloud, or could it be, was it a mystery even worse, something between the two, some hopeless no-man's land from which nothing could return but exhaustion. . . . I would not be permitted to flee the mystery. I was close to prayer then, I was very close, for what was prayer but a beseechment *not* to pursue the mystery. 'God,' I wanted to pray, 'let me love that girl, and become a father, and try to be a good man, and do some decent work.' Yes, 'God,' I was close to begging, 'do not make me go back and back again to the charnel house of the moon.' (p. 153)

Rojack's mind is open, vulnerable to all influences and unprotected. In Reichian terms this is a positive condition; like Rojack's persistent vomiting, it signifies purgation, release from emotional plague. His character 'armouring', the individual's defensive anxieties against libidinal impulses, has been penetrated and he has moved closer towards liberation and the natural flow of bodily feelings. But dissolving the superego is a frightening liberation (Mailer uses imagery relating to heights, parapets and abysses to dramatize this), since, as Philip Reiff points out, 'to experience the power of desires [is] enough to create a profound fear of satisfying them'.[35] Deracination precipitates visions of the unrepressed (in Rojack's case, of heaven and hell) and genuine moral choices. But dreams belittle history and ideological radicals find it difficult to accept such states of being. For Jean Malaquais, the notion of the revolutionary individual is a preposterous idealistic myth; the psychopath can only be a 'frustrated conformist' or 'frustrated rebel'.[36] His actions can never become broad-based or spiral into anything meaningfully social. At his most potent he still represents 'the avant garde of conformity'.[37] For Mailer, though, a radical role is ascribed to the unconscious, which is argued to have 'an enormous teleological sense'.[38] If its ultimate purpose is unknown, it is existential; if it is not a discourse learned from the external world, it is instinctive. Neither of these things diminishes the social: 'Once History inhabits a crazy house, egotism may be the last tool left to History.'[39]

For both Reich and Mailer the Russian Revolution represents a moumental failure because it did not spread, not just in Trotsky's sense of world revolution, but inwardly, proceeding from the ideological to the psychological level. Mailer did not ascribe to this view consciously in 1951, but *Barbary Shore* certainly illustrates this outward-inward tension, emerging, as he later noted, 'from the bombarded cellars' of his 'unconscious'.[40] Yet the novel failed to deliver what Mailer had hoped for, 'a kind of insane insight into the psychic mysteries of Stalinists, secret policemen, narcissists, children, lesbians, hysterics, revolutionaries'.[41] The characters' lives can only be made to symbolize the failure of the revolution because the novel does not include within its conspectus issues of individual repression and liberation at the psychological level. In 1951 Mailer did not have the conceptual hardware necessary to link history and psychology; he was 'trying for something at the very end of [his] reach, and then beyond it'. Only when Freud has been added to Marx does he desire to 'create a revolution in the consciousness of our time' rather than a materialistic transformation in the means of production. Once his socialism has 'gone completely psychological'[42] he becomes, like Reich, a 'political doctor',[43] obliged to attend to what Barney Kelly in *An American Dream* calls 'the general insanity of everything' (p. 218).

Mailer's fundamental disagreement with left radicalism in 'The White Negro' and *An American Dream* lies in his reversal of the Marxist axiom that history precedes consciousness, that consciousness reflects historical process. What the schismatic Reich and Mailer (after 1957) argue is that character structure can *create* social structure. Attacking economies, political regimes or establishments directly leaves the root (radix, radical) problem unaffected. Newer tyrannies are created from the ideological character structures that have remained intact, unchanged by socialist revolution. In Philip Reiff's description the pattern is classic: 'Revolutions freeze, lock themselves in. Heroism gives way to efficiency. Passion gives way to calculation. Thermidor follows Germinal. Stalin follows Lenin.' Mailer certainly seems aware of this by the end of *Barbary Shore* but he has little to offer in its place besides a return to theory and underground activity. However, in 'The White Negro' and *An American Dream* the individual, once he achieves a radical/rootless condition, can presage social change. It is not the working class but the psychopath that has the loop to history, as the 'perverted and dangerous front-runner of a new kind of personality which could become the central expression of human nature before the twentieth century is over'.[44] Rojack's marginalization produces in him a self-reflexive consciousness which he recognizes as a 'new contract' (p. 126) in culture, an intoxicating notion that shapes the politics of *An American Dream*. The seed of this idea is contained in a remark of Mailer's made two months before he began the novel:

> Sometimes I feel as if there's a vast guerilla war going on for the mind of man, communist against communist, capitalist against capitalist, artist against artist. And the stakes are huge. We will spoil the best secrets of life or will we help to free a new kind of man? It's intoxicating to think of that. There's something rich waiting if one of us is brave enough and good enough to get there.[45]

It is a radical heresy shared with Herbert Marcuse, for whom 'the concept of the new man as a transforming agent has been the great, real, transcending force, the *idée neuve* in the first powerful rebellion against the whole of existing society, the rebellion for the total transvaluation of values for qualitatively different ways of life'.[46]

The emphasis Mailer places on his new man is one of inwardness: 'inner universe', 'narcissistic detachment', 'inner certainty'.[47] His vocabulary suggests the buried or repressed life trying to get out, implying that there is something *in* the individual that needs to be preserved against corruption. As a model this is the exact opposite of behaviourism, and the reason why Mailer failed to demolish behaviourism in *The Naked and the Dead* was that he did not have an innateness argument at his disposal. The depths of personality could only be approached covertly, with critical caution. Rojack's sense of becoming, by contrast, embraces innateness. As Andrew Gordon notes, 'the entire novel is a testimony to the power of the repressed, which must always return'.[48] Killing Deborah triggers the self: 'I was feeling good, as if my life had just begun' (p. 43); 'Deborah's dying had given me new life' (p. 91). The modulation in consciousness that comes with release from repression is transcendental, and while in police custody Rojack undergoes an inward rebirth:

> I wondered if I were in fever for I had the impression now that I was letting go of some grip on my memory of the past, that now I was giving up my loyalty to every good moment I had

had with Deborah and surrendering the hard compacted anger
of every hour when she had spoiled my need. I felt as if I were
even saying goodbye to that night on the hill in Italy with my
four Germans under the moon, yes, I felt just as some creature
locked by fear to the border between earth and water (its grip
the accumulated experience of a thousand generations) might
feel on that second when its claw took hold, its body climbed
up from the sea, and its impulse took a leap over the edge
of mutation so that now and at last it was something new,
something better or worse, but never again what it had been on
the other side of the instant. I felt as if I had crossed a chasm
of time and was some new breed of man. What a fever I must
have been in. (p. 80)

The 'chasm of time' is the distance between history and mythical
Time. Reich's ideal, based on the model of the animal, is the
'unafraid individual', who has the capacity to satisfy 'his strong
libidinal needs even at the risk of social ostracism'.[49] Although
Rojack is, like most of us, in Reich's term, a 'mixed-type'[50] and
far from unafraid, he tries to obey libidinal imperatives, and in
moments of reverie 'on the border' he experiences a keen new
sensibility. His self takes a 'leap over the edge of mutation' into
a psychic transformation that implies heritable variation ('new
breed') and reintegration, coming back to his 'separate parts'
(p. 127).

Mailer's new man, as distinct from Reich's or Marcuse's,
is not the antithesis of a society perceived as oppressive.
Even in 'The White Negro', where Mailer is militantly alive
to the redemptive particularities of certain individuals, there
is a basic unwillingness to transfer responsibilities from self
to society or see these categories in crude opposition to each
other: 'No matter how crippled or perverted an image of man
was the society he had created, it was nonetheless his creation
(at least his collective creation from the past) and if society was so
murderous, then who could ignore the most hideous of questions
about his own nature?'[51] Despite their radical geography, Mailer
keeps self and society locked in to a close, tense, dialectical
relationship, and the lines of demarcation between them are
difficult to draw. Compared with Reich or Marcuse, Mailer
does not allow for absolute radical confidence in the buried self,
since the released inner condition of the individual is never free

of contamination by system. For Mailer the buried self is almost certainly a 'nest of personalities' (p. 95), corrupted and capable of further corruption, which is why he is so preoccupied with mystery and the epistemology of not knowing. The radical individual who deconstructs his repression is obliged to examine the complex network of influences in his own sensibility to discern what is corrupt and what is, in Marcuse's phrase, a genuine transvaluation of values. Ultimately Mailer does not have the unqualified confidence of Reich or Marcuse; he retains at the centre of his politics a fundamental doubt – and it is this spirit of uncertainty that makes the Mailerian individual's fate intriguing and potentially heroic.

Mailer's major and most controversial departure from the position held by the other psychoanalytic radicals lies specifically in the area of power. Reich's and Marcuse's definition of freedom rests on a completely negative view of power. For Reich, 'all power is pathological'.[52] Marcuse's vision is of a co-operative society arising out of repressive desublimation and the absence of power relations. Mailer's special contribution, on the other hand, is to take the opposite view. As Solotaroff points out, 'Although Mailer is egalitarian in celebrating the potential of each individual, his philosophy is no less power-orientated than Cummings's.'[53] He is in no way sympathetic to what Foucault has labelled the 'repression theory of power' or 'Reich hypothesis',[54] the attempt to get beyond power. Yet Mailer is widely misinterpreted on this point. Solotaroff insists that aggression in Mailer can only be interpreted negatively as the 'first new form that energy takes when it cannot find sexual relief'.[55] Jean Radford, siding with the Reich hypothesis, locates in Mailer a celebration of 'violence and repression in the name of a single form of "health"'.[56] Similarly Laura Adams insists that 'only through an act of violence' can Rojack be wrenched free of his 'false self'.[57] But Mailer is implying something much less limited than these glosses would suggest. Rojack, speaking for Mailer, feels that 'the root of neurosis is cowardice' (p. 235), the failure to exercise individual power in those testing circumstances that require action. Individual desublimation, 'the close call of the self',[58] demands personal demonstrations of physical and mental courage, which inevitably involves power processes.

In *An American Dream* brave actions are rewarded while cowardly actions lead to uncomfortable diminutions in one's sense of self.

Yet, as selfhood ebbs and flows, knowing exactly how courageous you are is no easy thing:

> I felt something begin to go out of the very light of my mind, as if the colours which lit the stage of my dreams would be more modest, now, something vital was ready to go away forever even as once, not thirty years ago, I had lost some other part of myself, it had streamed away on a voyage to the moon, launched out on that instant when I had been too fearful to jump, something had quit me forever, that ability of my soul to die in its place, take failure, go down honourably. Now something else was preparing to leave, some certainty of love was passing away, some knowledge it was the reward for which to live. . . . (p. 196)

Rather than arguing for a renunciation of power, Mailer involves a positive therapy based on power. The individual earns liberation through actions that dispel neurosis and desublimate repression. Each of Rojack's tests – with Deborah, the police, Shago Martin, Barney Kelly – requires from him expressions of power, both physical and psychic, which are purgative and liberate the quiescent self. The important distinction is not between power and its negation but between individual or micro acts of power and abstract, macro acts of power at the societal level:

> It seems to me that there are two kinds of violence and they are altogether different. One is personal violence – an act of violence by man or woman against other men or women. The second kind is social violence – concentration camps, nuclear warfare. If one wants to carry the notion far enough, there are subtler forms such as censorship, or excessively organized piety, or charity drives. Social violence creates personal violence as its antithesis. . . . Threatened with the extinction of our possibilities, we react with chronic rage. Violence begins, you see, as the desire to fight one's way out of a trap. . . . The first reaction, the heart of violence, is the protection of the self.[59]

For Reich and Marcuse, knowledge, health and liberation are associated with the renunciation of power (power can promote only ideology); but Mailer cannot treat the failure to exercise power with indifference. The absence of power at the micro-level is a symptom of repression, individual paralysis and cowardice. The potential consequence of this is a biopolitical 'revolt of the cells' (p. 20), cancer, a disease of the body and body politic stemming from the repressive social order: 'In some madness must come with breath . . . in some it goes up to the mind. Some take the madness and stop it with discipline. Madness is locked beneath. It goes into the tissues, is swallowed by the cells. The cells go mad. Cancer is their flag' (p. 249). In psychotherapeutic terms, cancer is a genuine medical symptom and a potent moral signifier of discord between the powerless micro-level and the excessive powers of the macro-level. Rojack suffers from cancer phobia, which psychoanalytic theory also links with power. As Otto Fenichel puts it, 'The psyche punishes itself, which is safer than punishing the hated person. This is experienced by the neurotic as a generalized fear of being attacked from the inside, being eaten by cancer'.[60] Mailer's power therapy is a strategy of resistance both to the disease and the social conditions which bring it into existence.

The sociological theorist Talcott Parsons complains about the 'utopian conception of an ideal society in which power does not play a part at all'.[61] Although the criticism is aimed primarily at C. Wright Mills, it applies equally to the anti-power positions of Reich and Marcuse. The flaw in their radical idealism is that it never distinguishes between types of power. According to Parsons, the radical in this position 'adopts one version of the concept without attempting to justify it. This is what may be called the "zero sum" concept: power, that is to say, is power *over* others'.[62] Mailer does not accept the 'zero sum' argument, but neither does he align himself with those, such as Parsons, who treat power as primarily a facility that makes possible the attainment of goals, which minimizes the presence of dominance, submission and power-over. With the murder of Deborah in *An American Dream*, Mailer actually leads the reader directly into the problem of power-over. Although freedom involves the exercise of an enabling micro-power, it is not allowed for us to speak of it only as a capacity. It is a position that rests finally on a scrupulous observation of numerous distinctions. In fact, Mailer's work in this period actually precedes and anticipates Foucault's recent complete re-examination of the philosophical and political question of power. Foucault, a non-Marxist radical, also attacks the weakness of the 'zero sum':

We must cease at once and for all to describe the effects of power in negative terms: it 'excludes', it 'represses', it 'censors', it 'abstracts', it 'masks', it 'conceals'. In fact power produces; it produces reality; it produces domains of objects and rituals of truth. The individual and the knowledge that may be gained of him belong to this production.[63]

What both Foucault and Mailer argue is that power is much more ambiguous than either Reich or Marcuse believes. Rojack, poised between power-*over* and power-*to*, between being a 'power subject' and a 'power holder',[64] between powers that simultaneously repress and produce, illustrates this essential ambiguity. Thus radical idealism's glib acceptance of the desublimated autonomous subject is undercut.

An American Dream presents a non-utopian critical consciousness which does not pursue the overthrow of society, only its radical regulation. Mailer may persist in speaking of revolution in the early 1960s, but his work is very short on the political pragmatism – the lingering Leninism – for bringing about such an event. The term is simply his radical inheritance, deployed rhetorically, without a theory of revolution or a strategy for its inception. The psychopath or new breed of man is an agent of social change (character structure can create social structure) but not economic or political revolutionary change. Mailer's counterpolitics, like Foucault's 'unpolitics',[65] augur local transformations following from the positive expression of micro-powers or acts of transgression that effectively circumvent the dead weight of conventional politics. We are in the sphere of regulatory rebellions which, though uncompromising and non-reformist, produce only fragments of any new order. The changes, principally of sensibility, involve only those who participate. It is primarily a politics of revelation.

III

One of the most important features of *An American Dream* is its integration of sexuality into power politics. Paul A. Robinson identifies Reich and Marcuse as primarily sexual radicals, whose defining characteristic is that they are convinced of the unparalleled significance of sex, both in individual psychology and in the evolution of civilization. In this they do not, I suppose, differ markedly from Freud himself. What makes them sexual radicals is their unqualified enthusiasm for sex, their belief that sexual pleasure is the ultimate measure of human happiness, and their pronounced hostility to the sexual repressiveness of modern civilization.[66]

The other crucial characteristic of sexual radicalism is the conviction that politics and sexuality are intimately connected, the radical component arising from 'regarding sexual repression as one of the principal mechanisms of political domination'.[67] In *An American Dream* Mailer fulfils both of Robinson's criteria and therefore makes his own contribution to sexual radicalism. More generally, Richard Poirier feels that sex is a natural point of interrogation for the clarification of a writer's vision, since it marks the interface between cultural and political realities: 'It might be asked why sexuality matters in a discussion of radicalism. The answer is that the key to any writer's idea of self and of society, or an inner, more or less unarticulated being and of an outer, overwhelmingly articulated system is probably best located in what can be deducted about the writer's idea of sexuality.'[68]

Mailer actually presents himself as a sexual radical in *The Deer Park*, but his first attempt to produce a novelistic *ars erotica* that will penetrate into repressed culture remains largely unachieved. However, in the preliminary sketch for *An American Dream*, 'The Time of Her Time', and the novel itself there are genuine initiations into pleasure and the meanings and consequences of pleasure. Rojack's encounters with Ruta (Deborah's German maid) and Cherry are yet further exercises in epistemology and power, revelations of truth to the reluctant radical. As Stanley Gutman observes, sex becomes the 'major battleground of existence, on which the individual makes himself and discovers himself'.[69] It puts him into contact with the sources of knowledge and establishes the limits of knowledge.

Reich narrows down the problem of alienation to the sexual sphere. 'As social and clinical sex economy have convincingly demonstrated,' he urges, 'the mechanism which makes the masses of people incapable of freedom is the social suppression of genital love life in children, adolescents, and adults'.[70] So extreme is Reich's biological treatment of social questions that Mark Shechner, among others, has argued that there is 'ample reason to look upon his system as a political neurobiology and not as a psychology'.[71] Placing sex on the leading edge of politics brings Mailer to a similar preoccupation with the genital and the somatic:

> a voice like a child's whisper on the breeze came up so faint I could hardly hear. 'Do you want her?' it asked.'Do you really want her, do you want to know something about love at last?' and I desired something I had never known before, and answered; it was as if my voice had reached to its roots; and, 'Yes,' I said, 'of course I do, I want love,' but like an urbane old gentleman, a dry tart portion of my mind added, 'Indeed, and what has one to lose?' and then the voice in a small terror, 'Oh you have more to lose than you will have lost already, fail at love and you lose more than you can know.' 'And if I do not fail?' I asked back. 'Do not ask,' said the voice, and some continent of dread speared wide in me, rising like a dragon, as if I knew the choice were real and in a lift of terror I opened my eyes and her face was beautiful beneath me in that rainy morning, her eyes were golden with light, and she said, 'Ah, honey, sure,' and I said sure to the voice in me, and felt love fly in like some great winged bird, some beating of wings at my back, and felt her will dissolve into tears, and some great deep sorrow like roses drowned in the salt of the sea came floating from her womb and washed into me like a sweet honey of balm for all the bitter sores of my soul and for the first time in my life without passing through fire or straining the stones of my will I came up from my body rather than down from my mind, I could not stop, some shield broke in me, bliss, and the honey she had given me I could only give back, all sweets to her womb, all come in her cunt.
>
> 'Son of a bitch,' I said, 'so that's what it's all about.' (pp. 122–3)

Rojack is initiated into a consciousness of the body. The essence of this therapy is that the ultimate corporeal experiences are free of mental imperative. But Mailer's epistemological urge requires that a linguistic correlative be found for these experiences, and, as the quoted passage aptly illustrates, he uses two techniques to achieve this. First, he uses the slightly awkward rhetorical device of inner voices (from the inner man, the buried self) to articulate bodily sensations. Secondly, he applies a highly metaphorical language so that something else can substitute for the elusive sensation that is without an appropriate signifier. The flight of fancy in passages such as this derives from the interplay of these techniques, and Ruta's reference to Rojack as a 'genius' (p. 49) alludes to his, or Mailer's, literary skill in evoking sexuality. To complain, as some critics have done, that Mailer's writing on sex is absurd is to underestimate his commitment to sex as physical release of political energies, and the stylistic difficulties this presents for the writer. In fact the particular achievement of *An American Dream* is that it succeeds, where *The Deer Park* had failed, in transmitting a language of body and a sense of the 'power of sex' (p. 57).

This consciousness of the body is not described passively. Mailer is concerned with the individual's redefinition of himself as a subject, with the body as a technique of self. In Reichian political neurobiology the relationship between power and the body is axiomatically repressive. Instinctive repression is a historical stage peculiar to authoritarian cultures and in Western societies obtains on behalf of capitalistic exploitation. Reichianism aims to be countervailing, an ideology of liberation that, in Mark Shechner's words, 'armed its adherents with basic interpretations and rigid internal dialectics that pointed the way to freedom through submission to a stern agenda of treatments'.[72] Mailer is not in profound disagreement with this analysis. As Richard Poirier has noticed, 'the influence of Wilhelm Reich on Mailer's radicalism is conspicuous'[73] in *An American Dream*. The book lays great emphasis on Protestantism as the origins of a capitalism that is excessively materialistic and corrupting of American idealism. It also follows Reich in the reduction of the political arena from society to the body, where gains in the form of localized therapies can be realized. But Mailer makes two crucial departures from the Reichian model. He is not as single-minded as Reich in his attitude towards sexuality (it's only one among a range of techniques of self), and, because he rejects the anti-power bias of therapeutic radicalism and confers qualified approval on the self's exercise of power, he does not wish to liberate sexuality from the arena of power. As a consequence, there is a critical difference between what Mailer and Reich conceive to be individual release or treatment.

In Reich, the body is released from the effects of power. Full genitality is achieved when the superego is neutralized. In Mailer, the self is always prey to powers, although a distinction is made between those powers that are dominating and repressive and those that are creative and liberating. Freedom comes from the satisfactory release of energies through the right kind of power. Thus the liberated self is initiated *into* rather than out of power, and the moral complexities that follow from this are illustrated by Rojack:

> I had had a bad year this last year, and for a while it got very bad; I may as well admit that for the first time in my life I had come to understand there was suicide in me. (Murder I had known was there for a long time.) It was the worst of discoveries, this suicide. Murder, after all, has exhilaration within it. I do not mean it is a state to entertain; the tension which develops within your body makes you sicken over a period, and I had my fill of walking about with a chest full of hatred and a brain jammed to burst, but there is something manly about containing your rage, it is so difficult, it is like carrying a two-hundred-pound safe up a cast-iron hill. The exhilaration comes I suppose from possessing such strength. Besides, murder offers the promise of vast relief. It is never unsexual. (p. 15)

Both murder and sexual gratification are acknowledged as potential mechanisms of release, the sternest of therapies. This is an inevitable consequence of Mailer's contribution to therapeutic radicalism, his acceptance of violence and acts of power as valid forms of release. His is an *ars erotica* that embraces power.

At the centre of Mailer's sexual radicalism is a celebration of orgasm, and in this area he acknowledges his debt to Reich:

> In the western literature with which I am familiar, classical, technical, and pornographic, I can remember – with the harsh radical exception of Wilhelm Reich – there is almost no incisive discussion of male orgasm. The very notion of 'good orgasm' . . . betrays the lack of examination we bring to it, for it assumes there are two domains, good orgasm and bad, each clearly set apart by a defense line of psychic dragon's teeth.

But the Hip argument, if one is to dredge it forth, would claim that even in orgasm which is *the most* there is always the vision of an outer wider wilder orgasm which is even more with it. The Nature of orgasm is a spectrum, perhaps intimately dialectical: in the worst orgasms there are nips of pleasure, in the best of orgasms some mannered containments denying pleasure beyond high pleasure, restraining the rarer liberations of energy for the next day.[74]

As in Reich, orgasm is a regulatory mechanism in the closed energy system of the individual. Mere ejaculation is what Mailer calls 'bad orgasm', while true orgasm modifies the whole sensibility. Mailer had tried to say as much in *The Deer Park* but produced only the abstract *aperçu* at the end of the book. In *An American Dream* orgiastic sex plunges Rojack into epistemological and ontological depths and communion with the mysterious forces to which the individual is exposed. Because the concern in 'The White Negro', 'The Time of Her Time' and *An American Dream* is principally with male individuals, Mailer *ars erotica* tends to be narrowed down to a single sex, although women are not excluded from radical therapy. Denise Gondelman in 'The Time of Her Time' is inducted into radicalism (from Freudianism) through the apocalyptic orgasm; Cherry Melanie is presented as Rojack's equal, his female counterpart. But Mailer is clearly aware of his limitations when it comes to doing justice to female vision and sexuality, and these things are rarely pre-eminent. The novel also has formal reasons to support this general exclusion. As a first-person narrative which perceives the world exclusively from Rojack's point of view, it is wholly involved with his consciousness. Deborah, Cherry and Ruta can be dealt with only in relation to Rojack's disposition. In this respect, each of the women occasions a different kind of orgiastic release: murder (Deborah), anal orgasm (Ruta) and full genital engagement (Cherry). Killing Deborah cancels Rojack's social contract with the 'dream' world of capitalist success, status and privilege. Buggering Ruta is a technique for absorbing her vast reservoir of energy, cunning and guile into his own body. Genital release with Cherry represents the perfect harmonious coupling: 'There was a child in her, and death, my death, my violent death would give some better heat to the embryo just created, that indeed I might even be created again, free of my past' (p. 138).

With Ruta, Rojack experiences what might be called an

epistemological orgasm; it creates a proliferation of data. His refusal to ejaculate into her vagina is on the grounds that it would fecundate the worst sort of worldliness. Ruta's 'Nazi' (p. 47) background, her talent for 'getting along in the world' (p. 45), links her to both primitive capitalism and the soldiers killed by Rojack. To choose her anus is to rebel against the Protestant notion of fatherhood and fruitful labour, and we learn later of Ruta's complicity, through sexual intercourse, with the ultimate evil in the novel, Barney Kelly. The German mind, Prostestantism and Kelly have combined to corrupt her personal culture. Yet her name implies she is somehow fundamental, that she is at the root of things (Rojack calls his penis a 'root' – p. 35). Thus she is a field of signs and symbols, an array of small offerings of meaning. Her anus contains 'knowledge'(p. 46), and successfully extracting this makes Rojack a 'great thief' (p. 47). With Cherry, whose name implies she is the opposite of Ruta, Rojack establishes full Reichian blood-consciousness. They meet as Reich's unafraid individuals:

> Her ass was indeed a prize – with my hands on her, life came back to me again across all the glaciers of my fatigue. But we did not meet as lovers, more like animals in a quiet mood, come across a track in the jungle to join in a clearing, we were equals. . . . I felt I could go on forever. Exhaustion had fired me. I was alive in some deep water below sex, some tunnel of the dream where effort was divorced at last from price. She was exquisitely sensitive. Again, I had expected no less. Some cool blonde sense of violet shadow lived in the turn of her flesh. I had never moved so well. It was impossible to make a mistake.
>
> (pp. 120–1)

Unlike Ruta, Cherry is the true counterpart of Rojack (she too is a murderer, having killed the lover responsible for her sister's suicide), and only with him is she able to experience her first 'good' orgasm. Together they arrive at sexual redemption, at love as a radical sacrament.

Locating these erotics of redemption at the individual level has a strong and obvious appeal. It strips away the wearisome volumes of politics from radicalism, removing the mundane problems that attend traditional radical activity: meetings, committees, canvassing factions, internecine power struggles, conflicting doctrines and appeals to the proletariat. Mailer is thus able to circumvent those questions of impersonal institutional power that have never stimulated his imagination. More importantly, he can disassociate himself from those conventional radical strategies that have been marked by unalloyed failure in the post-war American scene. Fastening onto the missing variables in prior revolutionary calculations – the self, the truth of sex, individual desublimation – Mailer can entertain at least the possibility of psychic rebirth. That element in each of us which, so the argument goes, has been repressed or stifled by conformity gives cause for celebration. In *An American Dream* Mailer becomes a spokesman for what Mark Shechner calls 'bioenergetic revivalism',[75] or what David Zane Mairowitz labels, less respectfully, the 'American Wet Dream'.[76]

IV

In the radical brew of *An American Dream* there are two further ingredients which, though they appear quite different, are inter-related manifestations of the same development. One is the neo-primitivist mode of perception Mailer creates for his radicalized hero (which Gutman considers 'the most striking achievement of the novel'[77]). The other is the argument made for the power of art to affect reality. Mailer goes much farther towards an ultimate pastoralism than any of the other therapeutic or sexual radicals. Reich may abandon his Enlightenment prejudices in favour of a view of religion as socially useful, a positive good which preserves the individual's awareness of life forces, but Mailer, evoking the second of America's two rivers, that of 'untapped ferocious lonely and romantic desires', takes completely seriously a whole range of occult phenomena associated with primitive religious experience: telepathy, demons, charms, communication with the dead, voices in the mind, psychic arrows, evil spirits, voodoo, vampires, and psychic emanations from people and things. Through Rojack, who comes to be steered by these prerational forces, Mailer reinstates the primitive in contemporary urban America. Instead of being in a profane history, the new breed of man exists in the concentrations of Time. Those critics who view this indulgence in magic as part of a metaphorical reality, as symbolism, underestimate just how radical are Mailer's intentions. As he later insisted to a bewildered Laura Adams, 'there wasn't a single phenomenon in that book that I considered dreamlike or fanciful or fantastical. To me, it was a realistic look at the place where extraordinary things are happening'[78]. What these extraordinary things add up to is a radical rupturing of culture, a strengthening of the anti-rationalist tendency of the Mailerian *ars erotica*.

Rojack travels backwards in time. Metaphors to do with jungle, swamp and ocean evoke the primordial, a world at the opposite end of the spectrum from the technological rationality Marcuse claims is the dominant ethic of post-war American society. It is a world presided over by the moon: 'its pale call, princess of the dead, I will never be free of her' (p. 23). What distinguishes Rojack from his Harvard contemporary John F. Kennedy is that he 'ended with too large an appreciation of the moon' (p. 100). Kennedy purged the influence of the irrational. By murdering Deborah, Rojack therefore reconnects with the 'secret frightened romance with the moon' (p. 179) begun with the killing of the four German soldiers. In fact the wartime incident provides the personal basis for Rojack's scholarship. As a professor of psychology he holds the thesis that 'magic, dread, and the perception of death [are] the roots of motivation' (p. 15):

> In contrast to the civilized view which elevates man above the animals, the primitive had instinctive belief that he was subservient to the primal pact between the beasts of the jungle and the beast of mystery.
>
> To the savage, dread was the natural result of any invasion of the supernatural: if man wished to steal the secrets of the gods, it was only to be supposed that the gods would defend themselves and destroy whichever man came too close. By this logic, civilization is the successful if imperfect theft of some cluster of these secrets, and the price we have paid is to accelerate our private sense of some enormous if not quite definable disaster which awaits us. (p. 150)

In the course of the novel's action this academic thesis is transformed into a critique of his own life. He begins to receive messages on the lower frequencies which depend on thought patterns that are remarkably similiar to primitive magic:

'I had come to believe in spirits and demons, in devils, warlocks, omens, wizards and fiends, in incubi and succubi' (p. 40). The awakening of this consciousness is not celebrated; it involves a terrifying and unwelcome expansion of reality:

> The metaphysics, however, was vast – buried in the twenty volumes I had not written. And I at this moment was buried in fear. I no longer had the confidence my thoughts were secret to myself. No, men were afraid of murder, but not from a terror of justice so much as the knowledge that a killer attracted the attention of the gods; then your mind was not your own, your anxiety ceased to be neurotic, your dread was real. Omens were as tangible as bread. (pp. 191–2)

The world is once again a dangerous place; signs and portents are everywhere and require interpretation. Each of Rojack's senses is hypersensitive, operating without the bureaucracy of rational organization. His experience is rendered permanently charismatic. Inaugurated by death (the German soldiers', Deborah's), it is a state of being that amounts to a flagrant contradiction of the civilized, capitalist, post-industrial West. What Mailer later terms honorifically a 'kill society' is brought about:

> we could easy say that we exist in a keep-everybody-alive society. Ironically, most of the cultures to exhibit great energy in history, the societies which produced our society, were, on the contrary, built on killing.
>   The idea common to all animals, and prehistoric and primitive man, even among civilized societies like the Greeks, the Romans, during the Middle Ages, and the Renaissance, the idea was still that if you didn't have enough right to live – in other words, if you were a drag upon the mood and the energy and the sustenance of other people – you were better off, Christ to the contrary, dead. These societies were kill societies. They got their neatness, their elegance, they got their style out of killing.
>   But we are a society which says in effect, 'Be sure you live. Life is our only gift. We're not going to get anything after this.' The kill societies, to the contrary, were religious. They believed in the immanence of God, or a devil, or in demons. Primitive man spent his time placating demons in every tree. If a wind

blew a sudden leaf past his face, he began to propitiate some spirit. They believed nothing was accidental. They were, in fact, more scientific than we are, for they believed that everything you can't explain is tremendously disturbing, whereas we prefer to ignore whatever we cannot dominate with our minds. We wipe out the artefacts of the past as if they have no curse.[79]

An American Dream shows Mailer working implicitly with a model of a kill society, and it puts Rojack's murder of Deborah into a clearer perspective. It has already been shown that Mailer's system endorses acts of power that abolish the individual's repression, but the more radical dynamic which underlies this is that the individual's right to life is not held automatically. This, the most outrageous element of an already controversial radicalism, is anathema not only to sexual and ideological perspectives but to the whole spectrum of twentieth-century thought from which Mailer arises. It is a rupture with modernity itself. It is the most extreme type of pastoralism imaginable, in which the pasture becomes an elemental landscape and the shepherd a primitive self. The nostalgia is for the primordial situation, whose potential recovery is presented as the radical alternative to the rationalist historical present. In this respect, both Mailer and Rojack become shamans. According to Mircea Eliade, in primitive societies

> mystical experience is generally the prerogative of a class of individuals who, by whatever name they are called, are *specialists in ecstasy*. The shamans, the medicine-men, magicians, healers, the ecstatic and the inspired of every description, are distinguished from the rest of the community by the intensity of their religious experience. They live the sacred side of life in a profounder and more personal manner than other people. In most cases they attract attention by some unusual behaviour, by the possession of occult powers, by having personal and secret relations with divine or demonic beings. . . . By general agreement these individuals are regarded as the equivalents, among 'primitives', of the religious elites and the mystics in other and more highly evolved cultures.[80]

Primitive magic is the key to Rojack's heightened sense experience. He has the magico-religious sensibility of one who has been chosen for 'mystic initiation',[81] a condition that only resembles the symptoms of madness or moral breakdown: 'Though we cannot ascribe shamanism to psychopathology, it remains true that this mystical vocation often enough involves a profound crisis, sometimes touching the borderline of "madness".' It is therefore the complex fate of the shaman to be mistaken for a madman. It is not hard to see the connection between these themes and the infamous incident on which *An American Dream* is based, in which Mailer stabbed his second wife and spent seventeen days in a mental hospital. The psychiatrist's report on Mailer reads, 'In my opinion, Norman Mailer is having an acute paranoid breakdown with delusional thinking and is both homicidal and suicidal. His admission to hospital is urgently advised.'[82] Mailer, though, at that time aware of his role as a shamanistic writer, defended his self-elected distinction from the rest of the community as a specialist in ecstasy:

> I have been upset, but I have never been out of my mental faculties. I only saw Dr. Rosenburg for thirty seconds or a minute. It's important for me not to be sent to a mental hospital, because my work in the future will be considered that of a distorted mind. My pride is that I can explore areas of experience that other men are afraid of. I insist that I am sane.[83]

Shamanistic 'madness', so the argument goes, performs a valuable mystic function; through it aspects of reality inaccessible to ordinary people are revealed for the public good. Only by entering these hidden dimensions of reality can the individual achieve mystical states of mind and make the transition to shaman.

This is the crucial importance of Rojack's exotic sense experience. As Mailer's reclamation of psychoanalytic concepts attempts to show, Rojack's apparent madness prepares for new creation. As Eliade says, shamanistic madness is a sign that 'the profane man is on the way to dissolution, and that a new personality is about to be born'.[84] Killing Deborah, responding to his crisis, has brought about changes of sensibility, an apprehension of the sacred. From the ranks of the profane he has been chosen. His various trials – with Deborah, Detective Roberts (the rationalist who doesn't know 'how to put demons on a police report' – p. 66), Cherry's black lover Shago and Barney Kelly ('there's nothing but magic at the top' – p. 230) – serve as Rojack's initiation

into dimensions of reality where subjective data are accepted
as true. They are encounters which permit him to 'blow up poor
old Freud' (p. 235) and integrate into new experiences:

> like a bird indeed in a cage in a darkened room, the passing
> flare of light from outside gave some memory of the forest,
> and I felt myself soaring out of the beating of my heart as if a
> climax of fear had begun which might race me through swells
> of excitement until everything burst, the heart burst and I flew
> out of my death . . . I knew at last the sweet panic of an animal
> who is being tracked, for if danger were close, if danger came
> out on the breeze, and one's nostrils had an awareness of the air
> as close as the first touch of tongue on your flesh, there was still
> such a tenderness for the hope one could stay alive. (p. 75)

As with the other aspects of Mailer's radical vision, there is
no naïve, unqualified acceptance of shamanism, and one of the
questions *An American Dream* addresses is whether the recovery of
charismatic selfhood is not too dangerous, too potent an activity.
As Richard Poirier says, Rojack 'lives at the divide of two kinds
of equally unacceptable power: of demonic social and economic
systems and of the demonic imaginations of himself as a kind
of *Übermensch*'.[85] By the end of the novel Rojack's heightened
perception is intolerable: '"Damn you," I thought, "I've lain
with madness long enough"' (p. 243). Repeatedly he implores
to be relieved of shamanistic selfhood: 'I wanted to be some
sort of rational man again, nailed tight to details, promiscuous,
reasonable, blind to the reach of the seas'(p. 238). A break with
the modern that will leave the self intact and undamaged is not
envisaged. The therapeutic value of such a recovery lies in the
temporary participation in hidden dimensions of reality, Time and
epistemological mysteries. The self returns from the margins of
human experience to the centre of culture to add to an ongoing
dialectic. On the final page of *An American Dream* Rojack is still
communicating with the dead (Cherry) but he is 'something like
sane again' (p. 252). The implication is that he has not quit the
radical enterprise, Mailer's dialectical frame, but is moving in the
direction of further refinements of primitive consciousness and
the pastoral dream 'on a long trip to Guatemala and Yucatán'.

Besides being an epistemology, mythopoeic perception is a
fulsome manifestation of the faculty of imagination, which is

the final part of Mailer's personal radical package. Philip Rieff has pointed out that artists find Reichian doctrine particularly attractive because it flatteringly associates art with the ideal genital character – the imagination is freed through sexual desublimation. For Mailer this liberating of the artistic imagination is a mythopoeic tonic which acts against prevailing repressions. The American writer Russell Hoban has perhaps best identified the macro-political consequences of the absence of the mythopoeic:

> The Soviet and US governments, with their monstrous phallic displays, both fail to perceive the bomb for what it is – it is the enemy of all of us and should be dealt with in that way. It's a failure of mythopoeic perception. If our myth-making faculties were not so shrivelled up and atrophied we could see it. The world has lost the faculty of recognizing monsters, demons and devils.[86]

As a writer, Mailer's purpose is nothing less than a restoration of these shrivelled-up and atrophied faculties, and his belief in the writer's mythic powers dates from as early as 1954, before the publication of *The Deer Park*, when aesthetics begin to displace socialism as a source of meaning:

> As serious artistic expression is the answer to the meaning of life for a few, so the passion for socialism is the only meaning I can conceive in the lives of those who are not artists; if one cannot create 'works', one may dream at least of an era when humans create humans and the satisfaction of the radical can come from the thought that he tries to keep the idea alive.[87]

In *The Deer Park*, for the first time in Mailer's fiction, specifically artistic values can take precedence over political considerations. Eitel holds the theory that 'the artist was always divided between his desire for power in the world and his desire for power over his work'.[88] He himself has sacrificed himself on the altar of immediate worldly desires, but his aspirations for Sergius, the writer-*manqué*, are art-centred:

> 'For you see,' he confessed in his mind, 'I have lost the final desire of the artist, the desire that tells us that when all else is lost and adventure, pride of self, and pity, there still remains

that world we may create, more real to us, more real to others
than the mummery of what happens, passes, and is gone. So, do
try, Sergius,' he thought, 'try for that other world, the real world,
where orphans burn orphans and nothing is more difficult to
discover than a simple fact. And with the pride of the artist,
you must blow against the walls of every power that exists, the
small trumpet of your defiance'.[89]

What is transmitted here is a belief in the 'created' world's
relevance for history. The 'pride of the artist' is defined against
all available political positions. By the end of the novel Sergius
has succeeded in producing the first tentative attempts at the
narrative we read: 'I had survived, I was finally able to keep in
some permanent form those parts of myself which were better
than me, and therefore I could have the comfort that I was
beginning to belong to that privileged world of orphans where
art is found.'[90] In terms of Mailer's emerging aestheticism, he is
empowered. *Advertisements for Myself* consolidates Mailer's status
as a shaman-writer. Through a range of psychological and literary
techniques of self–persona, mask, narrative voice – he moves to
the centre of his writing, seeking to 'jiggle his self for a style
which will have some relation to him'.[91] Foregrounded in the
text, organizing readers' impressions and responses, acting as a
critic of his own work, he creates a personality that binds a large
disparate collection of pieces together. He has the authoritative
tone of the 'psychic outlaw',[92] who on the one hand is 'running
for president in the privacy of [his] mind'[93] and on the other is
trying, in his definitive phrase, to 'create a revolution in the
consciousness'[94] of the age. A self-begetting culture hero, he
inevitably channels the resources of personality into the getting
of charisma.

Marxism, of course, permits no such view of art or the
artist. Artistic production, like all other production that is part
of the superstructure of capitalism, is repressively controlled by a
ruling class. Marx formulated the notion of ideological domination
in this way:

> The ideas of the ruling class are in every epoch the ruling
> ideas, i.e. the class which is the ruling material force of society
> is at the same time its ruling intellectual force. The class which
> has the means of material production at its disposal has control

at the same time of the means of mental production, so that generally speaking, the ideas of those who lack the means of mental production are subject to it.[95]

Herbert Marcuse, though, argues against the severity of this prescription of the power of ideology in the realm of art, claiming, to the chagrin of fellow Marxists, that modernism, the counterculture and Black American culture have a distinct radical potential. In *Eros and Civilization* Marcuse isolates the arts as a source of contradictory sublimated versions of man's former unhappiness. Because they rely heavily on the faculties of memory and fantasy, works of art remember or reconstruct the shadow impressions of liberation. Their radical potential comes from embodying, in however distorted a fashion, the possibility of alternative social systems rooted in the enormous chamber of the unconscious: 'promises and potentialities which are betrayed and even outlawed by the mature, civilized individual, but which had once been fulfilled in his dim past . . . are never entirely forgotten'.[96] For Marcuse, great humanist art of the past created sublimated fantasy worlds that 'raised pain and sorrow, desperation and loneliness, to the level of metaphysical powers'.[97] The redemptive value of this fantasy world lies in the fact that it contains 'not only the justification of the established form of existence, but also the pain of its establishment; not only quiescence about what is, but also remembrance of what could be'. No matter how temporary or distorted the therapeutic experience might be (the material world is not transformed, only briefly transcended), it remains a liberation, a recovery of a repressed utopian world. Thus the writer's work can be a vehicle for future liberation; it contains 'the first glimmer of a new culture'.[98]

The essential difference between Marcuse's and Mailer's relaxation of the rigidities of Marxism's attitude to art is that, while Marcuse finds value in its preserved, achieved qualities, Mailer is preoccupied with art as a process, an activity, a means of perception and a cultural role. And Mailer goes much further than Marcuse in the cause of aesthetics. The imaginative recovery of the 'dim past' is not an echo in *An American Dream*; it is evoked literally as transformed consciousness. The writing itself is a wilful demonstration of the power of the imagination, allowing the reader to participate directly in Rojack's desublimation and reconstruction of experience. Using a narrative voice developed only in the late pieces of *Advertisements for Myself* and in *The Presidential Papers*, Mailer is a constant presence in the novel's prose, self-consciously 'creating' the text. As Leo Bersani has pointed out, 'every menace becomes the occasion for a verbal performance, and [Rojack's] fluttering nervousness about being deprived of his "center" is rather humorously belied by the incredibly dense and diversified self which his language reveals and creates'.[99] Language and style predominate because, as Richard Poirier says, Rojack's 'hyperbolic imagination of himself and his psychotic powers occur in language'.[100] Mailer's sentences are long, flexible and flamboyant, with many dazzling bravura touches that are elaborate, improbable, even ludicrous – a style appropriate to a shaman. His extensive use of metaphor stimulates the mythopoeic perception of cryptic species of reality, fusing, as Robert Begiebing notes, the 'unconscious or intuitive organs of perception with those that are conscious and rational'.[101] Metaphor is thus an epistemological tool in *An American Dream* ('My metaphors explain more phenomena to me than any theology I can adopt'[102]), a technique for integrating levels of myth and historical experience. Focusing on the point where the two things connect, the book recalls the Hawthornian distinction between the novel's realism and the romance's right to 'present the truth under circumstances . . . of the writer's own choosing or creation'.[103] Hawthorne asserted that his own work occupied a neutral territory, somewhere between the real and imagined world, 'where the Actual and the Imaginary may meet, and each imbue itself with the nature of the other'.[104] Putting demons on police reports, cultivating the faculty of recognizing monsters, the shamanistic Mailer also occupies the neutral territory, producing in *An American Dream* a radical or libertarian romance, a realism prepared to take enormous liberties in the name of the counterpolitics of myth.

The radical position adopted in *An American Dream* is frequently misunderstood, and often rejected on the basis of misunderstanding, even by critics sympathetic to Mailer's work. For Stanley Gutman, Mailer's new morality is 'spurious, contrived, and predominantly infantile'.[105] Jean Radford claims that Mailer has based his richest novel on 'a highly questionable private philosophical system'; to her, he is 'bigoted, histrionic and reactionary'.[106]

Andrew Gordon laments Rojack's 'infantile delusions of power'.[107] In Philip Bufithis's view, the novel 'rejects conservatism in favour of radicalism for no political reason but because conservatism is order and radicalism is disorder'.[108] What I have tried to show in this chapter is that literary-based criticisms such as these inevitably involve misprisions. Mailer's politics cannot simply be put to one side, divided off from what is seen as the main thrust of his work. The radical fiction's truth function is always irreducible.

An American Dream concludes aptly with a trope for the radical geography of self and society, Rojack's 'long trip' to South America and the primitive margins of the world. He has already struck out to the mythical West, with its 'arid empty wild blind deserts' (p. 251), but beyond this lies the meta-frontier of the South. Here Mailer strikes a note that resonates in recent American literature, notably with William Burroughs' grail quest in *The Yage Letters*: 'I decided to go down to Columbia and search for yage. . . . I am ready to move on south and look for the uncut kick that opens out instead of narrowing down like junk.'[109] Mary McCarthy has called such movements in Burroughs' work 'statelessness'.[110] Rojack's statelessness, like Burroughs', is a flight from gathering forces in Northern civilization. As Mailer argued in *The Presidential Papers*,

> Tropical people are usually more sexual. It's easier to cohabit, it's easier to stay alive. If there's more time, more leisure, more – we'll use one of the machine words – more support-from-the-environment than there is in a northern country, then sex will tend to be more luxuriant. Northern countries try to build civilizations and tropical countries seek to proliferate *being*.[111]

It's an idea also to be found in Pynchon, who contrasts the stateless South with the state-ridden North. In the words of the critic Douglas Fowler, one of the polarities in *Gravity's Rainbow* is between 'the tropics and the North, and Pynchon again contrasts the harmonious organic life of the jungle and savanna, where man still lives in touch with the great Cycle of creation, with the Christian North, "death's region", the land of technology, repression, rationalized destruction'.[112]

However, equipped with his own radical vision, Mailer does not follow Rojack southwards. Instead he turns back, in true dialectical fashion, towards the extremities of the North and the natural wastes of the Alaskan landscape, where he locates the origins of technology, repression and rationalized destructiveness. Essaying liberation, he chooses tyranny, and the result is a fictional confrontation between radical enterprise and death's region of non-being.

5

Saving the Root: Old and New Circuits in the Electroworld of *Why Are We in Vietnam?*

I

During his arrest in *The Armies of the Night* Mailer refers to his 'twenty years of radical opinions',[1] implying that in 1968 he continues to perceive himself as an American radical of sorts. Yet in the short novel *Why Are We in Vietnam?*,[2] published in the previous year, the break with any recognizable radical position appears at first sight to be complete. In this novel there is no promotion of the political myth of the 'new breed of man', no attempt to explore the *ars erotica* so vividly cultivated in *An American Dream*, and there are no positive applications of the Mailerian therapy of power. In the context of what has been established about Mailer's radicalism in the 1960s, it is a curious work, an apparent *non sequitur*. And on this basis it is tempting to argue that *Why Are We in Vietnam?* is a post-radical novel which effectively marks the end of the line of development I have traced back to the Marxist structure and subjugated knowledge of *The Naked and the Dead*.

To understand how *Why Are We in Vietnam?* continues the power themes of *An American Dream*, it is important to appreciate how, from *The Deer Park* onwards, Mailer has inched closer and closer towards a radicalism that is essentially *sui generis*. Mailer himself has supplied hints as to how this process works: 'just as Christianity seemed to create the most unexpected saints, artists, geniuses, and great warriors out of its profound contradictions, so Communism seemed to create great heretics and innovators and converts (Sartre and Picasso for two) out of the irreducible majesty of Marx's mind (perhaps the greatest single tool for celebration Western man has ever produced)'.[3] Truer to dialectical thought than Marxism, Mailer has been propelled beyond heresy and innovation to the point of being an 'ex-revolutionary' constituted in the particulars of his own thought: 'there was no one in America who had a position remotely like his own'.[4] Most notably, within his own dialectic and logic of dissent, he is able to embrace both ends of the ideological perspective simultaneously: 'Mailer was a Left Conservative. So he had his own point of view. To himself he would suggest that he tried to think in the style of Marx in order to attain certain values suggested by Edmund Burke.'[5] In this capacity as a '*Left* Conservative, he believed that radical measures were sometimes necessary to save the root. The root in this case was the welfare of the nation'.[6] In other words, Mailer has moved from a broadly conventional radical position, Marxist in *The Naked and the Dead* and *Barbary Shore*, non-Marxist in 'The White Negro', *Advertisements for Myself* and *An American Dream*, of stimulating the advance of forthcoming new consciousness to a radical posture based on the protection and preservation of endangered values and a consciousness that is all but lost.

In the 'dialectric' (p. 153) of *Why Are We in Vietnam?* the redemptive power of mythopoeic perception and the faculty of imagination are again validated. Against the grain of an ultra-modern or post-modern consciousness, whose main characteristic is that it is stripped of everything atavistic, Mailer strives to keep the archaic alive. The enemy is what Pynchon has labelled the pervasive 'electroworld',[7] in which the franchise on consciousness has been taken over by those who manufacture the counterenvironments of media-dominated reality. Mailer is not the first writer to identify the disabling features of a technologically dominated culture and its incursions into the 'archeology of the Self'.[8] In fact, while he was agonizing over various schools of Marxism in the early 1950s, Marshall McLuhan had already outlined the same scenario:

striving constantly . . . to watch, anticipate, and control events on the inner, invisible stage of the collective dream, the ad agencies and Hollywood turn themselves unwittingly into a sort of collective novelist, whose characters, imagery, and situations are an intimate revelation of the passions of the age. But this huge collective novel can be read only by someone trained to use his eyes and ears, and in detachment from the visceral riot that this sensational fare tends to produce. The reader has to be a second Ulysses in order to withstand the siren onslaught. Or, to vary the image, the uncritical reader of this collective novel is like the person who looked directly at the face of Medusa without the mirror of conscious reflection. He stands in danger of being frozen into a helpless robot. Without the mirror of the mind, nobody can live a human life in the face of our mechanized dream.[9]

The purpose of McLuhan's early work was to restore vigilance about the unrecognized effects of modernity's siren onslaught, particularly in electronic media. In *Why Are We in Vietnam?* Mailer creates a fictional equivalent to siren onslaught and, at the same time, attempts the more difficult task of becoming a writer who is a second Ulysses:

Postulate a modern soul marooned in constipation, emptiness, boredom and a dull flat terror of death. A soul which takes antibiotics when ill, smokes filter cigarettes, drinks proteins, minerals, and vitamins in a liquid diet, takes seconal to go to sleep, benzedrine to awake and tranquilizers for poise. It is a deadened existence, afraid precisely of violence, cannibalism, loneliness, insanity, libidinousness, hell, perversion, and mess, because these are the states which must in some way be passed through, digested, transcended, if one is to make one's way back to life.[10]

If, as Mailer argues, 'the twentieth century was in the process of removing the last of man's powers from his senses in order to store power in piled banks of coded knowledge',[11] a massive restoration of inner power to the senses and to consciousness is the countervailing requirement. *Why Are We in Vietnam?* is thus a text in that radical tradition of books designed to make a political intervention into the reader's life. A recent classic of this tradition is *The Naked Lunch*, in which William Burroughs declares his political intentions: '*The Naked Lunch* is a blueprint, a How-To book. . . . How-To extend levels of experience by opening the door at the end of a long hall. . . . Doors that open only in *Silence*. . . . *Naked Lunch* demands Silence from the reader. Otherwise he is taking his own pulse.'[12] Mailer is highly conscious of his place in this tradition, and in the opening section of *Why Are We in Vietnam?*, 'Intro Beep 1', he makes a self-conscious statement of radical intent that highlights his affinity with Burroughs:

America this is your wandering troubadour brought right up to date, here to sell America its new handbook on how to live in this Electrolux Edison world, all programmed out, Prononzo! (this last being the name King Alonso gave to the Spanish royal condom.) Well, Huckleberry Finn is here to get you straight, and his asshole ain't itching, right? so listen to my words, One World, it's here for adolescents and overthirties – you'll know what it's all about when you and me are done. (p. 8)

Mailer, like Burroughs before him, demands silence from the reader so that the message of his handbook will be transmitted effectively. Uncoupling the reader from the privatized reading consciousness McLuhan links with the 'hot' uninvolving print media (in which the reader takes his own pulse), Mailer attempts to create a 'cool' text which arouses more of the senses and includes a vast spectrum of consciousness.

In fact the consciousness of *Why Are We in Vietnam?* can only be explained by Mailer's shamanism. I. M. Lewis defines a shaman as

a person of either sex who has mastered spirits and who can at will introduce them into his own body. Often, in fact, he permanently incarnates these spirits and can control their manifestations, going into controlled states of trance in appropriate circumstances. . . . the shaman's body is a 'placing' or receptacle for the spirits. It is in fact by his power over the spirits which he incarnates that the shaman is able to treat and control afflictions caused by pathogenic spirits in others. . . . This 'master of spirits' is essential to the well being of the clan, for he controls the clan's own ancestral spirits and other foreign spirits which have been adopted into its spirit hierarchy. In the free state, these spirits are extremely dangerous to man. Most are hostile and pathogenic and are regarded as the sources of the many diseases which affect [the culture].[13]

Increasingly Mailer's metaphors project his sense of himself as a culture doctor, a master of American spirits:

a physician half-blind, not so far from drunk, his nerve to be recommended not at every occasion, nor his hand to hold at each last bed, but a noble physician nonetheless, noble at least in his ideal, for he is certain there is a strange disease before him, an unknown illness, a phenomenon which partakes of mystery, nausea, and horror; if the nausea gives him pause and the horror fear, still the mystery summons, he is a physician, he must try to explore the mystery.[14]

In their different ways, both *The Armies of the Night* and *Why Are We in Vietnam?* explore this mystery. In the non-fiction work an invisible author records the epistemological responses of 'Norman Mailer', shows him 'grappling with his own piece of the plague'.[15] The novel attempts to create a controlled state of trance. The reader is brought 'face to face with a desperate but most rational effort from the deepest resources of the unconscious of us all to rescue civilization from the pit and plague of its bedding, that gutted swinish foul old bedding on which two centuries of imperialism, high finance, moral hypocrisy and horror have lain.'[16]

For the shaman in Mailer, writing possesses 'its own occult force',[17] and in the preface to an edition of *Why Are We in Vietnam?* he spells out the primitive activism of his work. It is not enough for the writer to be, in Bellow's phrase, the moralist of seeing. Mailer speculates that

> We will never now if primitive artists painted their caves to show a representation, or whether the moving hand was looking to placate the forces above and forces below. Sometimes I think the novelist fashions a totem just as much as an aesthetic, and his real aim, not even known necessarily to himself, is to create a diversion in the fields of dread, a sanctuary in some of the arenas of magic. . . . By such logic, the book before you is a totem, not empty of amulets for the author against curses, static, and the pervasive malignity of our electronic air.[18]

Again, the model for such artistic prophylaxis is provided by Burroughs:

> Once, years ago in Chicago, I was coming down with a bad cold. By accident, a friend took me to hear a jazz musician named Sun Ra who played 'space music'. The music was a

little like the sound of Ornette Coleman, but further out, outer space music, close to the EEEE of an electric drill at the centre of a harsh trumpet. My cold cleared up in five minutes. I swear it. The anger of the sound penetrated into some sprung-up rage which was burning fuel for the cold. Burroughs' pages have the same medicine. If a hundred patients on terminal cancer read *Naked Lunch*, one or two might find remission. Bet money on that. For Burroughs is the surgeon of the novel.[19]

Thus the radical promise of *Why Are We in Vietnam?* is that the reader will not only receive an adequate account of the way things are in America ('know what it's all about'), but also experience at the level of sensibility remission from the cultural plague which is 'an ultimate disease against which all other diseases are in design to protect us'.[20] The radicalized or 'shamanized'[21] reader, whose silence has been rewarded, participates in Mailer's attempt to reintegrate the old, now suppressed, human circuitry with the baneful new, saving at least the root from being 'programmed out' of existence.

II

Why Are We in Vietnam? provides a new answer to the perennial question that, according to Peter Clecak, presents itself to all radical perspectives:

Historical systems exist as dynamic wholes whose economic, social, political, and cultural parts, though of mixed weight and value, are inextricably bound together. How, then, does an opponent of the general drift of society address himself to those parts he wishes to aid in preserving? What stands are both politically and ethnically viable – immediately and over the long haul?[22]

Mailer's reply to this question is now located in an emboldened aesthetic capable of reconnecting the archaeological self to an abused though salvaging counterpolitics of the mythopoeic, which is designed, in Charlie Eitel's words, to oppose every power that exists. As Jean Radford rightly points out, 'the writing is itself intended to be restorative'.[23] The style of *An American Dream* transforms our sensibility through militant exhibitions of imagination; we enter Rojack's desublimated consciousness. *Why Are We in Vietnam?* extends this idea of a dense, diversified self created within language and sets about isolating consciousness from the dynamic whole of history in order to preserve it.

The novel is divided into 'chaps', which contain narrative, and 'intro beeps', which situate the narrative and allow the narrator, D. J., to address the reader directly. Contrary to appearances, the book is considered by Mailer to be cast in a type of realism, an exotic mythopoeic realism that through D. J.'s 'stream of conch' (p. 23) is adapted both to the unconscious and Mailer's insight that 'reality is no longer realistic'.[24] The aim therefore is to find a realism that is not implicitly bankrupt by Mailer's own standards: 'The work of realism was done for the nineteenth century, but whether it can be done for the middle of the twentieth century we shall indeed not know unless the attempt is made.'[25] The daring strategy of this novel is to write in the first person and achieve depth of consciousness while retaining the scope and access normally associated with third-person narrative. Mailer is 'deep into D. J.'s mind pattern' (p. 150) without the loss of contact with collective social experience that this technique normally involves. *Why Are We in Vietnam?* is a realistic novel designed to meet the needs of a post-McLuhan culture. In *Understanding Media*, published just three years before the Mailer novel, McLuhan specifically criticizes the realistic novel for encouraging the spread of sensory deprivation, marooning readers on private islands of introspection: 'Man in literate and homogenized society . . . acquires the illusion of the . . . "private point of view" as a part of the Narcissus fixation.'[26] *Why Are We in Vietnam?* violently disabuses the privatized reader of this illusion: 'whose consciousness you getting, overlap on the frequencies, Percival? Shit, D. J. is going to make you fly up your own ass before you get to read him right' (p. 133). As Laura Adams notes, the book doesn't yield itself to conventional textual analysis because 'it is designed to set the reader's teeth on edge, to jar him out of his complacency, to *change* him by his powers to communicate'.[27] Breaking down the customary assumptions about realism, the realistic novel is transformed into a heroic 'collective novel',[28] which goes beyond the translucence and discretion of objective language to embrace the modification of reality made by acts of perception, creating a reality constantly mediated by consciousness ('no such thing as a totally false perception' – p. 8).

Taking up McLuhan's idea that private identity is untenable, Mailer fashions a narrative consciousness that is trance-like, although one which is controlled and in appropriate circumstances. Barry Leeds is mistaken when he accuses Mailer of sloppiness of style and form, insisting that 'he has not retained even a semblance of . . . control'.[29] Rather, Mailer's 'I' does not imply point of view in the conventional sense; everything in the novel takes place in a mind that is hostage to spirits of the social environment. As D. J. announces, 'there is no security in this consciousness' (p. 134). Punning both on McLuhan and on shamanism, Mailer presents his narrator as a 'medium' through which runs the national consciousness of the United States like a species of electricity. Thus he is a 'message center' (p. 49) for culture, a 'Disc Jockey to the world' (p. 24), embracing all the dangerous pathogenic elements: 'D. J., your disc jockey is telling you where you go when you sleep' (p. 170). In *The Naked and the Dead* Mailer attempted to re-create the diversity of American culture using discrete blocks of stream-of-consciousness; *Why Are We in Vietnam?* achieves a totalizing post-literate synthesis, a narrative *e pluribus unum*, held together by a compound voice. Form, for Mailer, is now the 'record of a war',[30] and in this unstable, scrambled, dialectical voice no individual identity is present. The narrator merely 'calls himself D. J.' (p. 11) and, as Richard Poirier confirms, is really a 'composite mind',[31] a medium 'through which pass hundreds of identifiable voices that circulate in the nation (and in our literature')':[32]

> Think of something black-ass and terrible, black as a tumour in your brain, black as the black-ass consciousness of that crippled Harlem genius which D. J. shoves up for gambit as one possible embodiment for his remarkable brain . . . . am I the ideational heat of a real crazy-ass broken-legged Harlem Spade, and just think myself D. J. white boy genius Texan in Alaska imagining my opposite number in Harlem land, when in fact, Good Lord, when in fact, I, D. J., am trapped in a Harlem head which has gone so crazy that I think I sitting at a banquet in the Dallas ass white-ass manse remembering Alaska am in fact a figment of a Spade gone ape in the

mind from outrageous frustrates wasting him and so now living in an imaginary white brain, or is that ether-load man? (pp. 57–8)

This dialectic is not limited, as Jennifer Bailey suggests, to 'dual consciousness';[33] identity is multiple. And Stanley Gutman's belief that the novel's 'greatest weakness is D. J. himself',[34] because he does not have a 'believable voice',[35] fails to come to terms with the fact that D. J. is not a person and therefore, as Jean Radford correctly concludes, 'not reducible to psychological categories'.[36] The many-selved voice of D. J. arises from the ideas about agency circulating in *An American Dream* where the unconscious is seen as having a teleological purpose often unknown to the individual: 'The fact of the matter is that you're up tight with a mystery, me, and this mystery can't be solved because I'm the center of it and I don't comprehend, not necessarily' (p. 23). His state of not knowing is symptomatic of shamanistic trance; his consciousness is overloaded with spirits: 'I'm coming on like Holden Caulfield when I'm really Doctor Jekyll with balls. I mean I got a horror in me, honey' (p. 26). The precise nature of the horror that possesses him remains ambiguous. As he himself emphasizes, 'it's a wise man who knows *he* is the one who is doing the writer's writing – we are after all agents of Satan and the Lord' (p. 28). The effect this cultivation of the mysteries of agency has is to focus our attention in unusual ways; we are impelled, as Philip Bufithis argues, to 'concentrate on voice rather than character, on what consciousness is doing rather than on where it comes from'.[37]

Although D. J. can 'see right through shit' (p. 49), he is not emancipated (he is only a 'presumptive philosopher' – p. 93), and the reader has no alternative but to confront the narrative's white noise: 'Gather here footlings and specialists, hot shit artists, those who give head, and general drug addicts of the world, which means all you Hindus and professional football asshole buffs, and glom onto the confusion of my brain' (p. 24). But the confusion is of a special sort, since D. J. speaks with a 'friendLee voice' (p. 7), the reference being to William Burroughs' pseudonym William Lee. From the early 1960s to the early 1980s, Burroughs used language to create a radical alteration in the reader's consciousness. His cut-up method was a literary strategy for breaking down the cultural conspiracies that are embedded in the individual, a front line against determinism and conditioning. Acknowledging Burroughs as a direct influence, D. J. allies himself to the deconditioning enterprise, although the confusion in *Why Are We in Vietnam?* is not as all-consuming as it is in *The Naked Lunch*, and D. J.'s juxtapositions, unlike Burroughs', are rarely without copula. But the 'message of resistance'[38] implicit in the technique is the same in each book. In McLuhanistic terms both novels represent cool media ('make it cool', D. J. implores – p. 9). They act against the reinforcing of individual sensory poverty, promote release from restricted fields of awareness imposed by print, and even give McLuhan's descriptive 'probes' the political applications lacking in *Understanding Media*. Mailer makes this fairly plain – 'Old McLuhan's going to be breaking his fingernails all over again when he sees this' (p. 24) – but he is not as anarchic as Burroughs in his applications of cool confusion. The tendency towards the aleatoric in Burroughs leads him closer and closer to silence. He uses language to 'rub out the word'.[39] His technique reduces everything but the medium's message to junk, dreck, what D. J. calls 'mixed shit' (p. 180). Mailer, on the other hand, simulates Burroughs' cut-up effects, retains their cool qualities, while maintaining an active belief in language and the form of the novel. The deconditioning that takes place is within the structure of what D. J. insists is a 'narrative form' (p. 74), even if its 'sluggish' parts resemble 'scum, slime, pollen slick, floating twigs, and wet rotting leaves all meandering down a dead-ass stream' (p. 91).

Donald Barthelme speaks of books that 'have a lot of *dreck* in them, matter which presents itself as not wholly relevant (or indeed, at all relevant) but which carefully attended to, can supply a "sense" of what is going on'.[40] Barthelme recognizes that much of language is not communication but a species of cultural garbage, what Mailer calls 'scum', and as a writer he pays particular attention to 'those aspects of language that may be seen as a model of the trash phenomenon'.[41] Through resourceful rearrangements, writers such as Barthelme, Burroughs in his middle period and Mailer in *Why Are We in Vietnam?* transform the redundant wastes of language into magic, achieving an alchemical redemption of reality, creating, in Poirier's telling phrase, 'a world elsewhere'.[42] In the midst of the 'mixed shit' of cultural accumulation, style performs an epistemological function, 'attempts to perceive reality'.[43] Like the shaman who has available

to him a 'secret language',[44] Mailer creates an ecstasy of verbal
exuberance which transcends the social, replenishes sensibility
and initiates an increase in knowledge (Barthelme's 'sense') that
will then return to society.

At the core of Mailer's shamanistic secret language lies
obscenity, the most prominent form of linguistic dreck, and,
in the words of *The Deer Park*'s abandoned subtitle, *Why Are We
in Vietnam?* is a search for the obscene. As Mailer himself points
out in *The Armies of the Night*,

> he had kicked good-bye in his novel *Why Are We in Vietnam?*
> to the old literary corset of good taste, letting his sense of lan-
> guage play on obscenity as freely as it wished, so discovering
> that everything he knew about the American language (with its
> incommensurable resources) went flying in and out of the line
> of his prose with the happiest beatings of wings – it was the first
> time his style seemed at once very American to him and very
> literary in the best way.[45]

The practice of obscenity is restorative of old circuits. (According to Otto Fenichel, obscene words 'retain remnants of the
old magical power which language in general originally had'.[46])
Robert Begiebing is right when he notes that the profanity is not
purposeless, as some critics feel, but wrong to insist that it is
'satirically directed'.[47] The radical status of the obscenity and the
humour is founded on mythopoeic grounds. These elements are
'in the veins and the roots of the local history of every state and
county in America'.[48] They are part of that which requires preservation. For Mailer obscenity keeps consciousness dialectical,
and his cool narrative blends highbrow philosophical concerns
with their opposite to produce synergy: 'ever read *The Concept of
Dread* by Fyodor Kierkegaard? No, well neither has D. J. but now
he wants to know how many of you assholes ever knew, forgive
me, Good Lord, that Fyodor Kierkegaard has a real name, Soren
Kierkegaard. Contemplate that you ass' (p. 34).

The crucial political task of Mailer's style, functioning as
an epistemology, a vision and a consciousness, is to create a
medium that will oppose other media. In *The Armies of the Night*
Mailer presents himself as the antithesis of the American mass
media, which does not know that 'there is no history without
nuance'.[49] His charm against the media is his own text. In *Why*

Are We in Vietnam? the cutting edge of style is turned against not just the mass media but all generic systems for transmitting within 'technology land'.[50] D. J. is a medium whose identity is divided from itself yet connected to everything, a characteristic he shares with Shago Martin in *An American Dream*: 'I'm a lily-white devil in a black ass. I'm just the future, in love with myself, that's the future. I got twenty faces, I talk the tongues. . . . I'm cut off from my own lines.'[51] Mailer's sprawling sentences, often running for more than a page, are expansive (D. J. speaks as an urban black, corporation executive, Southern redneck, philosopher and media specialist), all-inclusive and composed of varieties of 'shit'. But these waste elements that inhere in consciousness are recycled to produce a content-as-resistance, a truth function, what Burroughs calls 'operation rewrite'.[52]

In McLuhan's general theory, preliterate or tribal man lived in a rich aural-oral world in which the modes of awareness were primarily tactile and auditory. Culture produced a unified, homogenous sensibility; values were communal and sacred. The technological innovation of print, the Gutenberg revolution, exploded this world, creating modern individualism, privacy, specialization and alienation. The individual became fragmented from the whole ('Fragments are the only forms I trust',[53] announces one Barthelme narrator) and now experiences sensory impoverishment. McLuhan's later work emphasizes the electronic revolution's ability to revive the aural-oral experience and liberate us from the tyrannies which spring from the print world. Unlike mechanical technology, electronic media invite individual participation in their 'environments'. They restore a social wholeness and harmony that encourages a retribalization of Western culture. Thus, for McLuhan, 'we may yet find salvation in a happy, active, outgoing sensorium in Paradise Regained'.[54]

One of the main literary-political conceits of *Why Are We in Vietnam?* is to accept McLuhan's insistence that 'in our time the sudden shift from the mechanical technology of the wheel to the technology of electrical circuitry represents one of the major shifts of all time',[55] and that reality is now the communications media. D. J.'s broadcast is thus playback material from a psychic-biological tape recorder 'in the deep of its mysterious unwindings' (p. 24): 'Do you know I think there's a tape recorder in heaven for each one of us? and all the while we're sleeping and talking and doing our daily acts, bonging the gong, blasting the ass, chewing the milch, milking the chinz, and working the jerk, why there is that tape recorder taking it all down' (p. 9). Here Mailer reverses Burroughs' image of control. The soft machine is not programmed from the outside so much as monitored as a result of the access that prevails in the post-Gutenberg collective consciousness:

> Did you ever know the seat of electricity? It's the asshole. But what then is the asshole of electricity? Why Creation, Catherine, that's what it is. I mean just think of the good Lord, Amen, and all the while we're sleeping and talking and eating and walking and pissing and fucking, excuse me, Lord, Amen! Amen! why, here's that Lord, slipping right into us making an *operation* in the bowels of Creation so there's a tiny little transistorized tape recorder not as big as a bat's gnat's nut, why a million angels can dance on the idiot pinhead of that tape recorder, DNA, RNA, right? and it takes it all down, it makes all the mountainous files of the FBI look like paper cuttings in a cat-shit box, and so there is the good Lord, king of the Rat Finks, I mean, Sultan of the Wrathful Things, forgive me, Lord, yeah, yeah, there He is getting a total tape record of each last one of us, wow, double wow, rumble woof, beet the tweeter, Vera Elvira, everything you ever thought and your accompanying systole and diastole and pisshole and golden asshole all recorded, your divine intuitions and cloacal glut, all being put down FOREVER on a piece of microfilm. (pp. 24–5)[56]

But, if *Why Are We in Vietnam?* operates on McLuhanistic principles and accepts McLuhan's description of the transforming power of the media, it does not share McLuhan's optimism. Numerous critics have pointed out that McLuhan comes to identify with the irrationality of the media he describes, but it is important to appreciate that his quarrel was only with industrialism, print and Protestantism. It was the industrial era that had 'eliminated nearly all the emotional and corporate family feeling'[57] that had characterized preindustrial society. Electronic media and the multinational corporations that control them promise to become the new, benign agencies of a return to collective life. Mailer's vision is much less utopian than McLuhan's: a media-based retribalization is unthinkable. His own framework of nostalgia is more uncompromising, truly rooted in the pre-Gutenberg, archaic perception of Time. D. J. is thus a medium that struggles against its own media characteristics, and aesthetic ecstasies are achieved despite the language's condition of being broken down into fragments (Eliot's shabby equipment, always deteriorating). In common with Ellison's invisible man, who is also 'invisible and without substance, a disembodied voice',[58] D. J. connects with the reader's chthonic consciousness; and on the 'lower frequencies'[59] he is, in Mailer's view, a spokesman for all our archaeological selves.

III

Mailer's aesthetics function in opposition to the media that have taken up residence inside us, the machine in the garden of the human body. But the occult force in Mailer's writing is also directed beyond this to the wider electroworld of technology-dominated reality, from which the archaeological self requires protection. In *Why Are We in Vietnam?* the 'radical sacred' of shamanism is pitted against the 'radical profane'[60] of contemporary scientific applications: 'Our scientists are only experts; those of the last decade are dull in person, dull as Jonas Salk, they write jargon, their minds are narrow before they are deep. Their knowledge of life is incarcerated.'[61] In the Texas of the novel, old and new circuits are in profound tension. The 'high technological nexus and underdeveloped civilization of a megacity like the Dallas-Fort Worth complex is halfway between civilization and a nature culture-primitive constellation (like Alaska, Man)' (pp. 91–2). Alaska itself, though, is a singular reality, a 'cold bare electric land of North, magnetic-electro fief of the dream' (p. 196), an utterly hostile region filled with an electronic magnetism that duplicates the effects of those media that possess the minds of the characters in the novel.

In the face of such a totalizing electroworld, the saving remnant of consciousness, the radical sacred, is beleaguered. Poirier has noticed that Mailer's fear about the power of technology is 'excited, prompted, and supported by literary culture. Indeed it can be said that to the extent that literature and the forms of imagination associated with it have become progressively *less* valuable to contemporary life, they have become insistently *more* valuable'[62] to Mailer. His obsessive fear of technology is extreme 'even within the radical spectrum'.[63] The radical geography of self and society posited that the vanguard were those least corrupted by technological values, and part of the counterpolitical argument against the left hinges on its complicity, as Mailer sees it, with the forces of oppression: 'the Left had been . . . the secret unwitting accomplice of every increase in the power of the technicians, bureaucrats, and labor leaders who ran the governmental military-industrial-complex of super-technology land'.[64] Only cultural radicals or left conservatives can appreciate the radical necessity of being, in Poirier's words, 'so finely conservative'[65] on this particular issue. Mailer has been moving towards this notion of a radically profane technological threat – inside the self, enveloping it – since his break with socialism and rational politics. In *Why Are We in Vietnam?* he is finally equipped to examine closely the consequences of technology that is corporate, whose environments create domains that extend to all areas of culture. The members of Mailer's hunting party in *Why Are We in Vietnam?* are agents of the 'Electrolux Edison World'. Overaccommodated with the surpluses of capitalist culture, the executive class reveals no urge towards an enabling 'power-to' in nature. Because primal instincts are sublimated, the 'mixed shit' produced by overstimulation and repression must be purged through technologically assisted demonstrations of 'power-over'. As D. J. punningly observes, 'Cop Turds are exploding psychic ecology all over the place' (p. 115). Even the hunters' guide, Big Luke, who possesses 'big man death guts charisma' (p. 66), has succumbed to technology's embrace, using a helicopter against his better judgement. The concept of the hunt is completely debased; animals are merely executed with bureaucratic efficiency using state-of-the-art weaponry, whose 'overspecific technical data' (p. 91) take up pages of description in the middle of the novel:

Rusty, well now he's got, well you be sure Rusty is holding, in fact D. J. is now canny to save him for later. So here's Luke and Ollie. Luke got a Model 70 Winchester .375 Magnum restocked (with maple Japanese Shigui finish) and remodeled by Griffin & Howe with a Unertl scope, and that little rifle and cartridge could knock down anything but an elephant, and if the elephant had just gotten fucked, it would knock him down too. Luke don't need that gun, he could hit and

take and flatten anything he wanted in Alaska with his second
gun, old Swedish Husqvarna .30-06, restocked and remodeled,
also Unertl scope (Luke was agent for Unertl for a while) which
handles a 180-grain bullet on a very flat trajectory, a real 300–400
yard bap of an ice picker, extra high up over 3 thou in velocity
delivered at the muzzle . . . . (pp. 77–8)

Rusty, D. J.'s father, is Mailer's fictional portrait of the corporate,
cannibal sensibility on the American right: 'What characterizes
the Cannibals is that most of them are born Christian, think of
Jesus as love, and get an erection from the thought of whippings,
blood, burning crosses, burning bodies, and screams in mass
graves.'[66] Under the conditions of the technological society
they help to promote, based on sexual sublimation, libidinal
urges are difficult to contain, and repression brings with it
distortions: 'D. J.'s father, Big Daddy, old Rusty has got the
dynamite. He don't come, he explodes, he's a geyser of love,
hot piss, shit, corporation pus, hate, and heart, baby he blasts,
he's Texas will power, hey, hey!' (p. 13). Rusty's lineage in
Mailer's fiction can be traced back through Barney Kelly and
Herman Teppis to General Cummings. Like his precursors, he
articulates a power system within which he has a hegemonic
role. 'Corporate power is cooking in Rusty's veins' (p. 53); he
is 'the highest grade of asshole made in America' (p. 37). In the
context of Mailer's preoccupation with individual selfhood and
epistemology, this makes him unequivocally the cultural enemy:
'He got a corporation mind' (p. 53).

Corporateness is the essence of the technological self, and
it evokes one of Mailer's longstanding interests, the opposition
between structuralistic and voluntaristic power. Axiomatically
the corporate individual possesses no power; he is merely a
conduit for external agencies. In *Why Are We in Vietnam?* the
middle manager assistants are called MAs or 'medium assholes'
(p. 85), who in 'corporation land are vacuum tubes, man, ideal
diodes, they are there to damp the waves in one direction, send
them out to the other, yes, yes, and act out all the no no no'
(p. 120). The corporate mind is non-dialectical: 'die, love die,
in a diode, cause love is dialectic, man, back and forth, hate
and sweet, leer-love, spit tickle, bite-lick, love is dialectic, and
corporation is DC, direct current, diehard charge, no dialectic
man, just one way street, they don't call it Washington D. C. for

nothing' (p. 126). The images used in *The Naked and the Dead* to evoke Major Dalleson's mind (the map, switchboard, crossword puzzle) are replaced here by the diode, a valvular device which allows electricity to pass through it unidirectionally. In this kind of mind – pervasive in our time, in Mailer's view – there is no content-as-resistance. Mailer illustrates this by giving us access to Rusty's mental life, which is an inert catalogue of banal anxieties:

(1) The women are free. They fuck too many to believe one man can do the job. (2) The Niggers are free, and the dues they got to be paid is no Texas virgin's delight. (3) The niggers and the women are fucking each other. (4) The yellow races are breaking loose. (5) Africa is breaking loose. (6) The adolescents are breaking loose including his own son. (7) The European nations hate America's guts. (8) The products are no fucking good anymore. (9) Communism is a system guaranteed to collect dues from all losers. (9a) More losers than winners. (9b) and out: Communism is going to defeat capitalism, unless promptly destroyed. (10) a. Fucking is king. b. Jerk-off dances are the royal road to the fuck. c. Rusty no great jerk-off dancer. d. Rusty disqualified from playing King Fuck. (11) The white men are no longer champions in boxing. (12) The great white athlete is being superseded by the great black athlete. (13) The Jews run the Eastern wing of the Democratic party. (14) Karate, a Jap sport, is now prerequisite to good street fighting. (15) The sons of the working class are running round America on motorcycles. (16) Church is out, LSD is in. (17) He, Rusty, is fucked unless he gets that bear, for if he don't, white men are fucked more and they can take no more. (pp. 110–11)

Without the mirror of conscious reflection that McLuhan spoke of, the corporate mind files each piece of information *received* into its discrete numbered compartment. Because he has embraced technology and corporate thinking, man has 'separated himself from those dire disciples of magic which might have enabled him to communicate with the cosmos'.[67] The purpose of the shamanistic artist is to bring divided knowledges together and restore the interior lines of communication that have ceased to function in the new circuits of the corporate mind. Politically he is therefore 'trying to blow up the base of technology',[68] break the 'technological chain of being'.[69] The return is to an indiscreet awareness in which, for example, 'the trees spoke to one, and the message of the trees was not agreeable, and worst of all the trees were right. The message one got from the trees was true. The storm they had told you about – that terrible storm which was going to make the river wash over its banks and destroy your hamlet in three weeks was true. What a terror. What a terror'.[70] Through technology man has done 'everything he could . . . to get away from that kind of intimacy with nature'; through art Mailer attempts to interpret the message of the trees.

What distinguishes Mailer's argument against the Vietnam War (alluded to in the improbable title of the novel) from liberal, left and conservative anti-Vietnam positions is that it arises from his opposition to technology. For Mailer, the issue at bottom is not foreign policy, colonialism, imperialism or the protection of markets; it is the 'transition to technological culture', the 'attempt to bring technology land to Asia'[71] by both communism and capitalism. His hubristic insistence is that his argument, unlike the others, 'begins at the root'. Critics of *The Armies of the Night* often complain that Mailer does not treat the war seriously enough, and not a few observers have found *Why Are We in Vietnam?* evasive. William Burroughs, when asked about his stand on Vietnam, drew back unashamedly: 'Once a problem has reached the political-military stage it is already insoluble.'[72] Mailer, though, in a chapter of *The Armies of the Night* entitled 'Why Are We in Vietnam?', considers carefully what role he might play, only to conclude that his first instincts were correct: 'When was everyone going to cut the nonsense and get to work, do their own real work? One's own literary work was the only answer to the war in Vietnam.'[73] This is not, as it might appear, a retreat, but a radical endorsement of the power of the artwork and the cutting edge of style upon national consciousness.

From Mailer's perspective, Vietnam is not a single issue, a question of good or bad policy, but a phenomenon that expresses the general drift of American society. D. J. explains that the society itself is corrupted; and the conclusion of *The Armies of the Night* is that 'the center of America might be insane. The country has been living with a controlled, even fiercely controlled, schizophrenia, which has been deepening with the years.'[74] Vietnam thus takes its place within a repression hypothesis:

Any man or woman who was devoutly Christian and worked for the American Corporation had been caught in an unseen vice whose pressure could split their minds from their soul. From the center of the corporation was a detestation of mystery, a worship of technology. Nothing was more intrinsically opposed to technology than the bleeding heart of Christ. The average American striving to do his duty, drove further every day into working for Christ, and drove equally further each day in the opposite direction – into working for the absolute computer of the corporation. Yes and no, 1 and 0. Everyday the average American drove himself further into schizophrenia; the average American believed in two opposites more profoundly apart than any previous schism in the Christian soul.

On this view, Vietnam releases the repressed violence of this cultural tension. It provides a 'temporary cure' without applying therapy to the root of the problem. But as treatment of sorts it is valued by the society:

> the average good Christian secretly loved the war in Vietnam. It opened his emotions. He felt compassion for the hardships and the sufferings of the American boys in Vietnam, even the Vietnamese orphans. And this view of the war could shift a little daily as he read the paper, the war connected him to his newspaper again: connexion to the outside world, and the small shift of opinions from day to day are the two nostrums of that apothecary where schizophrenia is treated. America needed the war. It would need the war so long as technology expanded on every road of communication, and the cities and corporations spread like cancer; the good Christian Americans needed the war or they would lose their Christ.[75]

The answer to the question of the novel's title is not direct, logical or responsible. Vietnam is mentioned only once in the text, on the last page. But, if the novel contains nothing resembling an analysis of the war, its plot, symbols, images and voice do carry forward a truth function, and once on Mailer's shamanistic wavelength the reader will not find it difficult to extrapolate the message. However, it is probably a mistake to conclude from Mailer's indirect handling of the subject that the basic action of the plot stands for the American presence in South

East Asia, that the hunt is an allegorical representation of the military-industrial complex. For Philip Bufithis, 'the parable is clear. The hunting party is the American military in miniature, replete with commanders and their GI subordinates. The crazed animals being annihilated by aerial machines are the people of Vietnam napalmed by the Air Force'.[76] But after the allegorical folly of *Barbary Shore* Mailer attempts no such formal exercise. At the same time, he does nothing to suppress the suggestion that the slain animals resemble the bombarded and napalmed Vietnamese or that the pathology affecting the hunters is similar to that manifested by US forces. These things are simply part of a text that bristles with references, allusions, homages and alternative meanings. The hunt itself resonates in a number of ways – Vietnam, the myth of the frontier, transcendentalism, *Moby Dick*, Hemingway, Faulkner, the anthropology of primitive culture – all of which are actively cultivated by Mailer. To insist, as some critics have done, on an allegorical purpose in the novel is to narrow authorial intention at precisely those points where it is at its most ambitious and expansive. Consequently, the hunting party can be no more or less than, as Robert Solotaroff says, 'a paradigm of society'.[77]

Nevertheless, one symbol stands out from the glittering array of images in *Why Are We in Vietnam?* At the very heart of the text, Rusty's unconsciously ironic description of the American eagle (the symbol and real creature) is the closest Mailer comes to political homily:

> Listen, know the worst thing I ever saw. It was a poor deer being killed by an eagle. Some hunter had wounded the deer – the eagle finished the job or was about to when I couldn't stand to watch no more and shot the eagle and put the poor deer out of its miz. But that eagle had swooped in, plucked out one eye of the deer, fluttered up a little you know like a Nigger strutting his ass feathers, an then plucked the other eye. It was going to go for the nuts next. Terrible creature the eagle. I've heard they even pull the intestine out of the carcass like a sailor pulling rope with his mouth. It got me so upset to recognize that E Pluribus Unum is in the hands of an eagle that I almost wrote an open letter to the Congress of America. Can you imagine your daddy getting that ape shit? But I think it's a secret crime that America, which is the greatest nation

ever lived, better read a lot of history to see how shit-and-sure a proposition that is, is nonetheless represented, indeed even symbolized by an eagle, the most miserable of the scavengers, worse than a crow. (p. 132)

Although this is certainly a comment on American foreign policy, the gloss refers to the whole historical enterprise of the United States. In a moment of political clarity unusual in so dense and refracted a novel, technology, capitalism and Americanism combine as the 'terrible creature' that destroys the ecology of the order of things. The shaman recognizes a monster loose on the world: 'the only explanation I can find for the war in Vietnam is that we are sinking into the swamps of a plague and the massacre of strange people seems to relieve this plague'.[78]

While critics such as Richard Poirier lament this repetitive, obsessive preoccupation with the meaning of technology, it may be that, on reflection, Mailer was right to cling to his obsessions. The fate of other cultural radicals of the period is instructive. The Yippies, for example, rejected ideological politics (bureaucracy, scholasticism and a tendency towards the endless refinement of theory) in search of new modes of opposing the American eagle, or what Abbie Hoffman called 'PIG NATION'.[79] Their quest, in common with Mailer's, was for an increase in authenticity and sense of self. But the Yippie impulse dispersed and became impotent very quickly. Fundamentally this was because its dialectic for liberation was only a by-product of an apocalyptic imagination. As Peter Clecak points out in *Radical Paradoxes*, it is 'the utopian corruption of political imagination' that 'impairs vision, distorts analysis and predictably ends in political disaster'.[80] The Yippies' attack on US society was all-inclusive; it failed to distinguish between different elements of society and therefore had no fix on individual social conditions. All it offered was total revolution. Their analysis was treacherously vague, went beyond the limits of plausibility and became what Clecak labels a 'destructive fiction'.[81] Mailer, with a very specific case against technology which he endlessly refines, avoids the analytical vagueness and all-or-nothing tactics of such fashionable, though short-lived, cultural radicalisms. As a seasoned radical in 1967, he knows it is never enough to express opposition to society in general. One must be able to distinguish the cultural root before attending to its salvage.

IV

The overall perspective emerging from *An American Dream* and *Why Are We in Vietnam?* is one shared by a spectrum of modern thinkers, not just Freudo-Marxist therapeutic radicals such as Reich and Marcuse, but historians of religion such as Mircea Eliade and founders of contemporary thought such as Nietzsche. Briefly, it states that the advent of history, of society, brought with it a constraint on man's animal nature. Natural outlets for the instincts became blocked and repression came into existence, bringing with it the guilt that arises from unreleased, forbidden urges. The body became thwarted because instincts could find only partial or distorted expression. The radical solution offered by all of these writers, and many more besides, is effectively the resurrection of the body. From the vantage point of the late 1980s, the thinker with whom Mailer seems to have most in common is Eliade. As a historian of primitive religious experience, it is Eliade's conviction that the way towards the resurrection of the body and a positive social dialectic is backwards to the archaic sacred, a return to the none-time of primordial beginnings. We have already seen how this is in fact one of the main ideas of *An American Dream*. In *Why Are We in Vietnam?* Mailer's discontent with the history of his own time, the new circuits of the electroworld of post-industrial America, persists undiminished, and the question of taking further the dialectic of the archaic sacred is even more pressing.

In this context it might be expected that Mailer's radical measures to save the root from the disenchantment of technological society would involve a pre-eminent role for nature, drawing on the conservative side of his left conservatism. And to an extent this is borne out. 'Syphilization' (p. 149), represented by the corporation mind that 'don't believe in nature' (p. 53), is contrasted with the wilderness as a source of meaning, 'the center of all significant knowledge' (p. 193). There is an awe of nature and its powers. But Mailer's pastoral impulse is odd: it involves a potent longing for things past and a search for a simple life free of the corruptions of technology, yet it does not extend to a yearning for lost innocence in which man existed in harmony with nature. Mailer does not subscribe to the golden age of primitive bliss, and he manages, on the whole, to avoid naïveté and utopianism. In fact, prior to *Why Are We in Vietnam?*, the only other novel of Mailer's to explore the subject of nature is *The Naked and the Dead*, where the environment is terrifyingly indifferent to humanity and the superiority of nature's force is acknowledged as man-breaking. Even Sergeant Croft, whose hunter's sense is instinctive, is thwarted finally by nature. The message of the novel is that the natural world is a 'No Man's Land'.[82]

In *Why Are We in Vietnam?*'s revised vision of nature, man and the natural world are not as clearly separated from each other as in the earlier work. The environment is permeated with 'mood' (p. 128), the hills are 'full of static charge' (p. 207). Nature does not stand in crude opposition to technology. The continent itself is alive with psychic force. D. J. 'got one breath of the sense of that *force* up in the North, of land North North above him' (p. 102), which is the super*natural* equivalent of an electro-magnetic field. This electro-magnetic radiation, or M. E. F., transmits signals to human beings through the antenna of the spinal cord. Thoughts from the spine lodge in the brain: 'one lightning leap from the bottom of his genius belt to the base of his brainpan' (p. 63). Alaska exposes Mailer's characters to signals in the charged atmosphere emanating from the Northern Lights: 'all the messages of North America go up to Brooks Range. The land above the Circle, man, is the land of the icy wilderness and the lost peaks and the unseen deeps and the spires, crystal receiver of the continent. Wait and hear. Goose your frequency' (p. 172). The elemental force of M. E. F. connects a circuit of communication between man and nature, but it is inherent in the environment rather than a product of culture, reminding us of Burroughs' claim in *The Naked Lunch* that 'America is not a young land: it is an old and dirty land, before the indians. The evil is there waiting.'[83] For Mailer, M. E. F. is a sort of *Ur*-technology, although it incorporates much psychic-electrical pollution from modern post-industrial society, and this condition makes it difficult for him to erect a sentimental myth of a return to nature. Nevertheless, he is unwilling to relinquish his dialectic of the sacred and the possibility of getting 'all the mixed shit and sludge out of [the individual's] system' (p. 180), and this makes his attitude to nature never less than ambivalent.

The animals in *Why Are We in Vietnam?* embody this ambivalence. According to Eliade, 'friendship with the animals and knowledge of their language belong to the paradisiac syndrome. In *illo tempore*, before the "fall", this friendship was constitutive of the primordial human condition'.[84] And to an extent the shaman returns to the paradisiac situation by recovering the animals' spontaneity, imitating their behaviour and language. At the beginning of the hunt, D. J. is 'uptight with the essential animal insanity of things' (p. 70). Later, when he kills a goat, he becomes connected to animal life: the pain of the goat's 'exploding heart shot like an arrow into D. J.'s heart, and the animal had gotten him, they were talking all around him now, communicating the unspoken unseen unmeasurable electromagnetism and wave of all the psychic circuits of all the wild of Alaska' (p. 100). But he is 'only part of them', since 'part he was of gasoline of Texas, the asshole sulfur smell of money-oil clinging to the helicopter'. Similarly, the idyllic image of a bear eating berries is qualified by the scene which follows it in which the bear cowardly rips open a caribou's entrails: 'griz right down on young beast and with one paw at the neck and the other on the flank, goes in with mouth open to rip her belly and get the living blood and taste of live entrail' (p. 192). Effectively this involvement with animals marks an end of innocence for D. J. and his companion/*alter ego* Tex Hyde. As in *Moby Dick, The Old Man and the Sea* and 'The Bear', the animals are monstrous embodiments of a natural world that is ambiguous at its essence, and yet, as Leslie Fiedler has qualified, they are 'sacred embodiments of power, taboo objects whose death is a blasphemy if it is not a rite'.[85] Of course, in *Why Are We in Vietnam?* the killing of animals is far from ritualized; it is a routinized catharsis for cultural repression, and the animals themselves are not allowed to set a pure example of the sacred. Thus, to Mailer, the bear's execution of the caribou is as profane as Rusty's decimation of the animal kingdom, and this in turn raises questions about exactly what is now recoverable from nature.

Simply to put man back in contact with nature is not one of Mailer's aims. Yet it is only through a profound experience of nature that D. J. and his 'blood brother' (p. 185) Tex Hyde can search for new principles. The myth of the hunt is all but totally corrupted, but at the climax of the novel hunting is supplanted by the more resonant ritual of the 'purification ceremony' (p. 175), an attempt to achieve what Eliade calls 'new psychic integration'.[86] In order to precipitate the necessary crisis, D. J. and Tex enter the wilderness without weapons: 'they're heating up all the foul talk to get rid of it in a hurry like bad air going up the flue and so be ready to enjoy good air and nature' (p. 180). They cultivate a dangerous state of openness and receptivity towards the ultimate power in nature: 'Mr. Sender, who sends out that Awe and Dread is up on their back clawing away like a cat because they *alone*, man, you dig? why they just dug, they all alone . . . ' (p. 187). Mailer emphasizes their need for cleansing, the sloughing-off of repressions: 'they each know . . . that this is how you get the fear, shit, disgust and mixed shit tapeworm out of fucked up guts and overcharged nerves' (p. 176). To get 'free of the mixed shit' (p. 201) an incubation from culture is sought, during which normal profane experience can be broken down (something the hunt did not achieve). What they pursue is not just an alteration of sensibility but the most representative mystical experience of archaic societies, that of shamanism. It betrays, in Eliade's words, 'the *Nostalgia for Paradise*, the desire to recover a state of freedom and beatitude before "the Fall", the will to restore communication between Earth and Heaven; in a word, to abolish all the changes made in the very structure of the Cosmos and in the human mode of being by that primordial disruption'.[87] The strange behaviour exhibited by D. J. and Tex in the closing chapters of the novel reflects their proximity to mythic initiation, their period of incubation, during which 'the young man . . . takes refuge in the forest, feeds upon the bark of trees, throws himself into the water or the fire or wounds himself with knives'.[88]

In William Faulkner's 'The Bear', which in some ways is the model for *Why Are We in Vietnam?*, the land is also cursed – tainted as a result of an ancient family evil relating to the commodification of nature and people – and Ike McCaslin, like D. J. and Tex, tries to break the pattern of cultural inheritance. Repudiating his family legacy, he seeks purification in the forest, a sacrament with nature. The climax of Ike's initiation is his first encounter with a bear, Old Ben. To glimpse the fabled creature, he equips himself with technology: a gun, watch and compass. When the exploration proceeds badly, he lays aside the gun. But this is not radical enough. He is 'still tainted',[89] and remains 'alien and lost' until he has 'relinquished completely'[90] his hold on civilization by giving up the watch and compass. Divested of these symbols of mastery over time and space, he is able to have an encounter with Old Ben. But this brings with it no permanent emancipation from historical fate. Dispossessed of Eden, Ike is initiated into what R. W. B. Lewis calls 'an actual world and an actual age'.[91] Faulkner himself seems to be sceptical of his own

idea of mythic return and, like the later Mailer, refuses to see
nature as a source of comfortable *Gemeinschaft* values: 'I don't hold
to the idea of a return. . . . We mustn't go back to a condition,
an idyllic condition, which the dream [made us think] we were
happy, were free of trouble and sin.'[92] For Faulkner it is neither
possible nor desirable to repeal primordial disruption.

When *Why Are We in Vietnam?* approaches the all-important
subject of the repeal of primordial disruption – the reconnection
of old circuits to the new – it takes on distinctly pessimistic
implications. Having opened up the prospect of psychic integration, Mailer proceeds to withdraw it: 'The hunting over? This
fine narrative of native Texas pluck and grits now to be laid back
into its rifle case while D. J.'s mind opens up another box of strict
inside goodies? Screw. The climax within Alaska is yet to come –
you will get rocks off you thought were buried forever' (p. 149).
Relinquishing their technology, D. J. and Tex experience nature
as unrefracted mystery, and the onset of initiation is sensed
when they go 'deep into that feeling of *release*' (p. 70), searching
for what Robert Begiebing calls 'the intrinsic power of increased
consciousness and self-definition'.[93] The reward for this cultural
divestment is the vision of twelve dall ram followed by the sighting
of a herd of caribou pursued by a bear. A moment of sublime
intensity is upon them:

> D. J. full of iron and fire and faith was nonetheless afraid of
> sleep, afraid of wolves, full of beauty, yeah, he unashamed,
> for across the fire and to their side the sun was setting to
> the west of the pond as they looked north, setting late in the
> evening in remembering echo of the endless summer evening
> in these woods in June when darkness never came for the
> light never left, but it was going now, September light not
> fading, no, ebbing, it went in steps and starts, like going
> down a stair from the light to the dark, sun golden red in
> its purple and purple red in the black of the trees, the water
> was dark green and gold, a sigh came out of the night as it
> came on, and D. J. could have wept for a secret was near,
> some mystery in the secret of things – why does the odor die
> last and by another route? – and he knew then the meaning of
> trees and forest all in dominion to one another and messages
> across the continent on the wave of their branches up to the
> sorrow of the North. . . . (p. 196)

But hearing the message of the trees is as far as the boys can go, and the initiation stops short of completion. The discovery that it is 'terrifying to be free of mixed shit' (p. 184) prevents their final liberation, in which, as Eliade says, 'one has to die to the profane "natural" existence constituted by the law of endless "condition-ings" (karma) and be re-born into an 'unconditional', that is, a perfectly free and autonomous existence'.[94] The rite of passage is effectively rerouted. Instead of exorcizing corporateness, the boys develop a spirit of competitiveness with each other and become murderous brothers, 'Killer I and Killer II' (p. 186). They come of age within a social structure of conditionings. The *status quo* is able to recapitulate itself. Thus in the final pages of *Why Are We in Vietnam?* D. J. and Tex are shown to be no better than the previous generation. Alaska is the place 'where the boys got their power' (p. 157), although it is not enabling, not 'power-to'. They have become vehicles for a pernicious institutionalized power of which Vietnam is a symptom and a symbol.

Making the most hopeful characters agents of a proliferating evil is a savage, gloomy irony on Mailer's part. The divine presence located in nature is a god who is a devouring cannibal creature:

Yeah God was here, and He was real and no man was He, but a beast, some beast of a giant jaw and cavernous mouth with a full cave's breath and fangs, and secret call: come to me. They could almost have got up and walked across the pond and into the north without their boots, going up to disappear and die and join that great beast . . . for God was a beast, not a man, and God said, 'Go out and kill – fulfill my will, go and kill', and they hung there each of them on the knife of the divide in all conflict of lust to own the other yet in fear of being killed by the other and as the hour went by and the lights shifted, something in the radiance of the North went into them, and owned their fear, some communion of telepathies and new powers, and they were twins, never to be near as lovers again, but killer brothers, owned by something, prince of darkness, lord of light, they did not know; they just knew telepathy was on them, they had been touched forever by the North and each bit a drop of blood from his own finger and touched them across and met, blood to blood, while the lights pulsated and glow of Arctic light was on the snow, and the deep beast whispering

Fulfil my will, go forth and kill, and they left an hour later in
the dark to go back to camp and knew on the way each mood of
emotion building in Rusty and Big Luke and Ollie and M. A. Bill
and Pete and their faces were etched just as they had foreseen
them and the older men's voices were filled with the same mix
of mixed old shit which they had heard before in the telepathic
vaults of their new Brooks Range electrified mind. (pp. 202–4)

The boys have been taken over, and this condition brings to
a resolution the problem of their apparent alienation. Radical
potential has been co-opted, pushed in other directions. The
failure to imagine the repeal of primordial disruption implies
that contemporary mystical experience is much inferior to that
of primitive culture, that the machine now dominates the garden.
Some cryptic species of reality are lost forever, some of the lower
frequencies can no longer be reached.

This pessimistic conclusion, though, links *Why Are We in
Vietnam?* to a distinctive line in American literature. Like Ishmael,
D. J. survives an ordeal in nature to tell his tale; like Huck Finn,
he gives 'civilization' another go. It illustrates Leslie Fiedler's
observation that at the end of classic American stories the
heroes are shown 'remanded to the world of reality',[95] or Richard
Poirier's companion insight that American writers are 'at some
point always forced to return their characters to prison. They
return them to "reality" from environments created by various
kinds of stylistic ingenuity'.[96] The attempt by radical means
to replenish consciousness of the archaeological self involves
learning what previous practitioners have repeatedly discovered:
to move backwards or sideways against historical process is to
arrive, eventually, at an untenable position.

Why Are We in Vietnam? contains no hint of radical change:
'North American shit heads stir in their sleep, digesting the
messages they sent out and get back' (p. 206). But the reader who
has understood the novel's strategies may experience remission
from cultural plague, a restoration in the senses, increases in
aesthetic and critical consciousness. The mirror of mind might
be established. For the most part, though, these possibilities exist
in the context of a deepening sense of limitation. Mailer may not
be able to fulfil his contract to (in his own words) 'restore men

and women by reproducing in them that sense of lost spell, as if the artist is some sort of magician or midwife between the lost life of the primitive and the modern world of technology'.[97] If the alienation from the sacred is now complete, the attempt to 'return to magic' is probably fated:

> I think the horror is that there's no one alive who can return us to anything. Our senses are so destroyed that we may be a light-year away from that primitive man. There may be no road back to him, none ever. We may not be able to begin to do – to comprehend where we lost the way, or where or how we can restore it. The artist may finally be some sort of extraordinary recorder of the failure.

And Mailer's intuition finds support from Thomas Altizer, a writer on Eliade: 'in so far as he exists as a profane being, modern man can only know the sacred as a Nothing. Moreover, the modern scholar can only discover the sacred as a reality that wholly inverts everything that modern man "knows" to be real: the sacred can only appear to us as the other, an other whose epiphany would dissolve our being in time'.[98]

It is the impossibility of this task that lies behind the outrageous comedy of *Why Are We in Vietnam?* Everything in the novel is filtered through a comic viewpoint and tainted with the spirit of comedy. Mailer is, to use Solotaroff's words, 'putting us on'.[99] Even his most cherished ideas are mocked. What makes this radical is not that it is a satire of America but that Mailer creates ironies in those places where seriousness would be expected to prevail. Restoring and thickening consciousness, humour acts as a compensatory device against the failure to *know* the sacred. Comedy is thus a vast distraction ('the way you make it is on the distractions', says D. J. – p. 8) from the hard realities of post-sacred existence. As Richard Poirier puts it, Mailer 'makes us almost regret that it is such a funny book, among the comic masterpieces, I think, of American literature. It is a book that makes us yearn for what it disposes of in its jokes. It endorses the wish that it were possible still to restore sincerity to the noble effort of the line of heroes stretching back from Faulkner to Emerson and Cooper'.[100]

The most that can be achieved is to save the root of radical vision. But no matter how quixotic the abolition or primordial disruption is acknowledged to be, Mailer is not prepared merely to record its failure to come about. In *The Crying of Lot 49* Pynchon offers teasing glimpses of the epiphanic possibility of 'one world's intrusion into another'[101] and the 'promise of hierophany'.[102] Mailer's next novel, his long awaited *magnum opus*, might well be described as the most sustained attempt imaginable to dissolve our being in time within a literary framework of nostalgia.

6
Making One's Way Back to Life in *Ancient Evenings*

I

At the present time there are no authoritative, detailed studies of *Ancient Evenings*.[1] It is still too early to say what the consensus on Mailer's attempt at a master narrative will be. For the time being, the foundation of the current discussion of the novel is provided by long, sympathetic and perceptive reviews by two critics who are, in their separate ways, ideally equipped to deal with what can only be called the phenomenon of Mailer's recent fiction: Richard Poirier and Harold Bloom. With the exception of these two commentators, there is every sign that the critical community remains baffled by *Ancient Evenings*.

Mailer himself anticipated the novel's effect in this respect: 'People are going to be immensely confused by the book. They are going to say, why did Mailer write it? What is he saying that means something to him? The man we know. What is this?'[2] He advertises it as a text for which there are no convenient map references: 'It's the most ambitious book I ever worked on. It's by far the most unusual work I've done, and it's out of category. I can think of no other novel that's remotely like it.'[3] Bloom, who has had scant regard for Mailer's previous work, does not dispute this claim: 'Our most conspicuous literary energy has generated its weirdest text, a book that defies usual aesthetic standards, even as it is beyond any conventional ideas of good and evil.'[4] Poirier, too, is quick to recognize the particular achievement of *Ancient Evenings*: 'Mailer has never before tried anything so perilous, and the prodigious demands he makes on the reader are a clue to his ambitions. This is at once his most accomplished and his most problematic work.'[5] Mailer's most triumphant fiction raises the thorniest questions about itself: 'I've taken more risks with the Egyptian novel than any other book I've ever written. It's the

149

most, dare I say it, audacious of the books I've done.'[6] While, as
George Stade has pointed out, *Ancient Evenings* provides the fullest
workings-out so far 'not only of Mailer's psychosomatics, but also
of his poetics'[7] (territory Mailer himself says he 'reconnoitered
years ago'[8]), it is nevertheless a novel without comparison. The
audacity of *Ancient Evenings* is that Mailer's old ideas are so
submerged in the particulars of his researched ancient materials
that they are hardly visible at all on the surface of the text. The
danger here is that Mailer will recede too far, that his novelistic
vision will be too radical for its own good. As a subtle 'alchemical
artist' he is under a heavy obligation to perform artistic magic, to
'produce an herb that will change all that is before us'. And many
critics will certainly argue that he has failed to find that herb, that
Ancient Evenings effectively marks the death of the subject in his
fiction, that he no longer has anything of relevance to say to the
contemporary reader.

Superficially this preoccupation with the distant non-American
past might seem to belong in the context of a number of recent
works, including Gore Vidal's *Creation*, Joseph Heller's *God Knows*
and Philip Glass's opera *Akhnaten*. On closer examination, though,
any similarity between *Ancient Evenings* and these works disap-
pears. Vidal is concerned with the philosophical origins of our
modern state in the classical world; Heller is drawn to the biblical
past of our official sacred literature; Glass is animated by the one
heretical religion from the ancient world with similar characteristics to Judaism and Christianity. Mailer's 'somber excavation of
our aboriginal and buried human nature'[9] is of a different order.
The historical agendas of Vidal, Heller and Glass all display a link
with modernity; Mailer, on the other hand, is fascinated by an
epistemological rupture with modern knowledge:

> what interested me was that I made one assumption that
> certain people will argue with and others will find natural. The
> assumption is that the Egyptians had minds that are easily as
> complex and interesting as our minds. They had an intellectual
> discipline that was highly unscientific from our point of view
> But I suspect no farther off the mark than ours. . . . The idea
> is to immerse yourself in another point of view when you are
> writing. Because when you do a lot of things come to you. . . I
> want people to realize, my God, there are wholly different points
> of view that can be as interesting as our own.[10]

As Harold Bloom insists, the novel is 'a wild, speculative work, but hard work nevertheless'.[11] It is 700 pages long and divided into seven large chapters or books: 'The Book of One Man Dead', 'The Book of the Gods', 'The Book of the Child', 'The Book of the Charioteer', 'The Book of Queens', 'The Book of the Pharaoh' and 'The Book of Secrets'. Loosely speaking, the narrative describes the adventures of a transmigrating soul in the afterlife of the Egypt of the pharaohs. But the central gestures of the narrative are those of telling and remembering. In Poirier's words, 'the scene of the novel is a scene of telling, of narration, of recollection'; each book 'spirals out of and back into the scene of telling'.[12] The text begins in the Land of the Dead and moves to a memory of Rameses IX (Ptah-nem-hotep). Within this memory there is a further remembrance, of a golden past during the reign of Rameses II (Usemare). Finally, the novel returns to the original or primal scene in the Land of the Dead. The exotic career of the novel's protagonist-narrator, Menenhetet, includes four lives and three incarnations.

If the truth function is clearly operating in *Ancient Evenings*, the book does not have a simple didactic mission. There is a much more enigmatic quality to the book which, so far, only Richard Poirier has attempted to account for:

Mailer offers none of the illusions . . . that there is something we want to know and that we will eventually know it, that a centre will be located in the wilderness of possibility, that the true shape of a person's life will emerge out of the mysteries that have structured it. The disaffection or impatience which many will feel with *Ancient Evenings* is likely to result from the fact that telling and listening have less to do with a desire to get somewhere (unless the reader is satisfied with being told that it has something to do with the saving of souls, and is meant to help Meni and Menenhetet pass through the Duad) but rather to get away from the loneliness, darkness, waste and dissolution which are, interestingly enough, the conditions Mailer has worried about since the mid-1950s as peculiar to the fate of the writer, especially the American writer, in the last half of the century.[13]

Yet, within the terms of this massive narrative distraction from modernity's condition of being severed from a usable past, Mailer is a serious believer in 'karmic roots'[14] and prescientific mind, and *Ancient Evenings* ought to be understood as a species of sacred text, an equivalent to the Pyramid Texts, the Coffin Texts, *The Book of the Dead* and *The Book of Him Who Is in the Nether World*. This is underscored by the epigraph, a statement by Yeats that links the narrative devices, apprehension of reality and religious values of the novel:

> I believe in the practice and philosophy of what we have agreed to call magic, in what I must call the evocation of spirits, though I do not know what they are, in the power of creating magical illusions, in the visions of truth in the depths of the mind when the eyes are closed; and I believe . . . that the borders of our mind are ever shifting and that many minds can flow into one another, as it were, and create or reveal a single mind, a single energy . . . and that our memories are part of one great memory, the memory of nature herself.

Telling stories, remembering, communication from mind to mind, the concept of reality, the concept of the writer and the religious notion of God form a matrix of associated and overlapping factors in Mailer's novelistic vision. Because of these sorts of ingredients, the novel does not yield to summary or to any sorting out of the various family lineages. As Bloom notes, 'there is a lot less story than any summary would indicate'.[15] Instead there is a blurring of distinctions and categories, and through the mist Mailer emerges as a godlike figure. Asked recently why fiction continues to be important for him, Mailer replied,

> Oh, because it's the place where art and philosophy and adventure finally come together. For me there's nothing more beautiful than a marvellous novel. I love the idea of the novel; to me a novel is better than a reality. . . . I mean there's something beautiful about one mind being able to come up with a vision that's not Godlike but close enough to the Godlike to give us a vision of how marvellous the Lord's mind might be. You know, when we read Proust or the best of Maugham or Stendhal or Joyce or any of the great novelists. We could name twenty of them, say, who give us this idea of God's mind being something like that. Don't you get that feeling when you read Proust – that one side of God's mind is like Proust? And that's the challenge.[16]

Ancient Evenings not only takes the possible 'god-like posture'[17] of the author literally; it also attempts to approximate the world as a single energy, one great memory or mind. Within this demiurgic effort at creativity, the categories of writer, society and god inevitably become purposefully intermingled. Their confusion, as Poirier points out, is strictly in the service of mystic intention. Embracing mystery, Mailer withholds lucid explanations of motive or rational accounting for strategy. However, the religious purpose of Mailer's dialectic of the sacred must be understood to be socially redemptive in a wilfully imprecise way. As the post-Freudian culture critic Norman O. Brown says, 'Jeremiads are useless unless we can point to a better way. Therefore the question confronting mankind is the abolition of repression – in a traditional Christian language, the resurrection of the body.'[18] In this respect, Brown recognizes a radical potential in art ('art, if its object is to undo repressions, and if civilization is essentially repressive, is in this sense subversive of civilization'[19]) but, like Mailer, he does not have a rational perception of how the mechanics of this work. For Brown, 'the whole nature of the "dialectical" or "poetical" imagination is another problem urgently needing examination'.[20] On such terms, it is easy to see how *Ancient Evenings* seduces the reader into the struggle against repressive civilization. Contemporary Western culture is subverted by vividly reinstating the ancient world through the action of dialectical imagination, and in doing this the 'vitalistic magus Mailer',[21] as Bloom calls him, is 'desperately trying to save our souls'.[22] Drawing readers into his sacred text, he turns them into 'religious vitalists' like himself and connects them up to the old circuitry of the great single energy.

Bloom appreciates that Mailer's most recent works 'strain at the limits of art' as they try to achieve Brown's *better way*. But the enormity of the novel's size, the tax it places on the reader, naturally generates suspicion and lack of sympathy. For a cynical English critic such as Ian Hamilton, 'the whole book bubbles with a desperate giganticism – indeed it is often pretty well deranged by it'.[23] Yet, where others see quantity, Mailer sees only pureness and resolution of form: 'The book certainly has the most complete architecture of any book I've written. It's in seven parts. Each of its parts, I would say, has a separate existence. The book continues from part to part, most definitely. But the nature of the book discloses itself part by part. When you've read part

one and part two, you won't have any clue at all what parts
six or seven are going to be like. It's as if the book moves in
a spiral.'[24] However, it is possible to accept both these views
simultaneously and see *Ancient Evenings* in the tradition of those
epic films that are the legends of the twentieth-century cinema
– Griffith's *Intolerance*, Von Stroheim's *Greed*, Gance's *Napoléon*,
Eisenstein's *Ivan the Terrible* and Bertolucci's *1900*. As the film
critic Pauline Kael says, none of these directors brought off one
of these visionary epics so that it connected with audiences in the
same way as the artist's previous work had done. Yet such works
should be appreciated because 'these legendary follies that break
the artists' backs are also amongst the great works of film history,
transforming the medium, discarding dead forms, and carrying on
an inspired lunatic tradition that is quite probably integral to the
nature of movies'.[25] *Ancient Evenings* undoubtedly belongs in this
lunatic company, and one can say of it what Kael says of *1900*,
that 'it is appalling, yet it has the grandeur of a classic visionary
folly. Next to it all the other [works] are like something you hold
up on the end of a toothpick'. It is the sentiment of Mailer's
favourite Marxist aphorism: quantity changes quality.

II

The Egyptians, it seems, lived apart from the rest of the
ancient world and very few of their legal and administrative
documents have survived. As a result of this scarcity of data,
Egyptian history remains shrouded in obscurity, and even today
the idea prevails that the Egyptians were different from the rest
of mankind, that their civilization is impenetrable. But cultural
isolation alone does not explain the obscurity of the Egyptian
Weltanschauung. It presents intrinsic obstacles to understanding
because it is a manifestation of the pre-Greek mind and therefore
beyond Western cultural frames of reference. As the historian
of Egyptian ideas H. Frankfort insists, the basic conventions of
the Egyptians are completely alien to us and 'we cannot evade
that difficulty, least of all by quasirational interpretation'.[26] No
translation can do justice to the Egyptian world view, since 'a
translation inevitably carries our point of view into a field of
thought that does not share our premises'.[27]

Mailer's initial preoccupation with this historical material was stimulated by an ancient Egyptian sacred text: 'I read A. Wallis Budge – a great British Egyptologist – *The Book of the Dead*, and I was a goner. Egypt it was, for eleven years.'[28] According to Budge, certain sections of the text appear to belong to an 'indefinitely remote and primeval time',[29] and as a whole it belongs 'to a very remote antiquity'.[30] Thus *The Book of the Dead* is double-edged, saturated with the life out of which it comes and yet a *terra incognita*. One scholar, James Henry Breasted, compares reading it to 'entering a vast primeval forest, a twilight jungle filled with strange forms and elusive shadows peopling a wilderness through which there is no path',[31] terms that recall *An American Dream*. For Breasted, Mailer's primary source text 'vaguely [discloses] to us a vanished world of thought and speech, the last of the unnumbered aeons through which prehistoric man has passed till he finally comes within hailing distance of us as he enters the historic age'.[32] But the crucial point here is that these ideas have not entered history, they constitute a forgotten epistemology. As another writer, R. T. Rundle Clark, puts it, 'The myths, symbols and social concepts of the Babylonians, Syrians and Jews were passed on from people to people to become part of the western heritage, whereas those of the Egyptians were never transmitted and so seem completely alien.'[33]

It is precisely this lack of historicity, this remoteness from modernity, that appeals to Mailer, who recognizes that the Egyptian world view offers a profound way of interrogating the ingrained styles of thought in the contemporary mind: 'It's one of the toughest cultures to understand. One of its greatest gods is a beetle. There's nothing for anyone from a Christian tradition to get hold of. But I felt that any culture whose eschatology was founded on such a notion as reincarnation was congenial to me.'[34] At the same time, Mailer is obliged to avoid unconsciously modernizing the material, thereby dissolving the vital sense of strangeness and cultural distance: 'One has to keep reminding oneself that this was before the Judeo-Christian era. We're dealing with pagans. The pagan mind is fascinating, but I found while I was writing the book that when I went through it, I had to keep making certain that there wasn't a single Judeo-Christian idea in it.'[35] The obscurity and intractability of Egyptian culture leaves room for Mailer to exploit the material but only at the risk of violating its integrity. He is therefore required to strike a balance between the alien and the familiar. In George Stade's view, *Ancient Evenings* finds the right balance: 'Representations of our repressed fears and desires seem alien because they are repressed; they seem familiar because they come from within us. The consistent atmosphere of the uncanny does not go away, even after you learn to think Egyptian.'[36] Benjamin De Mott concedes as much about the first section of the novel, which pulls the reader inside a consciousness unique in modern fiction:

A soul or body entombed is struggling to burst free, desperate not alone for light and air but for prayer and story – promised comforters that have been treacherously withheld or stolen. Dwelling within this consciousness we relive the 'experience' of an Egyptian body undergoing burial preparations, sense the god's overwhelming yearnings, within an unquiet grave, for healing that no physical treatment can provide. All is strange, dark, intense, mysteriously coherent.[37]

Nevertheless, there are problems for the reader in Mailer's presentation of the Egyptian mind. They are neatly summarized by De Mott in his ultimately hostile review:

Two problems beset this storytelling from the start. The first problem is that the mentality of the dynastic world, magically imagined in the book's opening pages, is replaced with fearful abruptness by the preoccupations and obsessions of the late twentieth century mind – Norman Mailer's – as soon as the narrator settles into his dinner party discourse. The second problem is that, in dramatizing those obsessions, Mailer relentlessly suppresses his own sense of the ridiculous – a deed few readers are likely to emulate.[38]

In De Mott's view, 'material in the Mel Brooks mode is repeatedly presented as though it were without comic dimension'.[39] But such ludicrous scenes are probably an inevitable side-effect of Mailer's determination to avoid the trap of rationally explaining the material. Other critics have recognized this. George Stade, for example, feels that the book becomes less ridiculous once Mailer has 'broken our embarrassed resistance'[40] to his exotic subject matter. Harold Bloom is even more enthusiastic on this point: the novel's 'peculiar and disturbing sincerity is its strength', and Mailer's religious seriousness is 'rather humorously unquestioned and unquestionable'.[41] In other words, if, as Frankfort claims, 'there is no short cut to an understanding of the ancients',[42] a tolerant view ought to be taken of scenes that seem, on the surface at least, 'pitiably foolish in conception'.[43] Although it may not be obvious, the lack of rationality in the more recalcitrantly Egyptian material is a willed intention, something under authorial control rather than a lapse in artistic judgement.

De Mott's other major criticism – that the Egyptian world view is supplemented by Mailer's own contemporary interests – suggests that Mailer uses his sources in order to recapitulate his personal vision. Ian Hamilton also suspects *Ancient Evenings* of this kind of opportunism: 'Except in rare flashes . . . all Mailer has done here is to "write-up" (i.e. Mailerishly empurple) the available texts and histories – from *The Book of the Dead* to the *Journal of Egyptian Archeology*.'[44] But, while there are numerous opportunities for creative licence, there are actually surprisingly few direct parallels drawn between the Egyptian material and Mailer's previous work. Only on comparatively minor matters are there direct internal Mailerian references:

> There came a time when I was obliged to ponder the qualities of the food we eat. Not only do we take our strength from it, but what we cannot use is cast out. Excrement is full of all that is too despicable for us, but it also may contain all that we cannot afford to take into ourselves – all that is too rich, too courageous, or too proud for our bearing. . . . (p. 216)

Although the reader may say, along with Ptah-nem-hotep, 'None of this is wholly strange to my ear' (p. 217), it is probable that Mailer's reading of *The Book of the Dead* alerted him to what are little more than analogies to his own ongoing obsessions, that he is interested in the Egyptian world view essentially on its own terms. As Richard Poirier notes, Mailer

> has imagined a culture that gives formal, and not merely anthropological, sanction to what in his other works often seems eccentric or plaintively metaphysical, like his obsession with 'psychic darts' and mind reading, with immortality, with battles of the gods (Liston and Patterson, it now seems, were latter versions of the Egyptian gods Horus and Set), with villainous homosexuality, with magic and sorcery, and with

excrement as an encoding of psychic failure or success. Having so often written as if the self had several versions, he is completely at ease with the Egyptian names for the seven spirits of the self that continue to exist in different degrees of intensity after death.[45]

Mailer has the strongest interest in retaining the authentic, original Egyptian quality because it performs a validating function with regard to his own body of work. 'Why are we in Egypt?' asks Harold Bloom, only to conclude, 'Where else could we be? Mailer's dialectics of sex and death have found their inevitable context.'[46] Mailer may add emphasis in such areas as scatology, buggery and the conflict between men and women, but the fundamental material, on the 'wavering border between the human and the divine, and on the world of the dead, is already there in Egyptian mythology for him to develop'.[47]

In fact, Mailer's preoccupations cannot be said to be unprecedented, even in American literature. Frankfort describes how 'the fabulous antiquity of Egyptian civilization and the stupendous ruins have always suggested a background of profound wisdom'.[48] In the United States an Egyptian revival coincided with the American Renaissance, during which time collections of antiquities began to amass and an Egyptian style of architecture began to take hold. In 1823 Edward Everett stated, 'Since the days of the Romans, who plundered Egypt of obelisks and transported whole collonades of marble pillars from Italy to Constantinople, this magnetized kind of robbery never flourished more than at the present moment.'[49] This popular interest in all things Egyptian was coupled with an academic concern with the decipherment of hieroglyphic writing. The critic John Irwin has shown how the major writers of the period, including Poe, Whitman and Melville, were influenced by the revival, arguing that the 'immense symbolic importance of the Egyptian hieroglyphics for the writers of the American Renaissance' lay primarily in the fact that the hieroglyphics represented an 'archetypal form of writing'.[50] Mailer's recent interest, though, is not logocentric, preoccupied with the meaning of symbols or writing, even if their roots are in sacred texts. *Ancient Evenings* is what Nicholas Shrimpton calls a 'total immersion course in ancient Egyptian culture',[51] a display of encyclopaedic knowledge of the society. The novel's abandoned subtitle, 'The

Egyptian Novel', is unnecessary since, as Poirier notes, Mailer 'luxuriates, sometimes to the limits of patience and beyond, in accounts of Egyptian low life, in the power put into play during a royal dinner party, in details of costume and . . . cuisine'.[52]

Frankfort chides his fellow writers on ancient Egypt: 'In reading their books you would never think that the gods they discuss once moved men to acts of worship.'[53] They fail to appreciate the gulf that exists between contemporary thought and the mythopoeic thought of the ancient world. Mailer, by contrast, is what Harold Bloom terms a 'figure of capable imagination',[54] a 'strong reader',[55] who appropriates for himself, bridging the gap between the rational and the mythopoeic to provide exciting insights into the Egyptian mind. As Poirier highlights, Mailer has become a naturalized Egyptian, 'so that he writes as if saturated with the mentality and the governing assumptions, some of which he revises rather freely, of a culture in which the idea of the human is markedly different from what it has been in the west for the last 1,500 years or so'.[56] Mailer's considerable internalizing ability (seen previously in his mastery of the technical data of an Apollo space mission, Bantu language and philosophy in Zaire, and the facts of the Gary Gilmore case) helps him become a belated ancient sensibility, what Bloom calls a 'latecomer'.[57] Like the shaman, who holds the key memories of the beginnings associated with perfection, Mailer has produced an artwork which affirms the prestige of origins.

The speaker within the narrative for much of the ancient evening is Menenhetet One, the great-grandfather of the sometime narrator Menenhetet Two, who, for the most part, frames the narrative and moves freely from his own consciousness into that of others (rather as D. J. does in *Why Are We in Vietnam?*). Menenhetet One is a former general, harem master, magician, priest and raconteur, and the story of his four lives and three incarnations (including recollections of a much earlier period under Rameses II) spans almost 1000 years. Most of the story is told by Menenhetet One to the reigning pharaoh, Rameses IX, during the night of banqueting which consumes over 500 pages of the book. The denseness of the text is part of its authenticity. In Poirier's words,

Meni [Menenhetet Two] needs to be told the intricate story of the gods, the Pharaoh needs to be told exhaustively about his ancestors, Menenhetet [One] needs to rehearse his lives because each of them is convinced that only a person who can remember and explain his deeds when alive, or when he somehow partook of the life of another, can pass out of the land of the Dead. And because of the endless mirroring of one life in another and in the lives of the gods, there is, for the anxious spirit, no limit to recollection, no ascertainable boundary.[58]

There is a temptation to see Menenhetet One as Mailer himself: 'his hair showed the silver of a virile maturity while the lines on his face had not yet become a myriad of wrinkles, terraces, and webs, but exhibited, instead, that look of character supported by triumph which comes to powerful men when they are sixty and still strong' (p. 101). But there is a similar incentive to identify Mailer with Menenhetet Two, whose description of himself ('I was used to relatives and servants recognizing that I was not an ordinary child' – pp. 102–3) uses exactly the same words as Mailer's mother has used to describe her young son.[59] Poirier resists the view that any single character carries Mailer's personality or that Menenhetet is meant to represent Hemingway, Mailer's 'precursor'.[60] Bloom, by contrast, is committed to making *Ancient Evenings* base, personal and autobiographical. In Bloom's notorious poetics, an extension of Freud's view that the boy is the rival and antagonist of the father, the apprentice artist is a son who has a poetic father among previous artists. The apprentice must overthrow his precursor. Thus, for Bloom, 'There are only two characters who matter in the book', and they are 'versions of Hemingway . . . and Mailer himself, the heroic precursor and his vitalistic follower and son'.[61]

The power relationship in Bloom's psychoanalytical allegory is very narrow and precisely formulated; everything is reduced to power, struggle, strength of will. The virtue of Poirier's conception of power is that it is diffuse, covers more of *Ancient Evenings* and refers us back to Mailer's all-important epigraph. For Poirier the novel only comes into focus when it is appreciated that it is only indirectly Mailer's most self-revealing text. Menenhetet One carries out the implications of Mailer's more direct autobiographical writing because 'even as he tells stories about himself he is by that very process trying to put himself together from several different remembered versions'.[62] In this model, as in Bloom's, Mailer contends rather than records, although not so much with Hemingway as with earlier versions of himself. Either way, the effort to distinguish between the two Menenhetets is highly problematic: 'Whether I am the Second or the First Menenhetet or the creature of our twice seven separate souls and lights, I would hardly declare, and so I do not know if I will labor in greed forever among the demonic or serve some noble purpose I cannot name' (p. 709). Yet the problem is clearly part of Mailer's intention, and in Poirier's interpretation we are meant to understand that 'multiple identities, identities that in their passage through time come to blend with one another are common among the fantastic array of Egyptian gods and therefore among those humans for whom the gods are a paradigm of moral existence'. The characters are simply not modern, individualized. In George Stade's description, 'Minds dissolve, reform, expand, contract, seep into each other, take in and send out those energies we call spirits of gods.'[63] The whole issue of identity is thrown into serious question. While this refers back to the consciousness of *Why Are We in Vietnam?*, it is also well-grounded in the Egyptian world view. According to Frankfort, 'The creations of the primitive mind are elusive. The concepts seem ill defined, or, rather, they defy limitations. Every relationship becomes a sharing of essentials. The part partakes of the whole, the name of the person, the shadow and effigy of the original. This "mystic participation" reduces the significance of distinctions while increasing that of every resemblance.'[64] It is a concept of self that subverts our most fundamental habits of thought. Using it, Mailer's language will not perform a normative function.

This mystic participation in a world of reduced distinctions implies an all pervasive religious faculty. For a radical such as Norman O. Brown, religion is important for the improvement of psychoanalysis as a knowledge system. Psychoanalysis must view religion 'both as neurosis and as that attempt to become conscious and to cure, inside the neurosis itself, on which Freud came at the end of his life to pin his hopes for therapy'.[65] Brown insists that psychoanalysis can only go beyond religion when it sees itself as completing religion's original intent to make the unconscious conscious. Only when this point is reached will psychoanalysis be in a position to define the error in religion. Writers such as Mailer and Bloom, though, are moving in the opposite direction on this point. *Ancient Evenings* is a fantasy in which religious beliefs are treated as psychic realities. As Bloom puts it, Mailer has 'gone back to the ancient evenings of the Egyptians in order to find the religious meaning of death, sex, and reincarnation, using an outrageous literalism, not metaphor'.[66] He is reclaiming for religion the territory now occupied by psychoanalysis. Frankfort criticizes secularizing writers on ancient Egypt who not only 'ignore religion as a phenomenon *sui generis*, but are unable to see the wood for the trees'.[67] In a culture where monotheism and polytheism existed simultaneously, the universe was perceived as alive from end to end: 'powers confront man wherever he moves'.[68] All divine power was immanent, since the Egyptians lived within the sphere of their gods' activities. There was no bureaucracy. According to Frankfort, officialdom 'retained at all times and in all, its strata the characteristics of personal authority. . . . This left great scope for energetic individuals.'[69] Mailer, of course, is the antithesis of the secularizing scholar, although some critics have been puzzled by the fact that a Jewish writer can make only one minor reference to the plight of the Jews in the ancient world. Ian Hamilton, for example, cannot understand how Mailer can 'eliminate the Jews'[70] from his account. Mailer's justification for this absence of Hebrew culture is ostensibly historical: 'it wasn't even a minor culture at the time. They were still a race of tribes and barbarians. They weren't taken seriously. Not at this period. Later they were.'[71] But the more compelling reason is that *Ancient Evenings* stands for religious revisionism. Mailer uses it to challenge Christianity and his own religious tradition. The Egyptian religious world view is intended as an affront to our sense of order, which Mailer considers false.

Mailer, though, is not religious in the sense of being a believer in a faith (such as Christianity, Judaism or Islam); his religious experience is private and overwhelmingly gnostic. According to Harold Bloom, Mailer has been developing 'a private version of an American Gnosis for some time now, in the sense that Gnosticism can be a doctrine insisting upon a divine spark in each adept that cannot die'.[72] Bloom associates Mailer not so much with the original Hellenistic gnostic systems as with a mode of interpretation, a 'timeless knowing, as available now as it was then, and available alike to those Christians, to those Jews and to those secular intellectuals who are not persuaded by orthodox or normative accounts or versions of religions, and who rightly scorn the many mindless, soft pseudo-transcendentalisms now swarming, but who know themselves as questers for God'.[73] As an epistemology gnosis is not rational; it is a 'more-than-rational knowledge'[74] which never 'yields to a rigorous working-through'.[75] Poetically expressed by Bloom, the space gnosticism claims for itself is 'a freedom for knowledge, and knowledge of something in the self, *not* in the psyche or soul, that is Godlike, and knowledge of God beyond the cosmos. But also it is a freedom to be known, to be known by God, by what is alien to everything created, by what is alien to and beyond the stars and the cosmic systems and our earth'.[76] Bloom acknowledges the link between *Ancient Evenings* and his own work, and he is happy to proclaim himself to be a 'Jewish Gnostic, trying to explore and develop a personal Gnosis and a possible Gnosticism, perhaps even one available to others'.[77] But neither Mailer nor Bloom is a historian of religion or a religious scholar; they are interested only in a '*religious* knowledge'[78] which they wish to share socially. Their highly individual mission is to be, in the critic Marilyn Butler's words, 'the carriers of divine or satanic messages from one corner of the world to another'.[79]

Mailer's extensive use of Egyptian religious materials demonstrates his shamanistic impulse to be a 'fictive theologian'.[80] One of the main ways of practising this is through telling: '"Tell another story," said Usermare, "and tell it well"'; '"Make this story long," said Usermare. "I like long stories better"' (p. 413). Much of *Ancient Evenings* is a collection of well-known stories from mythology. As Bloom says, readers will learn 'rather more ancient Egyptian mythology than they are likely to want or need, but the mythology is the book'.[81] Mailer recapitulates the core stories of Horus, Set, Isis and, most important of all, Osiris. However, the telling of these stories is no stale exercise, and the result impresses even such an unsympathetic reader as Benjamin De Mott:

> a second voice speaks. Offering a kind of haunting succour, it commences a story of the gods – the myths of Isis and Osiris which in this telling is made utterly new, indeed seems to have been given utterance by the strewn bones and limbs themselves. I looked up at the end of this section of the book, simultaneously moved and (I am speaking seriously) ashamed – troubled by my own habitual skepticism, my trained resistance to whatever is heavily promoted.[82]

The stories Mailer tells in 'The Book of the Gods' constitute what might be called the Egyptian gospels. As Menenhetet One points out to Menenhetet Two, the stories themselves are not factual accounts; they are interpretations, not authentications, of what they report. Retelling them allows Mailer to fold himself into the mythmaking process. For Ian Hamilton this means little more than that they are 'bloated and distorted by Mailer's infantile megalomania'.[83] But the practical aim is to connect us to a mythology alien to the West, which is rooted in the folk tales of Greek and Norse culture. To do this, Mailer packages the stories as coherent, sequential narratives, although he knows very well that the Egyptians did not do this: 'If you think of the story I told you of our Gods at the beginning of our travels, I will now confess that I imparted it to you in the way that these Romans and Greeks tell it to each other. That is why my tale was familiar yet different from what you know. For our Lord of the Dead now belongs to them . . . ' (p. 705). As Wallis Budge cautions, 'The story of Osiris is nowhere to be found in a connected form in Egyptian literature, but everywhere, and in texts of all periods, the life, sufferings, death and resurrection of Osiris are accepted as facts universally admitted'.[84] Piecing together the heap of narrative fragments, Mailer attaches us to historically repressed beginnings.

Mailer is a gnostic mediator between the prehistoric and the modern, fashioning his own sacred book in order to retextualize the myths in such a way as to enhance psychic belatedness. Rundle Clark provides something like scholarly grounds for this attempt:

> Egyptian gods are nearer the stark archetypes of the unconscious mind than the Greek ones and, in a sense, they are more intellectual too, for they are expressing ideas. Egyptian myths cannot be retold, for then they become meaningless or trivial; they can only be appreciated through the actual texts, and these are to be read not for their linguistic interest but for their religious and metaphysical penetration.[85]

Thus *Ancient Evenings* and the sacred texts tell the same stories of the gods and the afterlife, at the centre of which is the death, mutilation and resurrection of the god Osiris ('"It is the passion of Osiris," Menenhetet remarked, "to conquer chaos"' – p. 83). Living within the sphere of the gods meant that any Egyptian of high birth could consider himself as Osiris and find the pattern of his own life or past life in the story's details. In *Ancient Evenings* these myths again become keys to experience. As Poirier notices, there is a strong link between the characters and their mythology: 'The story of Osiris, Isis, and of the bitter buggery-ridden battles between their son Horus and his uncle Set is a phantasmagoric version of much that happens to Menenhetet as his story unfolds in subsequent books.'[86]

Beyond these sacred myths, almost the whole of Mailer's appropriation of the Egyptian religious world view relates to death. *Ancient Evenings* is, as Harold Bloom intuits, Mailer's own *Book of the Dead*, reflecting an 'obsession with the world of the dead'.[87] As with the myths, Mailer's use is interpretative, and the fact that Egyptian notions of 'the power of the unseen world'[88] are intrinsically imprecise provides ample room for Mailerian investigations. Wallis Budge describes the void into which Mailer writes himself after a 'strong' reading of *The Book of the Dead*: 'The home, origin and early history of the collection of ancient religious texts which have descended to us are, at present, unknown and all working theories regarding them, however strongly supported by well-ascertained facts, must be carefully distinguished as theories only.'[89] Mailer's highly evolved theoretical capacity is inspired by this funerary literature, which, strangely, is entirely consistent with ancient practice. According to Rundle Clark, death provided the 'opportunity for creative speculation and gave scope for the elaboration of mythical detail in the funerary literature'.[90] The real aim of such texts was the 'development of consciousness'. From his own point of view, Norman O. Brown also wants to put death on the agenda: 'The hard truth which psychoanalysis must insist upon is the acceptance of death, its reunification in consciousness with life.'[91] This can only be achieved on the abolition of the *repression* of death. What the Egyptians had, and what Mailer cultivates in *Ancient Evenings*, is a sort of psychology of the dead – an enterprise that is even more outrageous to modern sensibilities than Harold Bloom's attempts to psychoanalyse dead writers.

The Egyptian concept of an afterlife on a survival of the bodily image, which is an appealing doctrine for a radical preoccupied with the resurrection of the body. The corpse does not simply lie in the tomb. Through prayers and ceremonies it is endowed with the power of changing into a spiritual 'body'. Certain states of body thus indicate, as Wallis Budge says, the status of having 'obtained a degree of knowledge and power and glory whereby it becomes henceforth lasting and incorruptible'.[92] Death is a vitalizing force. John Irwin argues that Emerson and the writers he influenced – Thoreau, Whitman, Poe and Hawthorne – found in ancient Egypt an attractive vision of resurrection through rein-carnation or reappearance. *Ancient Evenings* extends this impulse to provide an American literary version of death which violates the conventions on the subject in Judaism and Christianity. Personal immortality is superseded by a psychic survival that enacts a revenge on Western ideas of time. Mailer clearly prefers this Egyptianized account of death. He has become, like Osiris himself, a champion of the dead, incorporating in the novel a religious view of the dead that emerged in Egypt from what Breasted labels the 'Osirianization of the hereafter'.[93] Osiris's suffering and death provided the basis for the Egyptian hope that the body might rise again in some transformed, glorified shape. He managed to conquer death and become the king of the other world. As Wallis Budge encapsulates it, 'What is done for Osiris is also done for the deceased; the state and condition of Osiris are the state and condition of the deceased; in a word the deceased is identified with Osiris. If Osiris liveth forever, the deceased will live forever.'[94] Mailer, the mythmaking novelist, becomes an 'Osiris of a man'[95] who walks among the living. His text marries the material world to its spiritual counterpart in death and allegorizes the fic-tion writer's quest for immortality. The central scene of the novel, from which all tale-telling is projected and to which it is returned, is in the Land of the Dead, and the central characters whose identities are so difficult to distinguish (the two Menenhetets) are not alive in any modern sense of the word: 'Crude thoughts and fierce forces are my state. I do not know who I am. Nor what I was' (p. 3). The narrator is the ka or surviving double of the dead Menenhetet Two. In the Land of the Dead he meets the khaibit or shadow of his great-grandfather, Menenhetet One, who has just died in his fourth life. The narrator's state of being is thus one of ontological crisis:

> For now I knew who I was, and that was no better than a ghost in a panic for food. I was nothing but the Ka of Menenhetet Two. And if the first gift to the dead was that they could add the name of the Lord to their own name, then I was the Ka of poor helpless Osiris Menenhetet Two, yes, the Ka, the most improperly buried and fearful Ka who now must live in the violated tomb, oh, where was I now that I knew where

I was? And the thought of the Lord of the Dead opened to me with all the recognition that I was but a seventh of what had been once the lights, faculties, and power of a living soul. Now I was no more than the Double of the dead man, and what was left of him was no more than the corpse of his badly wrapped body, and me. (p. 31)

The ka, as well as being the 'twin, double, or genius'[96] of the dead person, is an impalpable vital force. Frankfort says that 'the Ka *is* power';[97] and for Rundle Clark this includes 'male generative power'.[98] Wallis Budge perhaps gives us the clearest definition of the ka: 'In addition to the natural and spiritual bodies, man also had an abstract individuality or personality endowed with all his characteristic attributes. This abstract attribute had an absolutely independent existence. It could move freely from place to place, separating itself from, or uniting itself to, the body at will.'[99] And for Mailer this empowered essence of self is but a purified model of the self's perennial condition: 'The Egyptians believed . . . well, it's complex but the most important part of it was that when you died you had a double, Ka, and in your adventures in the underworld this was either destroyed or it could live to be seen again. Hence the Egyptian prayer "Do not let me die a second time." '[100]

The ka's existence makes each person the receiver of a divine power and places him within a field of powers. The self retains a gnostic identity in death. The body is resurrected, since the ka is not independent of the flesh. Even after death the individual required food, drink and the satisfaction of sensuous needs. As Menenhetet One exclaims, 'I had body again' (p. 5), or, later, 'Then was my Ka born, which is to say I was born again, and was it a day, a year, or not for the passing of ten kings. But I was up and myself again apart from Meni and his poor body in the coffin' (p. 31). The opening of *Ancient Evenings* finds the ka of Menenhetet Two discovering himself kneeling on the floor of the Pyramid of Khufu with the khaibit or ka of the elder Menenhetet's penis in his mouth. While the experience is clearly disgusting to him, he is aware that it is somehow important and part of the mysterious preparation for passage from the Land of the Dead. The scene, returned to in the final sequence of the novel, is the crucial framing trope for the stories that are told, and it is at least as important as they are. Poirier strikes the right balance when he argues that 'It is impossible to assume that the two forms remain fixed in this position . . . while they visualize the immensely long night of story telling, the Night of the Pig, when any truth can be told without the fear of retaliation, a millenium back at the palace of Rameses IX.'[101] The precise nature of the coupling has mythical resonance, symbolizing the essential image of the ka as described by John Irwin: 'Significantly, the hieroglyph for the Ka is a pair of uplifted hands . . . suggesting the Egyptian sense that the relationship between body and self is like the mutually constitutive opposition between left and right.'[102] If an embrace is, as Rundle Clark says, 'the act of Ka', then 'to put one's arms around another meant, to the ancients, to impart one's vital essence'. In this way the ka is a symbol of 'the transmission of life power.'[103]

Mailer's interpretation of the transmission of life power brings his preoccupations with magic and sex into alignment. The act of ka becomes an application of the concept of surplus erotic energy to the gnostic idea of passing on the vital spark. Everything has an influence on everything else in *Ancient Evenings*, since magic in Egypt, as described by Breasted, was total, all-enveloping:

> It is difficult for the modern mind to understand how completely the belief in magic penetrated the whole substance of life, dominating popular custom and constantly appearing in the simplest acts of the daily household routine, as much a matter of course as sleep or the preparation of food. It constituted the very atmosphere in which the men of the early Oriental world lived. Without the saving and salutary influence of such magical agencies constantly invoked, the life of an ancient household in the East was unthinkable. The destructive powers would otherwise have annihilated all.[104]

This public dimension is crucial; it makes magic social rather than a private transaction. For Mailer, Egypt is 'one of the places where magic was being converted into social equivalence, if effect used as an exchange'.[105] In the multiple consciousness (Meni/many) of Menenhetet (One and Two) all these elements combine so that we have, as Bloom says, 'the song, not of the executioner, but of the magician'.[106] Menenhetet is 'Master of the Secrets of the Things that Only One Man Sees' (p. 658).

In order to cultivate the idea of transmitting life power, which is recognizable as an extension of the rite-of-passage theme, Mailer recklessly expands his psychology of the dead to include sexual reincarnation:

> so did I come into the deepest secret of my family. For my mother's mind offered it up without a word, although her lips certainly trembled as these confessions poured from her mind. I learned – all at once! – that my great-grandfather had the power to escape death in a way no other had ever done. For he had been able, during an embrace, to ride his heart over the last ridge and breathe his last thoughts as he passed into the womb of the woman and thereby could begin a new life, a true continuation of himself; his body died, but not the memory of his life. Soon he would show fabulous powers in childhood. So I understood why my mother could no longer keep such knowledge from me. I too, showed such powers! (pp. 161–2)

But the art of being born out of oneself in the last minutes of life does not require heterosexual mating, and the conclusion of *Ancient Evenings*, which takes us to the verge of Mailer's ill-defined 'last ridge', allows for any kind of coupling. It is a vision that suggests Norman O. Brown's famous celebration of the polymorphous perverse:

> I did not wish to die a second time. Yet I did not know if I dared to enter the fundament of pain. For I was worthless, and my great-grandfather was damned and worthless, and we were beset by mighty curses. I felt the sorrow of his heart, however, come into me, and with a thought as beautiful as radiance itself: if the souls of the dead would try to reach the heavens of highest endeavour then they must look to mate with one another. But since the soul was no longer a man nor a woman, or to know it better, now contained all the men and women among whom one had lived, it might not matter in the Land of the Dead whether the vow was taken between a man or a woman, two men or two women, no, no more was required than that they would dare to share the same fate. (p. 708)

Although this occult performance of becoming one's own father by begetting one's next incarnation in dying orgasm can be seen, as Marilyn Butler sees it, as a 'witty variant of Bloom's theory of literary influence',[107] Mailer is aiming for a broader inclusiveness, a merging of categories, states of being and specific identities. In Menenhetet there are 'hints of voice from many a province' (p. 202); his is 'more than one man's voice'. The ka and khaibit of the two Menenhetets have become, in George Stade's words, 'as intertwined as the strands of a double helix, each the promise of the other's regeneration'.[108] And the final words of the novel hint at a resolution of this dialectic as 'Past and future come together on thunderheads and our dead hearts live with lightning in the wounds of the Gods' (p. 709).

Entering into 'the power of the word', Menenhetet's consciousness is transformed by Mailer's artistry into a belated sacred document. But, if the narrative achieves resolution, the novel as a whole remains confusing, and it is not difficult to appreciate Mailer's sensitivity about misunderstood intentions. The questions that inevitably arise from a completed reading of the book (What is to be made of such avowedly untranslatable ideas, of a culture not susceptible to rational explication? What, precisely, is the value of a text based on a fundamental disconnection from our lives?) mean that *Ancient Evenings* needs to be assessed against the criticism that, despite its obvious achievement, its inspiring sense of grandeur, it is ultimately no more than an epic exercise in nostalgia and a folly unworthy of accolade.

III

The subtitle of C. Vann Woodward's recent book *Thinking Back* – *'The Perils of Writing History'* - succinctly cautions against glib historicism. Both Mailer and Bloom attempt to avoid these perils by insisting that they do not approach the past as historians. Their work cannot be tested, proved or disproved against empirical data. Mailer protests his dislike of the historical novel and its presumptuous didacticism: 'Most historical novels perform a service or pretend to teach us something about today. And I will have failed if that's the way people react to my book.'[109] Reviewers, such as Ian Hamilton, who have treated *Ancient Evenings* historically have tended to seek contemporary relevance in the novel ('*Ancient Evenings* is set in ancient Egypt .. but an element of its otherworldliness does seem to spout, near plaintively, from

Brooklyn Heights'[110]) and then dismiss it for not taking the subject seriously. One reviewer notes that an Egyptologist has given Mailer 'mixed marks on his homework, particularly criticizing "his cannibalized or bastardized forms of good ancient Egyptian names"'.[111] The reviewer points to liberties taken with Egyptian beliefs in reincarnation and telepathy, but Mailer is interested neither in complete historical fidelity nor in immediate contemporary relevance. He deliberately avoided consulting scholars: 'I just never wanted to cross that bridge and go over to the museum and put myself in the hands of the curator.' At the same time, he purged his text of obvious references to the present. As the commentator Peter Prescott appreciates, 'Unlike most historical novelists, [Mailer] has shorn his story of any reference to ideas or cultural attitudes that came later. His people are not twentieth century figures in fancy dress; the metaphors they use develop from the life they know.'[112] However, within this Egyptian material Mailer is highly interpretative. Bloom speaks of the 'spiritual power in Mailer's fantasy (it is not the historical novel it masks itself as being)'.[113] The real connection between the past and present is psychic and religious, and on these terms Bloom is prepared to argue that in *Ancient Evenings* there is a 'relevance to current reality in America that actually surpasses that of Mailer's largest previous achievement, *The Executioner's Song*. More than before, Mailer's fantasies, now brutal and unpleasant, catch the precise accents of psychic realities within and between us'. Thus Mailer is thinking back as a gnostic historian, locating cryptic relevances for the end of the industrial era in a culture whose world view found significance only in that which is changeless.

The main peril of Mailer's historical writing is that its motives will be too cryptic for its own good. Those readers who do not appreciate the gnostic purpose will find it harder than Bloom to accept that *Ancient Egypt* is set in an Egypt 'all too like the United States in the 1970s' if measured on the psychic level, or that Mailer is 'probably aware that his Egyptian obsessions are in the main tradition of American literature, carrying on from much of the imagery of the major writers of the American renaissance'.[114] Many critics will undoubtedly be tempted to see *Ancient Evenings* as an ironic revival of the past in a post-modern context; and almost every critic will be able to detect some form of nostalgic impulse at work, from which it is difficult to draw positive implications. This is especially so in the current climate, identified most vividly by the cultural historian Christopher Lasch, in which 'nostalgia' has become the ultimate term of intellectual disdain:

> In the vocabulary of political abuse, 'nostalgia' – along with 'elitism', 'authoritarianism', and 'idealism' – now ranks near the top. No other term serves so effectively to deflate ideological opponents. To cling to the past is bad enough, but the victim of nostalgia clings to an idealized past, one that exists only in his head. He is worse than a reactionary; he is an incurable sentimentalist. Afraid of the future, he is also afraid to face the truth about the past.[115]

Tarring *Ancient Evenings* with the brush of nostalgia is made even easier if the turmoil of American social thought in the 1970s is taken into account. (The novel was written between 1972 and 1982.) Throughout the decade social critics of all ideological backgrounds became completely demoralized: radicals and left liberals were convinced that neo-conservatives and reactionary forces had registered major political and cultural victories; neo-conservatives pointed to the emergence of new classes in the United States with self-serving bureaucracies. Almost all the culture critics of the period (radical, conservative and liberal) felt compelled to view the present against their earlier expectations, and in doing so became pessimistic. Peter Clecak describes how critics, 'especially those radicals and left-liberals in descending phases of their influence, were apt to dwell on the failures of their particular visions'.[116] Many radicals lost their vision altogether: 'Disappointment, radical guilt, and the fear of deradicalization precluded sustained inquiry into the positive effects of liberal and conservative pressures on radical ideas and initiatives.'[117] Anxieties about the present and future grew out of the failure of specific ideologies, but this spiralled into a sense of inadequacy about all inherited visions on the grounds that they were flawed, lacked acceptance or lacked power. In response to this confusion about the present, critics of the seventies created and inhabited what Clecak calls a 'general framework of nostalgia'[118] which looked to a recollected past:

> By the middle of the seventies at least, the theme of nostalgia dominated popular culture: nostalgia for times past, for places either remote or undisfigured by technology, for family, and

for an experience of community. Caught in the transition from industrial to postindustrial society Americans in large numbers felt themselves losing their psychological, social and moral bearings – their sense of time, place and manner. In such circumstances the mood of nostalgia was appealing, for it sanctioned a tight, or what was more convenient, a loose hold on elements of the past.[119]

By the end of the seventies, this ascendant dialectic of pessimism and nostalgia was pervasive:

> The future appeared ill, perhaps terminally so, to many intellectuals. Rational maps to a usable future no longer seemed reliable, as faith in particular visions grew increasingly tepid. Socialist and Communist visions, which a generation of radical critics had abandoned in the thirties and forties, remained only feebly alive in the remnants of another postwar generation. Mainstream liberal projections seemed less plausible than ever in the decline of reformist visions of a vigorous private economy enhanced and regulated by a beneficent welfare state. . . . Finally, conservative proposals to restore economic and political vitality by strengthening laissez faire practices amounted to exercises in nostalgia, at least in so far as they were represented as comprehensive cures to economic ills.[120]

Although Clecak does not deal specifically with Mailer's contribution to this *Zeitgeist*, it is clear that *Ancient Evenings* might be taken as a classic example of the practice of envisioning contemporary developments through the screens of preferences rooted in the past. Mailer's discontent with modernity and tendency towards what Clecak calls 'other temporal perspectives'[121] is already well established. So isn't *Ancient Evenings* an epic exercise in the regressive psychology of finging refuge in a fantasy past, an evasive, irresponsible fiction from a writer who is a victim of nostalgia born of radical pessimism?

The cold unsentimental pose William Burroughs strikes towards past civilizations adds superficial support to this criticism of Mailer's practice. In those sections of *The Soft Machine* that re-create Mayan culture, Burroughs focuses on religion's power and control technologies. There are repeated descriptions of sacrificial fertility rites, parodies of orphic rites, cannibalism, vampirism and the ritual of eating the god-man. At the centre of the control system of this society is the Mayan calendar, which regulates agriculture and festivals. Constructing a fantasy out of these ancient historical materials, Burroughs presents a satire, as the critic Eric Mottram says, of man 'unregenerately addicted to sacrifice, priests, experts and gods. The Mayan calendar represents all states of thoughts and feeling and was used by priests . . . to reduce people to docility'.[122] For Burroughs these ancient societies are models of totalitarianism, and in *The Soft Machine* he describes an attempt to break the calendar, its control of time and manipulation through symbol. Burroughs' writing is itself a resistance action: 'Cut word lines – Cut mosaic lines – Smash the control images – smash the control machine – Burn the books – Kill the priests . . . .'[123] Burroughs is not just attacking what he thinks of as 'broken down old mythologies'[124] his aim is really, in Mottram's words, 'freedom from mythology – what Edward Dahlberg calls freedom from living mythically'.[125]

The purpose of Burroughs' anti-sacred texts is to achieve emancipation from the past and instigate the future. The purpose of *Ancient Evenings* is to make the mythical reappear in culture. What makes *Ancient Evenings* remarkable is that, while it shares none of Burroughs' cynicism about the ancient world and is sentimentally attached to the past, it remains a more complex statement than the general framework of nostalgia will permit. Ultimately Mailer's involvement with other temporal perspectives is individual enough to be considered within the context of his own unique vision rather than in the broad historical climate which surrounds its creation. On its own terms, *Ancient Evenings* wrestles with the problems of adaption, preservation and change, and it has to be said that this is the most immediately observable theme in the numerous transitions Mailer's radicalism makes between 1948 and 1983. Thus, on the one hand, Mailer insists that the Egyptian world is distant, remote and unavailable, but on the other he attempts to make that world continuous with the living present through an enormous literary act of remembering, a telling of remembrances from a forgotten past. In *American Hieroglyphics* John Irwin speaks of a 'wholesale loss of knowledge, a radical break in the continuity of historical memory, a collective act of forgetting'.[126] Mailer's revisionist impulse is to correct this historical amnesia by reinstating the past in the present. As Harold Bloom says, Mailer 'wishes us to learn how to live in America where he sees our bodies and spirits as becoming increasingly artificial, even plastic as he has often remarked. If our current realities, corporeal and psychic, manifest only lost connections, then Mailer's swarming, sex-and-death ridden ancient Egyptian evenings are intended at once to mirror our desperation and to contrast our evasions with the Egyptian rehearsal of the part of death'.[127] In the interest of nothing less than cultural survival (the practical problem from which nostalgia is in flight) Mailer conducts this re-examination and produces a collective act of remembering. The revisionist, in Bloom's prescription, 'strives to *see* again, so as to *esteem* and *estimate* differently, so as then to *aim* "correctly" '.[128]

Perhaps Mailer's revisionism fits better in the context of a picture of the 1970s other than Peter Clecak's. In his study *Decadence: Radical Nostalgia, Narcissism, and Decline in the Seventies*, Jim Hougan also anticipates the impending collapse of a demoralized present-tense culture: 'Incapable of resurrecting the past, and unable to effect to future – we're left in the present with the evidence of our decline.'[129] But Hougan, unlike Clecak, is disinclined to be dismissive of past-oriented perspectives. There are things in the past that can be acknowledged as worthy of retrieval; and it is at least hypothetically possible that 'With their roots blasted, traditions crushed, and culture coopted, people may be moved to seize back what has been stolen from them.'[130] Hougan labels this putative phenomenon revolutionary or radical nostalgia (which he readily concedes to be an odd notion) and distinguishes it from the ordinary, banal versions of nostalgia that mark the age:

> A radical nostalgia, a nostalgia worth capitalizing, would not merely mourn the loss of old values and ways, but would *take action* to have those values and ways reinstated. It would be the motive force behind what would amount to a reactionary renaissance. But for such a Nostalgia to emerge, Americans would first have to recognize the depths of their loss. They would have to realize that they are, as much as the Indians, resident upon a reservation, devoted primarily to their containment.[131]

Hougan fully recognizes that radical nostalgia is something of an absurdity, that, no matter how widespread ordinary nostalgia is, it is unlikely to reach the point of being able to stimulate Marcuse's transvaluation of values. It is much more likely to decay into a pervasive wistfulness, an escape from the present rather than a lever on a potential future. Yet, writing in the mid-seventies, Hougan is prepared to see this improbable concept as perhaps the only basis for continuing idealism:

> our only chance for survival would seem to rest with our ability to reinvent the past — to return. And yet, this too seems to be impossible. The people are used up, sapped and exhausted by the splendour and intricacy of America. A Refusal of the sort which Marcuse envisions demands an expenditure of energy that is, quite simply, beyond us. We're too civilized, too refined, to experience anything so intense as Radical Nostalgia. Continued 'progress' requires nothing more of us than a dead man's float towards the historical horizon. The retreat would involve an attack upon axioms, a long swim against the current of events. Why bother? It's far easier to accept America as our fate than it would be to remake it as our instrument. To be used, to be acted upon, requires only that we be. To act. . . . that is a different matter.[132]

These are precisely the kinds of rare energies we have seen at work in *Ancient Evenings*. Swimming against the current, the novel is a Marcusean Refusal. Armed with a gnosis the primary teaching of which is, as Bloom says, 'to deny that human existence is a historical existence',[133] Mailer has the basis of a denial that the present social world, as it is constituted, affects our lives at the deepest level. His gnosis is thus a performative knowledge, a 'praxis',[134] rather than a cognitive knowledge. Immersed in Egyptian culture, he becomes the man who has power over texts. In Bloomian terms, the 'strong' reading yields political dividends: 'When you read, you confront either yourself, or another, and in either confrontation you seek power. Power over yourself, or another, but power. And what is power? *Potentia*, the pathos of more life, or to speak reductively, the language of possession.'[135] At the more impersonal level, these restorations or appropriations of knowledge in *Ancient Evenings*, brought about by revisionist readings, extend outwards towards a social, collective salvation.

Simplified or distorted images of the past can be used as

uncritical modes of dissent against the present. Used in this way, nostalgia provides no mental map for the present situation, only a temporary defence against the shock of the new. Its practice is to deny the persistence of the past. As Christopher Lasch complains, nostalgia is 'all too eager to pronounce the past dead and gone and to shed a sentimental tear in its memory. It even derives a kind of comfort from the death of the past'.[136] In the final analysis, *Ancient Evenings* is not an expression of no confidence in the present or the future. Its radical nostalgia, rooted securely in its Egyptology, is a massive testimony against the death of the past, which itself is Osirianized. Richard Poirier is especially sensitive to the implications of this: 'Mailer's (and our) debts to the past, it is suggested, are enormous; they are also mysteriously entangled and untraceable.'[137] Menenhetet Two comes in the end to accept all the stories he has listened to, and with this the burdens of the past. He cannot disown any of it because, in Poirier's observation, 'he cannot even know for sure that he did not somehow father himself or father his own father, whoever that might be, as did Ra in Egyptian mythologies'. Mailer's radical nostalgia is thus a reckoning with a repressed set of values from which modernity only appears to have been liberated. The past is not evoked in order to be buried alive. However, it can only become a 'known' epistemology when it exists in relation to ourselves, when it obtains a positive persistence in our time. The achievement of *Ancient Evenings*, founded on Mailer's revisionist praxis, is, that is, a densely textured and totalizing penetration into the contemporary world of the reader. Going back, the novel says, can be a way of going forward. Remembering the modernisms of previous centuries is a way of pushing towards that always difficult to define future, the creation of a modernism for the end of the twentieth century. As the cultural historian Marshall Berman sees it, acts of remembering 'can help us bring modernism back to its roots, so that it can nourish and renew itself to confront the adventures and dangers that lie ahead. To appropriate the modernities of yesterday can be at once a critique of the modernities of today and an act of faith in the modernities – and in the modern men and women – of tomorrow and the day after tomorrow'.[138]

At the present time those critics who have responded to *Ancient Evenings* have on the whole been disinclined to acknowledge the novel on its gnostic or revisionist principles. For a mean-spirited English observer such as Ian Hamilton, Mailer is only a child 'contentedly playing with his toys: dressing them up, giving them funny voices, making them perform sudden improbable acts of violence, and so on'.[139] Benjamin De Mott, whose initial resistance to the novel was broken down by the quality and uniqueness of the first ninety pages, concludes that Mailer's complete jettisoning of self-criticism and 'critical activity'[140] seriously weakens the book's effects. Even George Stade, who is impressed by the architectonics of the novel, allows that 'if you do not buy his notions of magic and the unconscious . . . you will simply feel that Mailer and his novel are full of shit'.[141] But for the critic who avoids the 'shit' *Ancient Evenings* is merely the museum piece Mailer sought so scrupulously to avoid creating. Thus, to Nicholas Shrimpton, it seems 'unexpectedly close to the honestly didactic historical fiction which thinking parents urged upon their teenage children'.[142] Almost all the current commentators on *Ancient Evenings* seem to feel that Mailer simply ought not to have spent so much time and energy looking backwards, that his mind is not suited to this sort of task, and that the result is, to use Pauline Kael's word, folly.

Mailer, on the other hand, senses that he has produced a work which is at the limit of his imaginative reach: 'I think I've used every bit of inspiration I've had on this book. If the book is not good enough, then I'm not good enough. I feel that kind of peace about it.'[143] The implication is, I think, that Mailer's original ideas, drawn from his break with Marxist-inspired radicalism, have been worked to the point of dialectical resolution and have found a still centre in the changelessness at the heart of the Egyptian world view. Poirier would agree that this is the *summa*, the work which effectively explains Mailer: 'Of the twenty-three books Mailer has written so far, only *Ancient Evenings* achieves the magnitude which can give retrospective order and enhancement to everything else.'[144] Bloom, though, urges us not to be so impressed by size, by quantity: the novel 'goes on for seven-hundred large pages, yet gives every sign of truncation, as though its present form were merely its despair of finding its proper shape. The book could be half again as long, but no reader will wish it so.'[145] For Bloom, Mailer's real achievement is to have wrenched himself out of post-Enlightenment reality. Having so emancipated himself, he seems to be 'verging on a new metaphysic'.[146]

The concluding words of *Ancient Evenings* remain an opaque, enigmatic rhapsody on rebirth. They suggest a vision that would anticipate a religious marvel or the final apocalyptic phase of late capitalist post-industrial civilization. Mailer's agon thus continues to the end of the novel ('A pain is coming that will be like no pain felt before – p. 709), enlarged by the composite 'I' which emerges, incorporating, as Poirier says, 'the assembled strengths of Menenhetet, Meni, all the characters they have loved, the Egyptian gods, along with their latest manifestations in Christian mythology, and, not least, the now enriched figures of Mailer's earlier writings and earlier selves'.[147] But the wrestling in the work, the preoccupation with usable truths, is never finally done, and therefore the work can never be completely durable. Both Poirier and Bloom are correct: *Ancient Evenings* pulls up within itself all that has gone before, but is unlikely to be the last of Mailer's radical fictions. The abiding characteristic of his radicalism is that it is speculative, responsive and suggestive – more haymaking than missionary work – always a reply to cultural, social and political questions that are already on the agenda. As this study has attempted to show, Mailer is the least hermetic of writers, and it is this openness and receptivity to disparate influences, coupled with a strong personal vision, that makes him such an important historian of the present.

In a recent interview Mailer eloquently summed up his practice. Asked about his desire to create followers, believers in his work, he replied,

> I think I'm truly misunderstood there. I'm right and I'm wrong so often, so many times of the day, that I have no interest in having people think the way I think. What I'm interested in is that however people think they get better at it. That's what's important about one's work. In the work of good authors, if a book is good enough, one cannot predict how people are going to react to it. You shouldn't be able to. If it's good enough, it means it's not manipulative.
>
> In a certain sense one's ideas are expendable. If the best of my ideas succeed in changing the mind of someone who's more intelligent than myself, then that's fine. I'm a great believer in the idea that if you advance an idea as far as you can and it's overtaken by someone who argues the opposite of you, in effect you've improved your enemy's mind. Then someone will come

along on your side who will take your enemy's improvement of your idea and convert it back again. I'm nothing if not a believer in the dialectic. And to that extent one does the best one can.[148]

Or, alternatively, in terms drawn from *Ancient Evenings* that suggest the highest and lowest motives:

'The search should not be difficult,' said Isis. 'I have more power than ever before.'
'No,' said Osiris, 'there is always one more power to need.' (p. 60)

Notes

CHAPTER 1   THE DILEMMA OF POWER IN
THE NAKED AND THE DEAD

1. Norman Mailer, *The Naked and the Dead* (London: Panther, 1964). Page references are given parenthetically in the text.
2. Stanley T. Gutman, *Mankind in Barbary* (Hanover, NH: University Press of New England, 1975) p. 3.
3. Alfred Kazin (ed.), *Writers at Work: The Paris Review Interviews* (London: Secker and Warburg, 1967) pp. 251–78.
4. Robert Solotaroff, *Down Mailer's Way* (Urbana: University of Illinois Press, 1974) p. 3.
5. Philip H. Bufithis, *Norman Mailer* (New York: Frederick Unger, 1978) p. 16.
6. Solotaroff, *Down Mailer's Way*, p. 8.
7. Ibid., p. 4.
8. Ibid., p. 8.
9. Kazin, *Writers at Work*, p. 260.
10. Norman Mailer, *Advertisements for Myself* (London: Panther, 1968) p. 84.
11. Kazin, *Writers at Work*, p. 260.
12. Norman Mailer, *The Armies of the Night* (Harmondsworth: Penguin, 1968) p. 25.
13. Mailer, *Advertisements for Myself*, p. 27.
14. See Jerry H. Bryant, 'The Last of the Social Protest Writers', *Arizona Quarterly*, Winter 1963, pp. 315–25.
15. Solotaroff, *Down Mailer's Way*, p. 40.
16. Ibid., p. 14.
17. Bufithis, *Norman Mailer*, p. 19.
18. Barry H. Leeds, *The Structured Vision of Norman Mailer* (New York: New York University Press, 1969) p. 10. For an alternative view of the structure of *The Naked and the Dead*, see pp. 10–17 of *The Structured Vision*.
19. Quoted in Karl M. Schmidt, *Henry Wallace: Quixotic Crusade, 1948* (Syracuse, NY: New York University Press, 1966) p. 60.
20. Quoted in Richard J. Walton, *Henry Wallace, Harry Truman and the Cold War* (New York: Viking, 1976) p. 211.
21. Ibid., p. 210.
22. Ibid., p. 211.
23. Ibid., p. 210.
24. Hilary Mills, *Mailer: A Biography* (London: New English Library, 1983) p. 197.
25. Norman Podhoretz, *Breaking Ranks* (New York: Harper and Row, 1979) p. 44.
26. Quoted in Mills, *Mailer: A Biography*, p. 108.

27. In recent years William Burroughs has expressed a similar fear: 'I think the most likely change would be some sort of extreme rightist fascism, a takeover by the army, very likely to occur' – *The Job* (New York: Grove Press, 1974) p. 29.

28. Quoted in Mills, *Mailer: A Biography*, p. 123.

29. Michel Foucault, *Power/Knowledge* (New York: Pantheon, 1980) p. 139.

30. Gutman, *Mankind in Barbary*, p. 32.

31. Solotaroff, *Down Mailer's Way*, p. 17.

32. *New York Star Magazine*, 22 Aug 1948, p. 3.

33. B. F. Skinner, *The Behaviour of Organisms: An Experimental Analysis* (New York: Appleton-Century-Croft, 1938).

34. B. F. Skinner, *Walden Two* (New York: Macmillan, 1948).

35. Thomas Pynchon, *Gravity's Rainbow* (London: Picador, 1975) p. 55.

36. Ibid., p. 347.

37. Solotaroff, *Down Mailer's Way*, p. 19.

38. See Mills, *Mailer: A Biography*, pp. 38–72.

39. Leslie Fiedler, *Love and Death in the American Novel* (London: Paladin, 1970) p. 406.

40. James Baldwin has indicated that the mental process Mailer describes is the most sinister psychological effect of racism: the individual's internalization of the cultural stereotype purveyed by white supremacist society.

41. Leeds, *The Structured Vision of Norman Mailer*, p. 18.

42. Critics disagree on this issue. Leeds, for example, thinks Hearn's role is only structural: 'He comes off as less real, as well as less sympathetic, than most of the other characters' (ibid., p. 18).

43. Solotaroff, *Down Mailer's Way*, p. 21.

44. Jean Radford, *Norman Mailer: A Critical Study* (London: Macmillan, 1975) p. 7.

45. Leeds is content to see Hearn as an 'upper class liberal' (*The Structured Vision of Norman Mailer*, p. 18). Gutman thinks Hearn 'finds that the liberal philosophy he had picked up . . . is lacking' (*Mankind in Barbary*, p. 13). Radford, Bailey and Bufithis make similar errors. At the very least, Hearn is a radical liberal.

46. Solotaroff, *Down Mailer's Way*, p. 35.

47. Radford, *Mailer: A Critical Study*, p. 11.

48. Solotaroff, *Down Mailer's Way*, p. 39.

49. Ibid., p. 36.

50. Jennifer Bailey, *Norman Mailer: Quick-Change Artist* (London: Macmillan, 1979) p. 10.

51. Foucault, *Power/Knowledge*, p. 88.

52. Ibid., p. 90.

53. Gutman, *Mankind in Barbary*, p. 18.

54. Foucault, *Power/Knowledge*, p. 81.

55. Harold Kaplan, *Power and Order: Henry Adams and the Naturalist Tradition in American Fiction* (Chicago: University of Chicago Press 1981) p. 40.

56. Richard Poirier, *A World Elsewhere* (New York: Oxford University Press, 1966) p. 237.
57. Norman Podhoretz, 'Norman Mailer: The Embattled Vision', in Robert F. Lucid (ed.), *Norman Mailer and His Work* (Boston, Mass: Little, Brown, 1971) p. 66.
58. Interview in Harvey Breit, *The Writer Observed* (Cleveland: World Publishing, 1956) p. 199.
59. The best summary of this debate can be found in David Couzens Hoy, 'Power, Repression, Progress: Foucault, Lukes and the Frankfurt School', *Triquarterly*, 52 (1970) 43–63.
60. Mircea Eliade, *Myths, Dreams and Mysteries* (London: Collins, 1968) p. 199.
61. Ibid., p. 227.
62. Ibid., p. 124.
63. See Richard Poirier, *The Performing Self* (New York: Oxford University Press, 1971).
64. Podhoretz, *Breaking Ranks*, p. 67.
65. Bailey, *Mailer: Quick-Change Artist*, p. 10.
66. Solotaroff, *Down Mailer's Way*, p. 20.
67. T. W. Adorno, *The Authoritarian Personality* (New York: Harper and Row, 1950) p. 16.
68. Ibid., p. 23.
69. Ibid., p. 89.
70. Mailer, *Advertisements for Myself*, p. 20.
71. D. H. Lawrence, *Studies in Classic American Literature* (London: Heinemann, 1964) p. 59.
72. H. H. Gerth and C. Wright Mills (eds), *From Max Weber: Essays in Sociology* (New York: Oxford University Press, 1946) p. 246.
73. Yi-Fu Tuan, *Topophilia: A Study in Environmental Perception, Attitudes and Values* (Englewood Cliffs, NJ: Prentice-Hall, 1974) p. 70.
74. Mircea Eliade, *Images and Symbols* (New York: Sheed and Ward, 1961) p. 37.
75. Bailey, *Mailer: Quick-Change Artist*, p. 13.
76. Solotaroff, *Down Mailer's Way*, p. 7.
77. Podhoretz, in Lucid, *Mailer and His Work*, p. 69.
78. William H. Whyte, *The Organization Man* (New York: Simon and Schuster, 1956).
79. Radford, *Mailer: A Critical Study*, p. 50.
80. Solotaroff, *Down Mailer's Way*, p. 7.
81. Richard Poirier, *Mailer* (London: Collins, 1972) p. 37.

CHAPTER 2   MARXISMS ON TRIAL: *BARBARY SHORE*

1. Norman Mailer, *Barbary Shore* (London: Panther, 1972). Page references are given parenthetically in the text.
2. Gutman, *Mankind in Barbary*, p. 34.

3. Walter B. Rideout, *The Radical Novel in the United States* (London: Oxford University Press, 1956) p. 166.
4. Mailer, *Advertisements for Myself*, p. 80.
5. Kazin, *Writers at Work*, p. 262.
6. Mailer, *Advertisements for Myself*, p. 26.
7. See Mailer's tribute, 'My Friend Jean Malaquais', in *Pieces and Pontifications* (London: New English Library, 1983) pp. 97–105.
8. Quoted in Mills, *Mailer: A Biography*, p. 97.
9. Ibid., pp. 97–8.
10. Ibid., p. 99.
11. Ibid., p. 103.
12. Ibid., p. 101.
13. See plots of novels discussed in Rideout, *The Radical Novel in the United States*.
14. The name McLeod seems to be important to Mailer: a Major McLeod appears in *The Naked and the Dead*; one of Mailer's sons is called Stephen McLeod Mailer.
15. Mailer, *Advertisements for Myself*, p. 87.
16. Mailer, *The Naked and the Dead*, p. 327.
17. Dalleson's emergence brings *The Naked and the Dead* remarkably close in its feeling for the banal absurdity of military organization to Joseph Heller's *Catch 22* (London: Jonathan Cape, 1962), without Mailer being as bitterly funny as Heller. Dalleson is a prototype for Scheisskopf, the character who achieves the greatest power in *Catch 22*.
18. Mailer, *The Naked and the Dead*, p. 327.
19. Ruth Prigozy, 'The Liberal Novelist in the McCarthy Era', *Twentieth Century Literature*, 25, no. 3 (Oct 1975) p. 260.
20. Leeds, *The Structured Vision of Norman Mailer*, p. 61.
21. Andrew Gordon, *An American Dreamer* (Toronto: Associated University Press, 1980) p. 80.
22. Radford, *Mailer: A Critical Study*, p. 51.
23. Solotaroff, *Down Mailer's Way*, p. 49.
24. Bailey, *Mailer: Quick-Change Artist*, p. 25; Robert J. Begiebing, *Acts of Regeneration* (Columbia: University of Missouri Press, 1980) p. 24.
25. Bufithis, *Norman Mailer*, p. 72.
26. Gutman, *Mankind in Barbary*, p. 30.
27. See Norman Mailer, *The Presidential Papers* (London: Panther, 1976) pp. 76–94.
28. For a discussion of paranoia and the making of *Maidstone*, see James Toback, 'At Play in the Fields of the Bored', *Esquire*, Dec 1968, pp. 151–4.
29. Norman Mailer, *St. George and the Godfather* (New York: New American Library, 1972) p. 307.
30. Mills, *Mailer: A Biography*, p. 391.
31. Ibid., p. 394.
32. Norman Mailer, *Marilyn* (London: Hodder and Stoughton, 1974) p. 242.

33. Mailer, 'A Harlot High and Low', in *Pieces and Pontifications,* pp. 159–205.
34. Ibid., p. 160.
35. Radford, *Mailer: A Critical Study,* p. 16.
36. Mailer, *The Presidential Papers,* p. 80.
37. Mailer, *The Naked and the Dead,* p. 75.
38. Gerth and Mills, *From Max Weber: Essays in Sociology,* p. 235.
39. Ibid., p. 155.
40. Bernard de Jouvenal, *On Power* (Boston, Mass: Beacon Press, 1962) p. 4.
41. For a full discussion of the process Mailer describes, see Harry Magdoff, *The Age of Imperialism* (New York: Monthly Review Press, 1969) pp. 27–66.
42. Mailer, *The Naked and the Dead,* p. 74.
43. Radford, *Mailer: A Critical Study,* p. 53.
44. Thomas Pynchon, *The Crying of Lot 49* (London: Picador, 1979) pp. 124–5.
45. Frank D. McConnell, *Four Postwar American Novelists* (Chicago: University of Chicago Press, 1977) p. 174.
46. Thomas Pynchon, *Slow Learner* (Boston, Mass: Little, Brown, 1984) p. 7.
47. Gutman, *Mankind in Barbary,* p. 29.
48. Solotaroff, *Down Mailer's Way,* p. 40.
49. For a discussion of these terms, see Bertell Ollman, *Alienation: Marx's Concept of Man in Capitalist Society* (Cambridge: Cambridge University Press, 1971).
50. For an absurd overinterpretation of the traveller image, see Leeds, *The Structured Vision of Norman Mailer,* pp. 70–1.
51. Saul Bellow, *Dangling Man* (New York: New American Library, 1972) p. 191.
52. Ralph Ellison, *Invisible Man* (Harmondsworth: Penguin, 1965) p. 466.
53. Ibid., p. 7.
54. Ibid., p. 8.
55. Ibid., p. 7.
56. Ibid., p. 467.
57. Ibid., p. 468.
58. Ibid., p. 467.
59. Ibid., p. 466.
60. Chester Eisinger, *Fiction of the Forties* (Chicago: University of Chicago Press, 1963) p. 93.
61. Mailer, *Pieces and Pontifications,* p. 147.
62. Kazin, *Writers at Work,* p. 263.
63. For a comparison between *Barbary Shore* and Hawthorne's *The Blithedale Romance,* see Laura Adams, *Existential Battles: The Growth of Norman Mailer* (Athens, Ohio: Ohio University Press, 1976) p. 41.
64. Rideout, *The Radical Novel in the United States,* p. 287.
65. See Irving Howe, *Politics and the Novel,* passim.
66. Rideout, *The Radical Novel in the United States,* p. 230.

67. Howe, *Politics and the Novel*, p. 22.
68. William Gass, *Fiction and the Figures of Life* (New York: Alfred A. Knopf, 1970) p. 38.
69. Quoted in Larry McCaffery, *The Metafictional Muse* (Pittsburgh: University of Pittsburgh Press, 1982) p. 175.
70. Quoted in *Washington Book World*, 13 Feb 1980, p. 9.
71. Poirier, *Mailer*, p. 71.

CHAPTER 3   A FLIGHT FROM IDEOLOGY AND TRANSITS TO NARCISSUS IN *THE DEER PARK*

1. Norman Mailer, *The Deer Park* (London: Panther, 1976). Page references are given parenthetically in the text.
2. Gutman, *Mankind in Barbary*, p. 50.
3. Podhoretz, in Lucid, *Mailer and His Work*, p. 64.
4. Included in T. W. Adorno and Max Horkheimer, *The Dialectic of Enlightenment* (London: Verso, 1979).
5. Bailey, *Mailer: Quick-Change Artist*, p. 56.
6. Mailer, *Advertisements for Myself*, p. 184.
7. David Zane Mairowitz, *The Radical Soap Opera: An Impression of the American Left from 1917 to the Present* (London: Wildwood House, 1974) p. 93.
8. Ibid., p. 97.
9. Ibid., p. 96.
10. Mills, *Mailer: A Biography*, p. 120.
11. Mairowitz, *The Radical Soap Opera*, p. 101.
12. Ibid., p. 102.
13. Interview in *Movie Makers*, BBC Radio 3, 16 July 1985.
14. Radford, *Mailer: A Critical Study*, p. 55.
15. Ibid., p. 56.
16. Gutman, *Mankind in Barbary*, p. 35.
17. Ibid., p. 51.
18. Mailer, *The Naked and the Dead*, p. 71.
19. Mailer, *Barbary Shore*, p. 199.
20. Begiebing, *Acts of Regeneration*, p. 35.
21. Mailer, *The Armies of the Night*, p. 191.
22. Kenneth M. Dolbeare and Patricia Dolbeare, *American Ideologies* (Chicago: Markham, 1971) p. 1.
23. Mailer, *The Armies of the Night*, p. 34.
24. Kazin, *Writers at Work*, p. 261.
25. M. H. Abrams, *A Glossary of Literary Terms* (New York: Holt, Rinehart and Winston, 1957) p. 67.
26. Solotaroff, *Down Mailer's Way*, p. 61.
27. Ibid., p. 70.
28. Dolbeare and Dolbeare, *American Ideologies*, p. 91.
29. Arnold Kauffman, *The Radical Liberal* (New York: Atherton Press, 1968).

30. Dolbeare and Dolbeare, *American Ideologies*, p. 81.
31. Gordon, *An American Dreamer*, p. 98.
32. Gutman, *Mankind in Barbary*, p. 57.
33. Richard Foster, *Norman Mailer* (Minneapolis: University of Minnesota Press, 1968) p. 17.
34. Begiebing, *Acts of Regeneration*, p. 46.
35. Ibid., p. 41.
36. Laura Adams prefers to link Eitel's theory to Matthew Arnold's poem 'The Buried Life'. See Adams, *Existential Battles*, p. 45.
37. Fiedler, *Love and Death in the American Novel*, p. 36.
38. Gerth and Mills, *From Max Weber: Essays in Sociology*, p. 155.
39. Solotaroff, *Down Mailer's Way*, p. 73.
40. Gutman, *Mankind in Barbary*, p. 46.
41. David Riesman's concept from his classic *The Lonely Crowd: A Study of the Changing American Character* (New Haven, Conn.: Yale University Press, 1950).
42. Solotaroff, *Down Mailer's Way*, p. 61.
43. Begiebing, *Acts of Regeneration*, p. 49.
44. Radford, *Mailer: A Critical Study*, p. 26.
45. Ibid., p. 21.
46. Bailey, *Mailer: Quick-Change Artist*, p. 26.
47. Ibid., p. 27.
48. Kazin, *Writers at Work*, p. 262.
49. Solotaroff, *Down Mailer's Way*, p. 68.
50. Ibid., p. 56.
51. Mailer, *Advertisements for Myself*, p. 278.
52. Kazin, *Writers at Work*, p. 264.
53. Mailer, *Pieces and Pontifications*, p. 60.
54. Ibid., p. 59.
55. Ibid., p. 60.
56. Begiebing, *Acts of Regeneration*, p. 49.
57. Ibid., p. 50.
58. Faye does return, in Mailer's most experimental piece of fiction, 'On the Way Out' (*Advertisements for Myself*, pp. 422–42).
59. Ibid., p. 60.
60. Begiebing, *Actors of Regeneration*, p. 41.
61. Solotaroff, *Down Mailer's Way*, p. 64.
62. *The Collected Works of Ralph Waldo Emerson*, vol. I: *Nature, Addresses and Lectures*, ed. Robert F. Spiller and Alfred R. Ferguson (Cambridge, Mass: Harvard University Press, 1971) p. 23.
63. Mairowitz, *The Radical Soap Opera*, p. 71.
64. Solotaroff, *Down Mailer's Way*, p. 63.
65. Mailer, *Advertisements for Myself*, p. 109.
66. Ernest Hemingway, *A Farewell to Arms* (Harmondsworth: Penguin, 1975) p. 109.
67. Bailey, *Mailer: Quick-Change Artist*, p. 24.
68. Solotaroff, *Down Mailer's Way*, p. 70.
69. Begiebing, *Acts of Regeneration*, p. 51.
70. Ibid., p. 52.

71. Mailer, *Advertisements for Myself*, p. 69.
72. See Mills, *Mailer: A Biography*, p. 108.
73. Adams, *Existential Battles*, p. 49.
74. Gutman, *Mankind in Barbary*, p. 55.
75. Solotaroff, *Down Mailer's Way*, p. 59.
76. Bailey, *Mailer: Quick-Change Artist*, p. 28.
77. Begiebing, *Acts of Regeneration*, p. 36.
78. Ibid., p. 44.
79. Poirier, *Mailer*, p. 42.
80. Bailey, *Mailer: Quick-Change Artist*, p. 29.
81. Poirier, *Mailer*, p. 39.
82. Ibid., p. 38.
83. Günter Grass, *On Writing and Politics* (London: Secker and Warburg, 1985) p. 74.
84. Mailer, *Advertisements for Myself*, p. 188.
85. Poirier, *Mailer*, p. 47.
86. Mailer, *Advertisements for Myself*, p. 147.
87. Ibid., p. 232.
88. Solotaroff, *Down Mailer's Way*, p. 70.
89. Mailer, *Advertisements for Myself*, p. 116.
90. Quoted in Mills, *Mailer: A Biography*, p. 146.
91. Mailer, *Advertisements for Myself*, p. 78.

CHAPTER 4 · THE RADICAL GEOGRAPHY OF SELF AND SOCIETY IN *AN AMERICAN DREAM*

1. Mark Shechner, 'Reich and the Reichians', *Partisan Review*, 52 (Spring 1986) 98–108.
2. Norman Mailer, *An American Dream* (London: Panther, 1972). Page references are given parenthetically in the text.
3. Term used by Philip Rieff in *The Triumph of the Therapeutic* (New York: Harper and Row, 1966) p. 146.
4. Richard Poirier, *The Aesthetics of Contemporary American Radicalism* (Leicester: Leicester University Press, 1972) p. 12.
5. Mailer, *Advertisements for Myself*, p. 201.
6. Ibid., p. 176.
7. Ibid., p. 183.
8. Mailer, *The Presidential Papers*, p. 9.
9. Begiebing, *Acts of Regeneration*, p. 124.
10. Mailer, *The Presidential Papers*, p. 15.
11. Ibid., p. 17.
12. The term is Michel Foucault's. See *Power/Knowledge*.
13. Mailer, *Advertisements for Myself*, p. 296.
14. Ibid., p. 289.
15. Michel Foucault, *Language, Counter-Memory, Practice* (Ithaca, NY: Cornell University Press, 1977) p. 207.
16. Mailer, *Advertisements for Myself*, p. 277.

17. Ibid., p. 275.
18. Ibid., p. 278.
19. Gutman, *Mankind in Barbary*, p. 96.
20. C. Wright Mills, *The Power Elite* (New York: Oxford University Press, 1956).
21. Gordon, *An American Dreamer*, p. 168.
22. Bufithis, *Norman Mailer*, p. 65.
23. Wilhelm Reich, *Character-Analysis* (New York: Orgone Institute Press, 1949) p. 17.
24. Radford, *Mailer: A Critical Study*, pp. 33–4.
25. Gutman, *Mankind in Barbary*, p. 107.
26. Poirier, *Mailer*, p. 128.
27. Gordon, *An American Dreamer*, p. 133.
28. Mailer, *Pieces and Pontifications*, p. 163.
29. Ibid., p. 191.
30. For a misguided discussion of the influence of existentialist thought on Mailer, see Solotaroff, *Down Mailer's Way*, pp. 99–102. According to Raymond Williams, 'the use of existential with a wide variety of nouns of feeling and of action' has become 'extended beyond any deliberate position' – *Keywords* (London: Fontana, 1976) p. 101.
31. Mailer, *Pieces and Pontifications*, p. 84.
32. Mailer, *The Presidential Papers*, p. 216.
33. Mailer, *Advertisements for Myself*, p. 275.
34. Mailer, *Pieces and Pontifications*, p. 176.
35. Rieff, *The Triumph of the Therapeutic*, p. 152.
36. Mailer, *Advertisements for Myself*, p. 292.
37. Ibid., p. 293.
38. Ibid., p. 314.
39. Mailer, *The Armies of the Night*, p. 65.
40. Mailer, *Advertisements for Myself*, p. 309.
41. Ibid., p. 71.
42. Rieff, *The Triumph of the Therapeutic*, p. 149.
43. Ibid., p. 150.
44. Mailer, *Advertisements for Myself*, p. 277.
45. Kazin, *Writers at Work*, p. 58.
46. Herbert Marcuse, *An Essay in Liberation* (Boston, Mass: Beacon Press, 1969) p. 38.
47. Mailer, *Advertisements for Myself*, p. 275.
48. Gordon, *An American Dreamer*, p. 167.
49. Reich, *Character-Analysis*, p. 161.
50. Ibid., p. 165.
51. Mailer, *Advertisements for Myself*, p. 83.
52. Rieff, *The Triumph of the Therapeutic*, p. 151.
53. Solotaroff, *Down Mailer's Way*, p. 108.
54. Foucault, *Power/Knowledge*, p. 81.
55. Solotaroff, *Down Mailer's Way*, p. 95.
56. Radford, *Mailer: A Critical Study*, p. 155.
57. Adams, *Existential Battles*, p. 75.

58. Mailer, *Advertisements for Myself*, p. 304.
59. Mailer, *Pieces and Pontifications*, pp. 28–31.
60. Otto Fenichel, *The Psychoanalytic Theory of Neurosis* (New York: Norton, 1945) p. 398.
61. Talcott Parsons, *Politics and the Social Structure* (New York: The Free Press, 1969) p. 201.
62. Ibid., p. 199.
63. Michel Foucault, *Discipline and Punish: The Birth of the Prison* (New York: Pantheon, 1977) p. 194.
64. A useful distinction made by Dennis Wrong in *Power: Its Forms, Bases and Uses* (Oxford: Basil Blackwell, 1979).
65. J. G. Merquior, *Foucault* (London: Fontana, 1985) p. 118.
66. Paul A. Robinson, *The Sexual Radicals* (London: Granada, 1972) p. 15.
67. Ibid., p. 16.
68. Poirier, *The Aesthetics of Contemporary American Radicalism*, p. 14.
69. Gutman, *Mankind in Barbary*, p. 109.
70. Wilhelm Reich, *The Mass Psychology of Fascism* (New York: Farrar, Straus and Giroux, 1970) p. 73.
71. Shechner, in *Partisan Review*, 52, p. 100.
72. Ibid., p. 108.
73. Poirier, *The Aesthetics of Contemporary American Radicalism*, p. 10.
74. Mailer, *Advertisements for Myself*, p. 300.
75. Shechner, in *Partisan Review*, 52, p. 105.
76. Mairowitz, *The Radical Soap Opera*, p. 199.
77. Gutman, *Mankind in Barbary*, p. 96.
78. Mailer, *Pieces and Pontifications*, pp. 82–3.
79. Ibid., pp. 62–3.
80. Eliade, *Myths, Dreams and Mysteries*, p. 72.
81. Ibid., p. 78.
82. Mills, *Mailer: A Biography*, p. 225.
83. Ibid., pp. 225–6.
84. Eliade, *Myths, Dreams and Mysteries*, p. 80.
85. Poirier, *Mailer*, p. 127.
86. *The Guardian*, 20 Feb 1986, p. 10.
87. Mailer, *Advertisements for Myself*, p. 184.
88. Mailer, *The Deer Park*, p. 126.
89. Ibid., p. 368.
90. Ibid., p. 344.
91. Mailer, *Advertisements for Myself*, p. 17.
92. Ibid., p. 201.
93. Ibid., p. 213.
94. Ibid., p. 162.
95. Karl Marx and Frederick Engels, *The German Ideology, Part One*, ed. C. J. Arthur (London: Lawrence and Wishart, 1974) p. 64.
96. Herbert Marcuse, *Eros and Civilization* (Boston, Mass: Beacon Press, 1974) p. 17.
97. Herbert Marcuse, *Negatives* (Harmondsworth: Penguin, 1972) pp. 98–9.

98.   Ibid., p. 117.
99.   Leo Bersani, 'The Interpretation of Dreams', *Partisan Review*, 32 (Fall 1965) 606–14.
100. Poirier, *Mailer*, p. 128.
101. Begiebing, *Acts of Regeneration*, p. 118.
102. Mailer, *Pieces and Pontifications*, p. 83.
103. Nathaniel Hawthorne, *The House of Seven Gables* (Boston, Mass: Houghton Mifflin, 1897) p. 13.
104. Nathaniel Hawthorne, *The Scarlet Letter* (Harmondsworth, Penguin, 1970) p. 66.
105. Gutman, *Mankind in Barbary*, p. 131.
106. Radford, *Mailer: A Critical Study*, p. 155.
107. Gordon, *An American Dreamer*, p. 168.
108. Bufithis, *Norman Mailer*, p. 72.
109. William Burroughs, *The Yage Letters* (San Francisco: City Lights, 1963) p. 68.
110. Mary McCarthy, *The Writing on the Wall* (Harmondsworth: Penguin, 1973) p. 113.
111. Mailer, *The Presidential Papers*, p. 17.
112. Douglas Fowler, *A Reader's Guide to Gravity's Rainbow* (Ann Arbor, Mich.: Ardis, 1980) p. 19.

CHAPTER 5   SAVING THE ROOT: OLD AND NEW CIRCUITS IN THE ELECTROWORLD OF *WHY ARE WE IN VIETNAM?*

1.   Mailer, *The Armies of the Night*, p. 166.
2.   Norman Mailer, *Why Are We in Vietnam?* (London: Weidenfeld and Nicolson, 1969). Page references are given parenthetically in the text.
3.   Mailer, *The Armies of the Night*, p. 198.
4.   Ibid., p. 192.
5.   Ibid., p. 196.
6.   Ibid., p. 199.
7.   Pynchon, *Gravity's Rainbow*, pp. 698–9. This passage, with its allusions to the father–son relationship, the idea of a vacation and return to 'Realityland', reads like a parody of *Why Are We in Vietnam?*
8.   Norman Mailer, *Cannibals and Christians* (London: André Deutsch, 1967) p. 285.
9.   Marshall McLuhan, *The Mechanical Bride: Folklore and Industrial Man* (London: Routledge and Kegan Paul, 1967) p. 97.
10. Mailer, *Cannibals and Christians*, pp. 269–70.
11. Mailer, *The Armies of the Night*, p. 104.
12. William Burroughs, *The Naked Lunch* (London: Corgi, 1968) pp. 250–1.
13. I. M. Lewis, *Ecstatic Religion: An Anthropological Study of Spirit Possession and Shamanism* (Harmondsworth: Penguin, 1971) p. 51.

14. Mailer, *Cannibals and Christians*, p. 5.
15. Ibid., p. 3.
16. Ibid., p. 2.
17. Mailer, *Pieces and Pontifications*, p. 11.
18. Ibid., p. 12.
19. Mailer, *Cannibals and Christians*, p. 116.
20. Ibid., p. 2.
21. Lewis, *Ecstatic Religion*, p. 53.
22. Peter Clecak, *Radical Paradoxes: Dilemmas of the American Left, 1945–1970* (New York: Harper and Row, 1973) p. 8.
23. Radford, *Mailer: A Critical Study*, p. 98.
24. Mailer, *Advertisements for Myself*, p. 97.
25. Mailer, *Cannibals and Christians*, p. 137.
26. Marshall McLuhan, *Understanding Media* (London: Routledge and Kegan Paul, 1969) p. 19.
27. Adams, *Existential Battles*, p. 120.
28. Mailer, *Cannibals and Christians*, p. 137.
29. Leeds, *The Structured Vision of Norman Mailer*, p. 198.
30. Mailer, *Cannibals and Christians*, p. 370.
31. Poirier, *Mailer*, p. 152.
32. Ibid., p. 143.
33. Bailey, *Mailer: Quick-Change Artist*, p. 79.
34. Gutman, *Mankind in Barbary*, p. 134.
35. Ibid., p. 213.
36. Radford, *Mailer: A Critical Study*, p. 116.
37. Bufithis, *Norman Mailer*, p. 77.
38. Burroughs, *The Job*, p. 34.
39. Quoted in Tony Tanner, *City of Words* (London: Jonathan Cape, 1976) p. 131.
40. Donald Barthelme, *Snow White* (London: Jonathan Cape, 1968) p. 83.
41. Ibid., p. 97.
42. Poirier, *A World Elsewhere*.
43. Mailer, *Cannibals and Christians*, p. 137.
44. Eliade, *Myths, Dreams and Mysteries*, p. 74.
45. Mailer, *The Armies of the Night*, pp. 58–9.
46. Fenichel, *The Psychoanalytic Theory of Neurosis*, p. 350.
47. Begiebing, *Acts of Regeneration*, p. 92.
48. Mailer, *The Armies of the Night*, p. 58.
49. Ibid., p. 60.
50. Ibid., p. 50.
51. Mailer, *An American Dream*, p. 178.
52. William Burroughs, *The Ticket that Exploded* (New York: Grove Press, 1967) p. 49.
53. Donald Barthelme, *Unspeakable Practices, Unnatural Acts* (New York: Simon and Schuster, 1978) p. 160.
54. Quoted in Henry H. Crosby and George P. Bond (eds), *The McLuhan Explosion* (New York: American Book Company, 1968) p. 79.

55. Marshall McLuhan, *The Gutenberg Galaxy* (London: Routledge and Kegan Paul, 1962) p. 18.
56. Mailer anticipates Burroughs' essay 'Playback from Eden to Watergate', in *The Job*, pp. 11–20, where God is described as 'prowling around like a house dick with a tape recorder' (p. 11).
57. McLuhan, *Understanding Media*, p. 82.
58. Ellison, *Invisible Man*, p. 469.
59. Ibid., p. 468.
60. Terms used by Thomas Altizer in *Mircea Eliade and the Dialectic of the Sacred* (Westport, Conn.: Greenwood Press, 1975) p. 195.
61. Mailer, *Cannibals and Christians*, p. 307.
62. Poirier, *The Aesthetics of Contemporary American Radicalism*, p. 5.
63. Ibid., p. 13.
64. Mailer, *The Armies of the Night*, p. 105.
65. Poirier, *The Aesthetics of Contemporary American Radicalism*, p. 23.
66. Mailer, *Cannibals and Christians*, p. 4.
67. Mailer, *Pieces and Pontifications*, p. 49.
68. Ibid., p. 48.
69. Ibid., p. 50.
70. Ibid., p. 49.
71. Mailer, *The Armies of the Night*, p. 199.
72. Burroughs, *The Job*, p. 79.
73. Mailer, *The Armies of the Night*, p. 19.
74. Ibid., p. 200.
75. Ibid., p. 201.
76. Bufithis, *Norman Mailer*, p. 26.
77. Solotaroff, *Down Mailer's Way*, p. 196.
78. Mailer, *Cannibals and Christians*, p. 91.
79. Abbie Hoffman, *Woodstock Nation: A Talk-Rock Album* (New York: Random House, 1969) *passim*. Peter Clecak refers to Hoffman as a 'Little League Norman Mailer' (*Radical Paradoxes*, p. 264).
80. Clecak, *Radical Paradoxes*, p. 275.
81. Ibid, p. 299.
82. Mailer, *The Naked and the Dead*, p. 61.
83. Burroughs, *The Naked Lunch*, p. 77.
84. Eliade, *Myths, Dreams and Mysteries*, p. 61.
85. Fiedler, *Love and Death in the American Novel*, p. 333.
86. Eliade, *Myths, Dreams and Mysteries*, p. 76.
87. Ibid., p. 64.
88. Ibid., p. 74.
89. William Faulkner, 'The Bear', in *Go Down Moses* (Harmondsworth: Penguin, 1960) p. 149.
90. Ibid., p. 232.
91. R. W. B. Lewis, *American Adam* (Chicago: University of Chicago Press, 1955) p. 89.
92. Quoted in R. A. Jellille (ed.), *Faulkner at Nagano* (Tokyo: Kenkyusha, 1956) pp. 77–8.
93. Begiebing, *Acts of Regeneration*, p. 94.

94. Eliade, *Myths, Dreams and Mysteries*, p. 90.
95. Fiedler, *Love and Death in the American Novel*, p. 327.
96. Poirier, *A World Elsewhere*, p. 28.
97. Mailer, *Pieces and Pontifications*, p. 54.
98. Altizer, *Eliade and the Dialectic of the Sacred*, p. 27.
99. Solotaroff, *Down Mailer's Way*, p. 134.
100. Poirier, *Mailer*, p. 142.
101. Pynchon, *The Crying of Lot 49*, p. 12.
102. Ibid., p. 66.

CHAPTER 6 MAKING ONE'S WAY BACK TO LIFE IN *ANCIENT EVENINGS*

1. Norman Mailer, *Ancient Evenings* (London: Macmillan, 1983) Page references are given parenthetically in the text.
2. *Dialogue*, 62 (Apr 1983) 61.
3. Ibid., p. 60.
4. Harold Bloom, 'Norman in Egypt', *New York Review of Books*, 28 Apr 1983, p. 3.
5. Richard Poirier, 'In Pyramid and Palace', *The Times Literary Supplement*, 10 June 1983, pp. 591–2.
6. *Dialogue*, 62, p. 61.
7. George Stade, in *The New Republic*, 2 May 1983, pp. 32–6.
8. *New York Times Book Review*, 6 June 1982, p. 57.
9. Stade, in *The New Republic*, 2 May 1983, p. 36.
10. *Dialogue*, 62, pp. 61–2.
11. Bloom, in *New York Review of Books*, 28 Apr 1983, p. 3.
12. Poirier, in *The Times Literary Supplement*, 10 June 1983, p. 591.
13. Ibid., pp. 591–2.
14. Ibid., pp. 591.
15. Bloom, in *New York Review of Books*, 28 Apr 1983, p. 3.
16. *The Listener*, 15 Nov 1979, p. 662.
17. *The Sunday Times Magazine*, 12 June 1983, p. 18.
18. Norman O. Brown, *Life against Death: the Psychoanalytical Meaning of History* (Middletown, Conn.: Wesleyan University Press, 1985) p. 307.
19. Ibid., p. 63.
20. Ibid., p. 320.
21. Bloom, in *New York Review of Books*, 28 Apr 1983, p. 5.
22. Ibid., p. 3.
23. Ian Hamilton, 'Mummies', *London Review of Books*, 16 June–6 July 1983, p. 6.
24. *Dialogue*, 62, p. 62.
25. Pauline Kael, *When the Lights Go Down* (New York: Holt, Rinehart and Winston, 1980) p. 324.
26. H. Frankfort, *Ancient Egyptian Religion: An Interpretation* (New York: Columbia University Press, 1948) p. 31.

27. H. Frankfort, *Kingship and the Gods* (Chicago: University of Chicago Press, 1948) p. 78.
28. *The Sunday Times Magazine*, 12 June 1983, p. 19.
29. A. E. Wallis Budge, *The Book of the Dead: The Papyrus of Ani* (New York: Dover, 1967) p. xii.
30. Ibid., p. xxii.
31. James Henry Breasted, *Development of Religion and Thought in Ancient Egypt* (London: Hodder and Stoughton, 1972) p. 90.
32. Ibid., p. 91.
33. R. T. Rundle Clark, *Myth and Man: Myth and Symbol in Ancient Egypt* (London: Thames and Hudson, 1959) p. 11.
34. *The Sunday Times Magazine*, 12 June 1983, p. 19.
35. *Dialogue*, 62, p. 62.
36. Stade, in *The New Republic*, 2 May 1983, p. 34.
37. Benjamin De Mott, 'Norman Mailer's Egyptian Novel', *New York Times Book Review*, 10 Apr 1983, p. 1.
38. Ibid., p. 34.
39. Ibid., p. 35.
40. Strade, in *The New Republic*, 2 May 1983, p. 34.
41. Bloom, in *New York Review of Books*, 28 Apr 1983, p. 3.
42. Frankfort, *Kingship and the Gods*, p. 78.
43. De Mott, in *New York Times Book Review*, 10 Apr 1983, p. 34.
44. Hamilton, in *London Review of Books*, 16 June – 16 July 1983, p. 6.
45. Poirier, in *The Times Literary Supplement*, 10 June 1983, p. 591.
46. Bloom, in *New York Review of Books*, 28 Apr 1983, p. 4.
47. Ibid., p. 3.
48. Frankfort, *Ancient Egyptian Religion*, p. v.
49. Edward Everett, 'The Zodiac of Denderah', *North American Review* 17 (1823) p. 233.
50. John Irwin, *American Hieroglyphics: The Symbol of Egyptian Hieroglyphics in the American Renaissance* (New Haven, Conn.: Yale University Press, 1980), p. 98.
51. Nicholas Shrimpton, 'The Riddle of the Sphincter', *The Sunday Times*, 12 June 1983, p. 44.
52. Poirier, in *The Times Literary Supplement*, 10 June 1983, p. 591.
53. Frankfort, *Ancient Egyptian Religion*, p. vi.
54. For a discussion of this, see Harold Bloom, *The Anxiety of Influence: A Theory of Poetry* (New York: Oxford University Press, 1973).
55. Harold Bloom, *A Map of Misreading* (New York: Oxford University Press, 1975) p. 38.
56. Poirier, in *The Times Literary Supplement*, 10 June 1983, p. 591.
57. Bloom, *The Anxiety of Influence*, p. 8.
58. Poirier, in *The Times Literary Supplement*, 10 June 1983, p. 591.
59. Quoted in Mills, *Mailer: A Biography*, p. 102.
60. Poirier, in *The Times Literary Supplement*, 10 June 1983, p. 592.
61. Bloom, in *New York Review of Books*, 28 Apr 1983, p. 3.
62. Poirier, in *The Times Literary Supplement*, 10 June 1983, p. 591.
63. Stade, in *The New Republic*, 2 May 1983, p. 34.

64. Frankfort, *Kingship and the Gods*, p. vii.
65. Brown, *Life against Death*, p. 13.
66. Bloom, in *New York Review of Books*, 28 Apr 1983, p. 3.
67. Frankfort, *Ancient Egyptian Religion*, p. vii.
68. Ibid., p. 4.
69. Ibid., p. 36.
70. Hamilton, in *London Review of Books*, 16 June – 6 July 1983, p. 6.
71. *Dialogue*, 62, p. 62.
72. Bloom, in *New York Review of Books*, 28 Apr 1983, p. 3.
73. Bloom, *Agon: Towards a Theory of Revisionism* (New York: Oxford University Press, 1982) p. 4.
74. Ibid., p. 5.
75. Ibid., p. 12.
76. Ibid., p. 4.
77. Ibid., p. 5.
78. Ibid., p. 12.
79. Marilyn Butler, *The Cult of the Exotic*, BBC Radio Three, 19 June 1986.
80. Bloom, *New York Review of Books*, 28 Apr 1983, p. 4.
81. Ibid., p. 3.
82. De Mott, in *New York Times Book Review*, 10 Apr 1983, p. 34.
83. Hamilton, in *London Review of Books*, 16 June–6 July 1983, p. 6.
84. Budge, *The Book of the Dead*, p. xlix.
85. Rundle Clark, *Myth and Man*, p. 12.
86. Poirier, in *The Times Literary Supplement*, 10 June 1983, p. 591.
87. Bloom, in *New York Review of Books*, 28 Apr 1983, p. 3.
88. Rundle Clark, *Myth and Man*, p. 31.
89. Budge, *The Book of the Dead*, p. xi.
90. Rundle Clark, *Myth and Man*, p. 33.
91. Brown, *Life against Death*, pp. 108–9.
92. Budge, *The Book of the Dead*, p. 1x.
93. Breasted, *Development of Religion and Thought in Ancient Egypt*, p. 142.
94. Budge, *The Book of the Dead*, pp. 1i-1ii.
95. Ibid., p. 1xx.
96. Frankfort, *Kingship and the Gods*, p. 72.
97. Ibid., p. 64.
98. Rundle Clark, *Myth and Man*, p. 232.
99. Budge, *The Book of the Dead*, pp. 1xi–1xii.
100. *The Sunday Times Magazine*, 12 June 1983, p. 19.
101. Poirier, in *The Times Literary Supplement*, 10 June 1983, p. 591.
102. Irwin, *American Hieroglyphics*, p. 146.
103. Rundle Clark, *Myth and Man*, p. 231.
104. Breasted, *Development of Religion and Thought in Ancient Egypt*, p. 290.
105. *Dialogue*, 62, p. 61.
106. Bloom, in *New York Review of Books*, 28 Apr 1983, p. 3.
107. Butler, *The Cult of the Exotic*.
108. Stade, in *The New Republic*, 2 May 1983, p. 36.
109. *Dialogue*, 62, p. 62.
110. Hamilton, in *London Review of Books*, 16 June–6 July, 1983 p. 6.
111. 'The Impish Iconoclast at 60', *Time*, 18 Apr 1983, p. 83.

112. Peter Prescott, 'Tales from beyond the Tomb', *Newsweek*, 18 Apr 1983, p. 82.
113. Bloom, in *New York Review of Books*, 28 Apr 1983, p. 3.
114. Ibid., p. 4.
115. Christopher Lasch, 'The Politics of Nostalgia: Losing History in the Mists of Ideology', *Harper's*, Nov 1984, pp. 65–70.
116. Peter Clecak, *America's Quest for the Ideal Self: Dissent and Fulfillment in the 60s and 70s* (New York: Oxford University Press, 1983) p. 96.
117. Ibid., p. 60.
118. Ibid., p. 44.
119. Ibid., p. 93.
120. Ibid., p. 42.
121. Ibid., p. 39.
122. Eric Mottram, *William Burroughs: The Algebra of Need* (London: Marion Boyars, 1977) p. 68.
123. Burroughs, *The Soft Machine* (London: Calder and Boyars, 1968) p. 79.
124. Burroughs, *Snack* (London: Aloes Books, 1975) p. 16.
125. Mottram, *Burroughs*, p. 78.
126. Irwin, *American Hieroglyphics*, p. 174.
127. Bloom, *New York Review of Books*, 28 Apr 1983, p. 5.
128. Bloom, *A Map of Misreading*, p. 4.
129. Jim Hougan, *Decadence: Radical Nostalgia, Narcissism, and the Decline in the Seventies* (New York: William Morrow, 1975) p. 196.
130. Ibid., p. 193.
131. Ibid., p. 194.
132. Ibid., p. 196.
133. Bloom, *Agon*, p. 177.
134. Ibid., p. 13.
135. Harold Bloom, *The Breaking of Vessels* (Chicago: University of Chicago Press, 1982) p. 13.
136. Lasch, in *Harper's*, Nov 1984, pp. 69–70.
137. Poirier, in *The Times Literary Supplement*, 10 June 1983, p. 592.
138. Marshall Berman, *All That is Solid Melts into Air: The Experience of Modernity* (London: Verso, 1983) p. 36.
139. Hamilton, *London Review of Books*, 16 June–6 July 1983, p. 6.
140. De Mott, in *New York Times Book Review*, 10 Apr 1983, p. 36.
141. Stade, in *The New Republic*, 2 May 1983, p. 34.
142. Shrimpton, in *The Sunday Times*, 12 June 1983, p. 44.
143. *Dialogue*, 62, p. 61.
144. Poirier, in *The Times Literary Supplement*, 10 June 1983, p. 591.
145. Bloom, in *New York Review of Books*, 28 Apr 1983, p. 3.
146. Ibid., p. 4.
147. Poirier, in *The Times Literary Supplement*, 10 June 1983, p. 592.
148. *Dialogue*, 62, p. 62.

Bibliography

BOOKS BY NORMAN MAILER CITED

The Naked and the Dead (New York: Rinehart, 1948; London: Panther, 1964).
Barbary Shore (New York: Rinehart, 1951; London: Panther, 1972).
The Deer Park (New York: Putnam's, 1955; London: Panther, 1976).
Advertisements for Myself (New York: Putnam's 1959; London: Panther, 1968).
The Presidential Papers (New York: Putnam's, 1963; London: Panther, 1976).
An American Dream (New York: Dial Press, 1965; London: Panther, 1972).
Cannibals and Christians (New York: Dial Press, 1966; London: André Deutsch, 1967).
Why Are We in Vietnam? (New York: Putnam's, 1967; London: Weidenfeld and Nicolson, 1969).
The Armies of the Night (New York: New American Library, 1968; Harmondsworth: Penguin, 1968).
The Prisoner of Sex (Boston, Mass.: Little, Brown, 1971).
St George and the Godfather (New York: New American Library, 1972).
Marilyn (New York: Grosset and Dunlap, 1973; London: Hodder and Stoughton, 1974).
Pieces and Pontifications (Boston, Mass.: Little, Brown, 1982; London: New English Library, 1983).
Ancient Evenings (Boston, Mass.: Little, Brown, 1983; London: Macmillan, 1983).

OTHER BOOKS CITED

Abrams, M. H., *Glossary of Literary Terms* (New York: Holt, Rinehart and Winston, 1957).
Adams, Laura, *Existential Battles: The Growth of Norman Mailer* (Athens, Ohio: University of Ohio Press, 1976).
Adorno, T. W., *et al.*, *The Authoritarian Personality* (New York: Harper and Row, 1950).
Adorno, T. W. and Horkheimer, Max, *The Dialectic of Enlightenment* (London: Verso, 1979).
Altizer, Thomas, *Mircea Eliade and the Dialectic of the Sacred* (Westport, Conn.: Greenwood Press, 1975).
Bailey, Jennifer, *Norman Mailer: Quick-Change Artist* (London: Macmillan, 1979).
Barthelme, Donald, *Snow White* (London: Jonathan Cape, 1968).
——, *Unspeakable Practices, Unnatural Acts* (New York: Simon and Schuster, 1978).
Begiebing, Robert J., *Acts of Regeneration* (Columbia: University of Missouri Press, 1980).

Bellow, Saul, *Dangling Man* (New York: New American Library, 1972).
——, *Herzog* (New York: Viking, 1964).
Berman, Marshall, *All That is Solid Melts into Air: The Experience of Modernity* (London: Verso, 1983).
Bloom, Harold, *The Anxiety of Influence: A Theory of Poetry* (New York: Oxford University Press, 1973).
——, *A Map of Misreading* (New York: Oxford University Press, 1975).
——, *Agon: Towards a Theory of Revisionism* (New York: Oxford University Press, 1982).
——, *The Breaking of the Vessels* (Chicago: University of Chicago Press, 1982).
Breasted, James Henry, *Development of Religion and Thought in Ancient Egypt* (London: Hodder and Stoughton, 1912).
Breit, Harvey, *The Writer Observed* (Cleveland: World Publishing, 1956).
Brown, Norman O., *Life against Death: The Psychoanalytic Meaning of History* (Middletown, Conn.: Wesleyan University Press, 1985).
Budge, E. A. Wallis, *The Book of the Dead: The Papyrus of Ani* (New York: Dover, 1967).
Bufithis, Philip H., *Norman Mailer* (New York: Frederick Unger, 1978).
Burroughs, William, *The Naked Lunch* (London: Corgi, 1968).
——, *The Yage Letters* (San Francisco: City Lights, 1963).
——, *The Ticket that Exploded* (New York: Grove Press, 1967).
——, *The Soft Machine* (London: Calder and Boyars, 1968).
——, *The Job* (New York: Grove Press, 1974).
Clecak, Peter, *Radical Paradoxes: Dilemmas of the American Left, 1945–1970* (New York: Harper and Row, 1973).
——, *America's Quest for the Ideal Self: Dissent and Fulfillment in the 60s and 70s* (New York: Oxford University Press, 1983).
Dolbeare, Kenneth M., and Patricia, *American Ideologies* (Chicago: Markham, 1971).
Eisinger, Chester, *Fiction and the Forties* (Chicago: University of Chicago Press, 1963).
Eliade, Mircea, *Images and Symbols* (New York: Sheed and Ward, 1961).
——, *Myths, Dreams and Mysteries* (London: Collins, 1968).
Ellison, Ralph, *Invisible Man* (Harmondsworth: Penguin, 1965).
Emerson, Ralph Waldo, *The Collected Works of Ralph Waldo Emerson*, vol. I: *Nature, Addresses and Lectures*, ed. Robert E. Spiller and Alfred R. Ferguson (Cambridge, Mass.: Harvard University Press, 1971).
Faulkner, William, *Go Down Moses* (Harmondsworth: Penguin, 1960).
Fenichel, Otto, *The Psychoanalytic Theory of Neurosis* (New York: Norton, 1945).
Fiedler, Leslie, *Love and Death in the American Novel* (London: Paladin, 1970).
Foster, Richard, *Norman Mailer* (Minneapolis: University of Minnesota Press, 1968).
Foucault, Michel, *Discipline and Punish: The Birth of the Prison* (New York: Pantheon, 1977).
——, *Power/Knowledge: Selected Interviews and Other Writings, 1972–1977* (New York: Pantheon, 1980).

——, *Language, Counter-Memory, Practice* (Ithaca, NY: Cornell University Press, 1977).

Fowler, Douglas, *A Reader's Guide to Gravity's Rainbow* (Ann Arbor, Mich.: Ardis, 1980).

Frankfort, H., *Ancient Egyptian Religion: An Interpretation* (New York: Columbia University Press, 1948).

——, *Kingship and the Gods* (Chicago: University of Chicago Press, 1948).

Gass, William, *Fiction and the Figures of Life* (New York: Alfred A. Knopf, 1970).

Gerth, H. H., and Mills, C. Wright (eds), *From Max Weber: Essays in Sociology* (New York: Oxford University Press, 1946).

Gordon, Andrew, *An American Dreamer* (Toronto: Associated University Press, 1980).

Gutman, Stanley T., *Mankind in Barbary* (Hanover, NH: University Press of New England, 1975).

Hawthorne, Nathaniel, *The Complete Short Stories of Nathaniel Hawthorne* (New York: Hanover House, 1959).

——, *The House of Seven Gables* (Boston, Mass.: Houghton Mifflin, 1897).

——, *The Scarlet Letter and Selected Tales* (Harmondsworth: Penguin, 1970).

Hemingway, Ernest, *A Farewell to Arms* (Harmondsworth: Penguin, 1935).

Hoffman, Abbie, *Woodstock Nation: A Talk-Rock Album* (New York: Random House, 1969).

Hougan, Jim, *Decadence: Radical Nostalgia, Narcissism, and Decline in the Seventies* (New York: William Morrow, 1975).

Howe, Irving, *Politics and the Novel* (New York: Books for Libraries Press, 1970).

Irwin, John, *American Hieroglyphics: The Symbol of the Egyptian Hieroglyphics in the American Renaissance* (New Haven, Conn.: Yale University Press, 1980).

Jellille, R. A. (ed.), *Faulkner at Nagano* (Tokyo: Kenkyusha, 1956).

Jouvenal, Bernard de, *On Power* (Boston, Mass.: Beacon Press, 1962).

Kael, Pauline, *When the Lights Go Down* (New York: Holt, Rinehart and Winston, 1980).

Kaplan, Harold, *Power and Order: Henry Adams and the Naturalist Tradition in American Fiction* (Chicago: University of Chicago Press, 1981).

Kauffman, Arnold, *The Radical Liberal* (New York: Atherton Press, 1968).

Kazin, Alfred (ed.), *Writers at Work: The Paris Review Interviews* (London: Secker and Warburg, 1967).

Lasch, Christopher, *The New Radicalism in America* (New York: Alfred A. Knopf, 1965).

Lawrence, D. H., *Studies in Classic American Literature* (London: Heinemann, 1964).

Leeds, Barry H., *The Structured Vision of Norman Mailer* (New York: New York University Press, 1969).

Lewis, I. M., *Ecstatic Religion: An Anthropological Study of Spirit Possession and Shamanism* (Harmondsworth: Penguin, 1971).

Lewis, R. W. B., *American Adam* (Chicago: Chicago University Press, 1955).

McCaffery, Larry, *The Metafictional Muse* (Pittsburgh: University of Pittsburgh Press, 1982).

McCarthy, Mary, *The Writing on the Wall* (Harmondsworth: Penguin, 1973).

McLuhan, Marshall, *The Mechanical Bride: Folklore and Industrial Man* (London: Routledge and Kegan Paul, 1967).

——, *The Gutenberg Galaxy* (London: Routledge and Kegan Paul, 1962).

——, *Understanding Media* (London: Routledge and Kegan Paul, 1969).

McConnell, Frank D., *Four Postwar American Novelists* (Chicago: University of Chicago Press, 1977).

Magdoff, Harry, *The Age of Imperialism* (New York: Monthly Review Press, 1969).

Mairowitz, David Zane, *The Radical Soap Opera: An Impression of the American Left from 1917 to the Present* (London: Wildwood House, 1974).

Marcuse, Herbert, *An Essay in Liberation* (Boston, Mass.: Beacon Press, 1969).

——, *Negatives* (Harmondsworth: Penguin, 1972).

——, *Eros and Civilization* (Boston, Mass.: Beacon Press, 1974).

Marx, Karl, and Engels, Frederick, *The German Ideology, Part One*, ed. C. J. Arthur (London: Lawrence and Wishart, 1974).

Merquior, J. G., *Foucault* (London: Fontana, 1985).

Miller, Jonathan, *McLuhan* (London: Collins, 1971).

Mills, C. Wright, *The Power Elite* (New York: Oxford University Press, 1956).

Mills, Hilary, *Mailer: A Biography* (London: New English Library, 1983).

Mottram, Eric, *William Burroughs: The Algebra of Need* (London: Marion Boyars, 1977).

Ollman, Bertell, *Alienation: Marx's Concept of Man in Capitalist Society* (Cambridge: Cambridge University Press, 1971).

Parsons, Talcott, *Politics and the Social Structure* (New York: The Free Press, 1969).

Podhoretz, Norman, *Breaking Ranks* (New York: Harper and Row, 1979).

Poirier, Richard, *A World Elsewhere* (New York: Oxford University Press, 1966).

——, *The Performing Self* (New York: Oxford University Press, 1971).

——, *Mailer* (London: Collins, 1972).

——, *The Aesthetic of Contemporary American Radicalism* (Leicester: Leicester University Press, 1972).

Pynchon, Thomas, *The Crying of Lot 49* (London: Picador, 1979).

——, *Gravity's Rainbow* (London: Picador, 1975).

——, *Slow Learner* (Boston, Mass.: Little, Brown, 1984).

Radford, Jean, *Norman Mailer: A Critical Study* (London: Macmillan, 1975).

Reich, Wilhelm, *Character-Analysis* (New York: Orgone Institute Press, 1949).

——, *The Mass Psychology of Fascism* (New York: Farrar, Straus and Giroux, 1970).

Rideout, Walter B., *The Radical Novel in the United States* (London: Oxford University Press, 1956).

Rieff, Philip, *The Triumph of the Therapeutic* (New York: Harper and Row, 1966).

Robinson, Paul A., *The Sexual Radicals* (London: Granada, 1972).

Riesman, David, *The Lonely Crowd: A Study of the Changing American Character* (New Haven, Con.: Yale University Press, 1950).

Clark Rundle, R. T., *Myth and Man: Myth and Symbol in Ancient Egypt* (London: Thames and Hudson, 1959).

Schmidt, Karl M., *Henry Wallace: Quixotic Crusade, 1948* (Syracuse, NY: New York University Press, 1966).

Skinner, B. F., *The Behaviour of Organisms: An Experimental Analysis* (New York: Appleton-Century-Croft, 1938).

———: *Walden Two* (New York) Macmillan, 1948).

Solotaroff, Robert, *Down Mailer's Way* (Urbana: University of Illinois Press, 1974).

Tanner, Tony, *City of Words* (London: Jonathan Cape, 1976).

Tuan, Yi-Fu, *Topophilia: A Study in Environmental Perception, Attitudes and Values* (Englewood Cliffs, NJ: Prentice-Hall, 1974).

Walton, Richard J., *Henry Wallace, Harry Truman and the Cold War* (New York: Viking, 1976).

Whyte, Willian H., *The Organization Man* (New York: Simon and Schuster, 1956).

Williams, Raymond, *Keywords: A Vocabulary of Culture and Society* (London: Fontana, 1976).

Wrong, Dennis, *Power: Its Forms, Bases and Uses* (Oxford: Basil Blackwell, 1979).

ARTICLES CITED

Bersani, Leo, 'The Interpretation of Dreams', *Partisan Review*, 32 (Fall 1965) pp. 606–14.

Bloom, Harold, 'Norman in Egypt', *New York Review of Books*, 28 Apr 1983, pp. 3–5.

Bragg, Melvyn, interview with Mailer in *The Listener*, 15 November 1979, pp. 660–2.

———, interview with Mailer in *The Sunday Times Magazine*, 12 June 1983, pp. 18–19.

Bryant, Jerry H., 'The Last of the Social Protest Writers', *Arizona Quarterly*, Winter 1963, pp. 315–25.

De Mott, Benjamin, 'Norman Mailer's Egyptian Novel', *New York Times Book Review*, 10 Apr 1983, pp. 34–6.

Dupee, F. W., 'The American Norman Mailer', *Commentary*, Feb 1960, p. 132.

Everett, Edward, 'The Zodiac of Denderah', *North American Review*, 17 (1823) 233.

Hamilton, Ian, 'Mummies', *London Review of Books*, 16 June – 6 July 1983, p. 6.

Hoy, David Couzens, 'Power, Repression, Progress: Foucault, Lukes, and the Frankfurt School', *Triquarterly*, 52 (1900) 43–63.

Lasch, Christopher, 'The Politics of Nostalgia: Losing History in the Mists of Ideology', *Harper's*, Nov 1984, pp. 65–80.

Podhoretz, Norman, 'Norman Mailer: The Embattled Vision', in Robert E. Lucid (ed.) *Norman Mailer and His Work* (Boston, Mass.: Little, Brown, 1971) pp. 60–85.

Poirier, Richard, 'In Pyramid and Palace', *The Times Literary Supplement*, 10 June 1983, pp. 591–2.

Prigozy, Ruth, 'The Liberal Novelist in the McCarthy Era', *Twentieth Century Literature*, 23, no.3 (Oct 1975) 260.

Prescott, Peter, 'Tales From Beyond the Tomb', *Newsweek*, 18 Apr 1983, p. 82.

Shechner, Mark, 'Reich and the Reichians,' *Partisan Review*, 52 (Spring 1986) 98–108.

Shrimpton, Nicholas, 'The Riddle of the Sphincter', *The Sunday Times*, 12 June 1983, p. 44.

Stade, George, in *The New Republic*, 2 May 1983, pp. 32–6.

Toback, James, 'At Play in the Fields of the Bored', *Esquire*, Dec 1968, pp. 151–4.

Dialogue, 62 (Apr 1983) 57–64.

The Guardian, 20 Feb 1986, p. 10.

New York Star Magazine, 22 Aug 1948, p. 3.

Washington Post Book World, 13 Feb 1980, p. 9.

New York Times Book Review, 6 June 1982, p. 3 and 42–3.

MEDIA

Butler, Marilyn, *The Cult of the Exotic*, BBC Radio Three, 19 June 1986.

Marowitz, Charles, *Movie Makers*, BBC Radio Three, 16 July 1985.

Index